GW01034616

ISBN: 9781313123372

Published by:
HardPress Publishing
8345 NW 66TH ST #2561
MIAMI FL 33166-2626

Email: info@hardpress.net
Web: http://www.hardpress.net

INTERNAL COMBUSTION ENGINES *and* TRACTORS

THEIR DEVELOPMENT, DESIGN, CONSTRUCTION, FUNCTION *and* MAINTENANCE

Notes of a Series of Lectures
Delivered by

MAJOR OLIVER B. ZIMMERMAN
U. S. R. Engineer Corps

OF THE ENGINEERING STAFF
INTERNATIONAL HARVESTER COMPANY
Chicago USA

A298-*I*—1-30 Fourth Edition.

CONTENTS

For Complete Index See Page 163.

This is a view of the great Tractor Works at Chicago where Mogul tractors and engines are manufactured. This photograph was taken from the large International Harvester warehouse, and shows in back of the principal manufacturing buildings the testing track on which all Mogul tractors are tested before being shipped. A second large manufacturing plant devoted to tractors and engines is located at Milwaukee. In the Milwaukee plant is built the famous Titan line of engines and tractors.

Chapter I

The Development of Internal Combustion Engines

Those of us who are familiar with the crude designs in which the internal combustion engine first appeared in the early nineties, marvel at the progress that has since been made in refinement of design and the perfecting of mechanical efficiency. Although these engines twenty years ago were extremely uncertain in operation and control, there were men who had faith enough in this type of motive power to continue its manufacture, experimenting and improving until they developed the present excellent engines with which we are now so familiar.

The final result of this sifting-out process is the development and specialization of different types, designed to meet some particular need in some certain specialized field. Because of this specialization we have today the automobile engine, the aeroplane, the marine, the stationary, and the tractor engine, each with its characteristic qualities and advantages for its special work.

Another complication, requiring more specialization, arose just as the gasoline engine reached the point of development where it became a satisfactory power producer mechanically. Manufacturers found themselves facing an entirely new problem—an insufficient supply of gasoline which threatened to become a chronic condition in the fuel oil business. This shortage of gasoline introduced a new stage in the development of the internal combustion motor—an endeavor to produce an engine that would run with positive certainty and economy on the lower grade fuels such as kerosene and distillate, the abundance and cheapness of which made them very desirable fuels. This fact has had an important influence on farm engine and tractor designs.

The Modern Farm Tractor

Of all the users of internal combustion engines, the farmer had the greatest variety of work to be done. As a consequence, a large amount of capital has been invested to build engines to meet the farmer's special demands.

The first farm engine was a small stationary engine usable for belt work only. Then a portable outfit was demanded, and finally a self-propelling vehicle to move itself from place to place. Thus the tractor industry came into being because, of all the power needed by the farmer, tractor power to take the place of animal power proved to be his most urgent need.

The Value of Experience

Though at this writing there are on the market fully one hundred and fifty makes of tractors, a glance over their outlines causes one to realize that the basic ideas of tractor design are not yet uniformly crystalized. Closer examination, however, shows that in this host of machines there is a rather clear division, one class representing correct ideas as the result of experience, and the other, incorrect ideas as the result of inexperience, either in manufacturing or designing, or both.

No machine manufactured has to meet such a wide variety of extreme conditions as the tractor; the heat of the desert, the cold of the arctic, the dry, dusty conditions of summer, the wet and mud of the spring, the skilled engine operator in America, or the unmechanical operator from Arabia, good or poor fuel, suitable or unsuitable lubricating oil, soft rain water or dirty hard water, short intermittent operation or long sustained maximum efforts, operating on the level plain without a stone or on the steep hillside, plowing on firm footing or the floating marsh, soft mellow land or the tough sticky clay, shallow scaling the top surface or plowing to a depth beyond reason.

From these indications it is not to be wondered at that one machine might fulfill one set of conditions perfectly and still fail under another set of conditions. It is easy to see that experience is necessary and valuable in the production of a general purpose tractor, one designed to do satisfactory work under all conditions.

Conditions Affecting Tractor Design

Assuming that we are about to design and build a tractor for every day use on an average farm, let us determine which features or what type of construction would be most desirable in the light of a comprehensive mechanical knowledge and an extensive experience in tractor field work. Our mechanical knowledge must tell us just what is going on within the cylinder, what temperatures and pressures are produced, and what parts they particularly affect, so that we can design all those parts accordingly. Our knowledge must give us definite information of liquid fuels, their production, chemical composition and action within the engine, so that we can design all parts in accordance with the laws that govern the combustion of these fuels. We must know the qualities of various materials and the changes that are produced by various heat processes, so that we may select only those most suitable.

Through our field experience we should know just what is expected of a tractor, and which of the many designs and constructions that it might be possible to use will prove most desirable.

Chapter II

Basic Features in Internal Combustion Engine Design

Influence of Purpose on Design

The purpose for which an engine is to be used has a great deal to do with its design. An engine for indoor stationary work need not have the feature of enclosure from dust and dirt as pronounced in its design as one intended for work in the rain and mud. An engine that is to be used in an electric light plant, must be designed for very steady operation so that the lights will not flicker. This implies exceptionally close speed regulation. One meant to serve as power for a motor boat, should occupy as little room and weigh as little as possible. In an engine designed for automobile service, certain other features must be given special attention. Likewise an aeroplane engine must be designed for lightness, running in clean, cold air at high altitudes. It must also be as near mechanically perfect in its design and operation as possible, so that no mishap will occur to endanger the operator.

Just so experience tells us that certain features are exceptionally desirable in a tractor engine—reasonable weight, not too heavy nor too light, low center of gravity so that the machine will work on hillsides and on rough land without danger of upsetting, ample protection from dust, dirt, water and mud, and generous bearings to insure long life and maximum power. No internal combustion engine intended for other purposes requires identically the same features, nor could be used in a tractor with equal efficiency, as a specially designed tractor engine.

Determining the Design of a Tractor Engine

It is evident that the designer of a tractor has many points to decide before he can make a real tractor engine, and only if he chooses wisely in the main points will his product be a success. He must determine whether the engine shall be two-, four-, or six-cycle; the type of ignition; the number of cylinders and their design; the speed at which the engine is to operate; the amount of compression to be provided in the cylinders. In order to ascertain the most sensible set of conditions for tractor use, he will analyze and review generally the points in design enumerated above as applied to various types of engines in order to better determine which features are desirable for tractor design and which features are positively undesirable.

Two-, Four- and Six-cycle Methods of Developing Power

Internal combustion engines as manufactured today present three customary ways of developing power from the fuels. The three ways have their own peculiarities and are commonly known as the two-cycle, four-cycle and six cycle types.

All of these use a cylinder with a moving piston to receive the pressure formed during the explosion of the fuel and air in the cylinder and turn this pressure into useful rotation of a crankshaft.

The term "cycle" indicates a repeating of some operation. In engine practice we use it to indicate the operation that takes place in the engine. This operation repeating itself, we say that from one repetition to the next is a cycle.

In the two-cycle engine, there is a repetition of the explosion in the cylinder for every two strokes of the piston, so it is more correct to use the term "two-stroke cycle."

In the four-stroke cycle, there is an explosion for every fourth stroke of the piston.

With the six-stroke cycle, an explosion occurs at every sixth stroke.

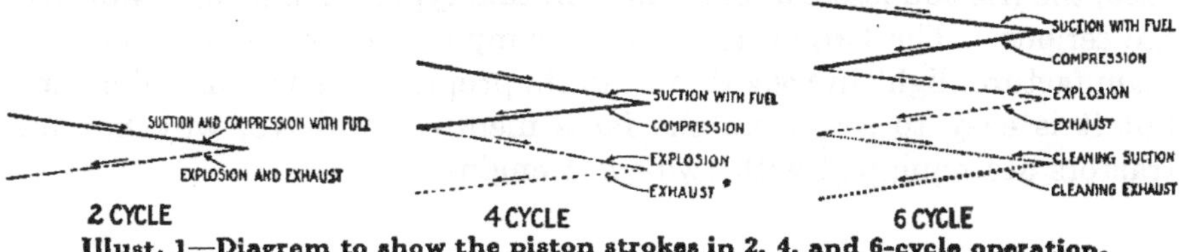

Illust. 1—Diagram to show the piston strokes in 2, 4, and 6-cycle operation.

As the engineer or designer has to choose one of these three combinations as the base of his engine design, it may be well to see which one best fits the requirements of the tractor engine.

The Two-Stroke Cycle Engine

Here we have an explosion in the engine for every forward stroke of the piston or for every revolution of the crank shaft. Fuel mixture is admitted into the crank case through a check valve on the inward stroke of the piston at the same time the charge in the cylinder is compressed and ignited. On the outward stroke of the piston the mixture in the crank case is slightly compressed and at practically the end of the stroke the inlet port is opened, allowing the partially compressed mixture to enter the cylinder. This is possible because the exhaust port is uncovered just previous to the opening of the inlet port.

As the fuel is admitted to the crank case through a check valve, fuel mixture proportions are hard to control because the bearings will wear, permitting excess air to enter, causing a slow burning mixture which is indicated by crank case explosions. Loose bearings and heat created in crank case also tend to destroy lubrication.

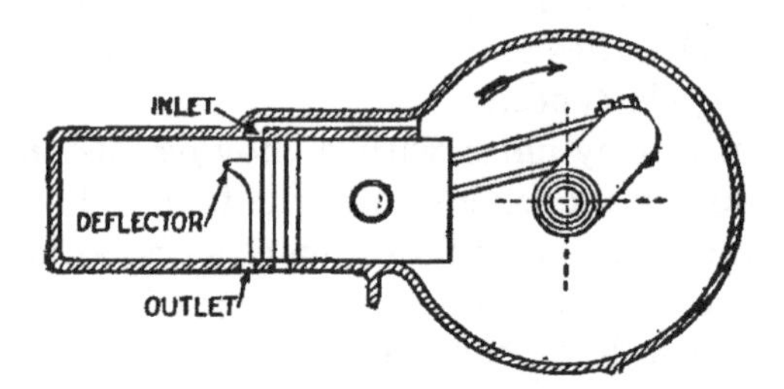

Illust. 2. Diagram showing the operation of a 2-stroke cycle engine.

Other disadvantages of the two-stroke cycle as a tractor engine are its inability to operate well under the violent changes of load usual on tractors; its lack of simple control; its high fuel cost. As the exhaust port is open just before the inlet, we find, especially in small engines, that it is quite impossible to avoid wasting fuel through the exhaust. Also, the friction losses average high in this type. These disadvantages are serious. The two-cycle engine is simple in construction, cheap to manufacture, light in weight, and in its proper place is a useful engine, but it is easy to see, from the facts mentioned above, why but few tractors are equipped with two-cycle engines.

The Four-Stroke Cycle Engine

In this type of engine the first stroke is used to draw into the engine the charge of air and fuel. The second stroke compresses the charge ready for the explosion. The third stroke transmits to the crankshaft the force of the explosion and expansion. The fourth stroke gets rid of the burned gases.

Four-cycle construction is simple and more easily controlled even though more parts are used than in the two-cycle. This type will be discussed fully later on.

The Six-Stroke Cycle Engine

This engine embodies the efforts of designers to obtain still greater economy of fuel by more thoroughly clearing the cylinder of burned gases, and thus burning very completely the fuel and air taken in.

The strokes are as follows:

First —Taking in the clean air and a fuel charge.
Second—Compressing this charge for firing and igniting.
Third —Exploding and expanding of gases.
Fourth—Exhausting burned gases.
Fifth —Taking in fresh air for cleaning out gases left after exhaust.
Sixth —Discharging the mixed gases and clean air.

The six-cycle is the best of the three in fuel economy, but this is its only advantage. Its fuel mixture is 97% burnable, as against 80% in the four and 50% to 70% in the two-cycle type. This advantage must be weighed against three disadvantages of the six-cycle type as a tractor engine:

1. The two extra strokes of each cycle use up considerable power in friction losses.
2. The extra cleaning stroke chills the cylinder, making this type less desirable for the burning of low grade fuels, which a tractor engine must use.
3. The six-cycle engine is heavier than either a two or four of the same power.

Considering these, especially the first and second, we must conclude that the six-cycle type is hardly adaptable to the best tractor engine design.

Since the two-cycle wastes fuel, and the six-cycle wastes energy' while the four seems to furnish a happy medium, let us consider the four-cycle engine in greater detail to see if we can adapt its features to the design of a practical tractor engine. Four of these features immediately suggest themselves—the number of cylinders—the speed of the engine—its weight—the compression it employs.

Illust. 2a. This shows the testing track at the Mogul Tractor Works. Every Mogul tractor, before it is shipped, undergoes several tests in the factory, and then to make doubly sure that it will deliver the goods, it is given a work-out on this track, pulling a load in keeping with its rating.

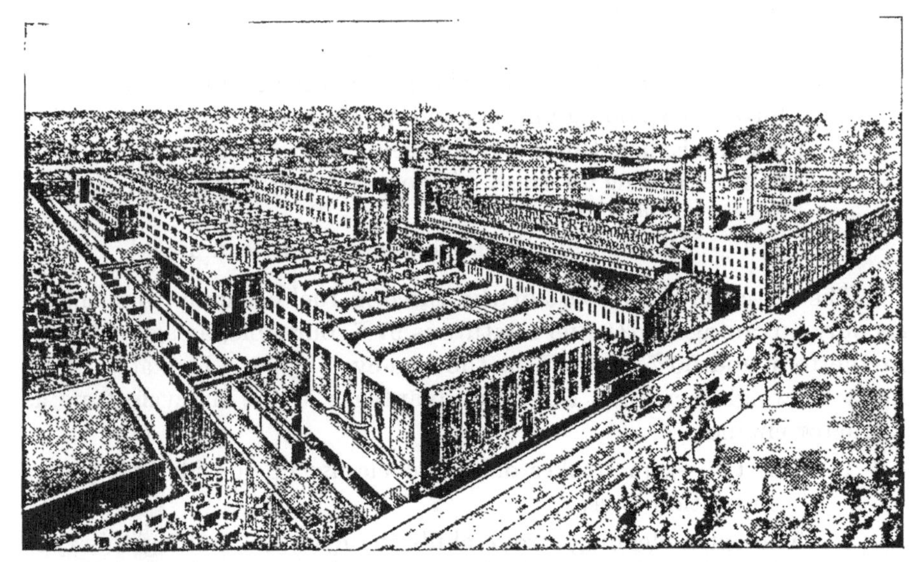

Illust. 2b. This is the big engine and tractor works at Milwaukee, Wisconsin, where Titan tractors and engines are made. This works ranks as one of the best equipped engine factories in the United States. The foundry is modern in every respect, and has an enormous capacity of the finest engine castings that it is possible to make. All departments in this plant are equipped with modern automatic machinery to insure highest class production.

Engine Speeds

Internal combustion engines now on the market range in speeds from 200 r.p.m. to 3,600 r.p.m. In a tractor we are governed by the speed we wish to go, the lowest speeds being for plowing, ranging from 2 to 2½ miles per hour. Our engine, then, should be designed for a speed which will deliver ample power to the drive wheels at their useful rate of travel. Since this must be done through gears or chains, the larger the difference between the engine speed and the revolutions of the rear wheels, the more gears and bearings we shall have to supply and care for, and the more power will be lost through gear friction. Later we shall see how important these losses are. Every argument is in favor of keeping the engine speed down.

Engine Weight

The proper weight for a tractor engine lies somewhere between the large stationary engine with one cylinder weighing as much as 500 lbs. for each horse power it can deliver and the lightest, highest type of aeroplane engine as low in weight as 2⅝ lbs. per horse power. The first mentioned weight for a 20-h.p. stationary engine would give the engine alone a weight of 10,000 lbs.—much too heavy for any modern tractor. The latter would make it too light. As engine weight and engine speed are interdependent, this subject will be discussed under another heading.

Compression

In all internal combustion engines we try to get the greatest amount of power from the least amount of fuel, and successful operation on any liquid or gaseous fuel requires that before the mixture of air and fuel is fired, it should be compressed[1]. Since the degree of compression depends on what fuel is used, some fuels requiring more compression than others, we find among the various engines compressions from 45 lbs. up to 500 lbs. per square inch. Most gasoline tractor engines

NOTE 1.—Care of Engine Valves to Insure Compression

Valves and valve seats must always be kept well fitted in order to obtain proper compression. It is easy to detect leaky valves by turning the engine over on the compression stroke. If it does not require the usual amount of strength then you may know that there is a leak somewhere, allowing compression to escape.

The first place to look for this trouble is the exhaust valve. This valve is subjected to extreme heat and is the vent through which all burned gases and carbon must be forced out on the scavenging stroke of the piston. If this valve is properly seated, then the trouble may be found in the intake valve, or there may be a leak around the piston. There is no doubt, however, that at least nine-tenths of the cause of poor compression is found in improper seating of the valves.

When you have determined that the valve is really leaking compression, the first step is to see if it is not due to a deposit of carbon or some other foreign substance resting either upon the valve or valve seat which prevents it from closing at the proper time. Such a deposit can quite often be removed by simply turning the valve on the seat by means of a pair of pliers or a wrench, which, under the pressure of the valve spring, will pulverize and can be removed by tapping the valve off the seat, thus removing this obstruction. If this does not remedy the trouble, then it will be necessary to regrind the valves.

Regrinding Mogul and Titan Valves

To regrind the valves is not a difficult thing. The cylinder head or the valve cages should be removed, the valve springs taken off, and the valve and valve seat cleaned with kerosene. Make sure also that the valve stem and the sleeve through which the valve stem works is washed free from burnt oil and other gummy sub stances which tend to slow up the valve action.

The best composition for grinding valves is made of emery dust and oil. Such compounds can usually be purchased from a machine shop or a garage where repair run on compressions between 60 lbs. and 70 lbs. per square inch. For good economy and controllability, the most sensible compression for a kerosene engine using water is from 75 lbs. to 85 lbs. and when not using water about 65 lbs. A further discussion of compression will be given under Fuels.

---

work of this sort is done on automobiles. Apply some of this composition to that part of the valve which should rest upon the valve seat. Then put the valve in place and with a carpenter's brace and screwdriver bit the valve grinding operation can begin.

The valve should be revolved not more than one-quarter or one-half turn, with only a small amount of pressure, then back in the opposite direction. Continue this operation ten or fifteen times, then lift the valve off the seat and give it about half a turn before placing it back upon the seat. Repeat the oscillating motion with the brace again. Be sure that the oscillations overlap one another. This operation should be continued until all parts of the valve and valve seat are in contact. This can be determined by removing the valve, cleaning it and observing the surface that is ground bright.

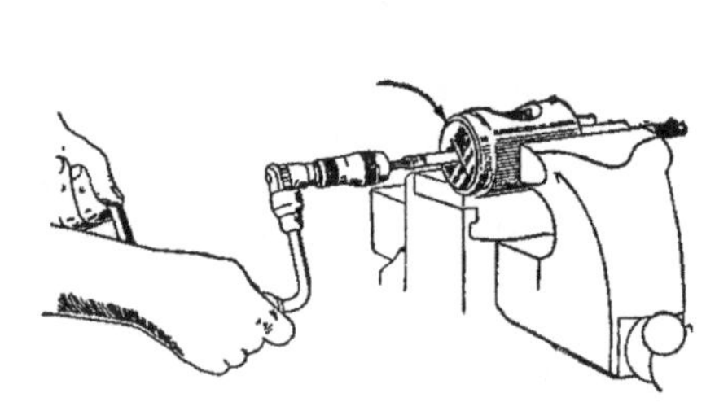

Illust. 3. If the valves are in cages, remove the cage, put it in a vice, and grind the valves as shown in the illustration. In all cases be sure that the valves seat on inner or edge next to compression chamber.

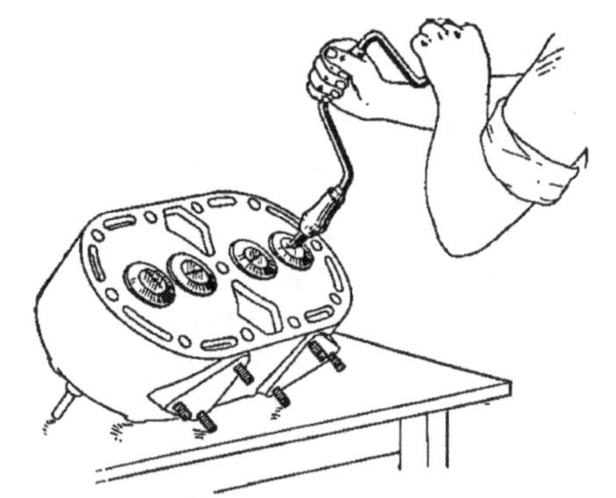

Illust. 4. If the valves are contained in the cylinder head, remove the head, place on a table, and proceed to grind the valves as shown in the illustration.

The bright ring or ground surface should extend continuously around the valve and valve seat.

As soon as the valve has been properly fitted, then all of the grinding compound should be cleaned off the valve, the valve seat, and all other parts of the cylinder head or valve cage. Be sure and test valves after grinding by pouring gasoline in port, revolving valve and looking for seepage.

The reason why the oscillating motion is better than a complete revolution in grinding is that in making complete turns with the valve upon the valve seat there is a tendency for the grinding compound to cut rings completely around on the valve and valve seat, which tend to increase valve troubles rather than diminish them.

Chapter III

What is Going On Within the Cylinder

Having determined that our tractor engine should be of the four-cycle type, with either one, two, or four cylinders, of reasonable engine speed and weight, it is next necessary to determine the details of construction which will produce the desirable features mentioned above.

Before we can do this, however, it is necessary to understand clearly just what is going on within the engine cylinder. We must know what temperatures and pressures are produced and their effect on the material of which engines are built, otherwise our design may prove a failure through inability to withstand temperatures and pressures we had not figured on. Let us see what happens within the cylinder at each stroke of the piston.

First or Suction Stroke

We see how the air and fuel go into the cylinder from the outside during the first stroke of the machine. The inlet valve E is open and as the piston recedes, the air follows in through the intake pipe, to fill the partial vacuum formed within the cylinder. As this air goes through the mixer or carburetor it picks up fuel, and forms, through a proper setting of the fuel needle-valve, an explosive mixture of air and fuel.

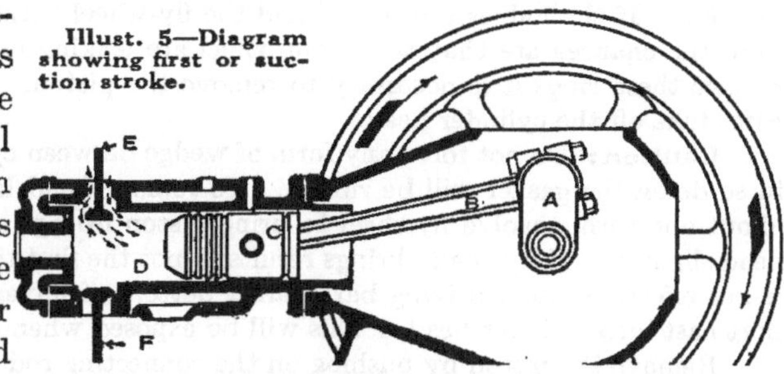

Illust. 5—Diagram showing first or suction stroke.

Points to be Watched During Suction Stroke

It is readily noted here that if the intake valve E is not freely open, or an obstruction is placed in the intake pipe, there will be trouble in getting the air into the cylinder; also, if the exhaust valve F is not tight on its seat, burned gases will be drawn back into the engine and spoil the charge.[1] Also, if the cylinder head gasket is leaky,[2] enough

NOTE 1—See page 12, Note 1, care of engine valves to insure compression.

NOTE 2—Tight Gasket Joint

If gasket leaks, tighten the bolts, and if that does not remedy the trouble, remove the cylinder head, clean the gasket and all surfaces coming in contact with it before replacing.

water may get into the cylinder to spoil the explosion. Again, it is plain that the suction of the engine depends upon the accurate fitting of the piston and rings and upon sufficient and complete lubrication of the piston and rings. If these points are faulty trouble in starting is sure to result.[1]

Each cylinder of a multiple cylinder engine must therefore be watched separately for these points.

Second or Compression Stroke

The mixture thus drawn in is not in condition to develop its greatest power without first being compressed. Hence a second step in the operation of the engine is to compress the charge or explosive mixture to the correct point for the fuel used. (See page 81.)

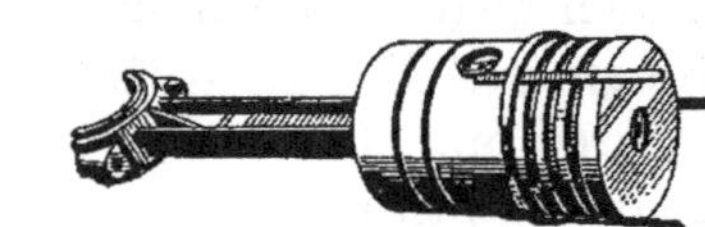

Illust. 6. Replacing Piston Rings.

NOTE 1—Leaky Piston Rings

To determine if piston rings are tight, turn the fly-wheel over against compression. If the valves are seated and the fly-wheel turns easily against compression, the chances are that the piston rings are leaking compression. To clean or replace these rings it is necessary to remove the piston. Proceed in this manner: First take off the cylinder head.

Caution: Do not force any form of wedge between cylinder and head because in so doing the gasket will be ruined. To remove head loosen cylinder head nuts about one turn, revolve flywheel to bring piston up against compression, and tap head slightly. This usually brings results, if not the first time, try it again. If this is not effective, use a driving bar against bottom of mixer or against edge of inlet port cast into cylinder head. This will be exposed when mixer is removed.

Remove the piston by pushing on the connecting rod or place a block of wood between the connecting rod and crankshaft, then turn flywheel against block, which will help to force out the piston. When disconnecting crank pin bearings be careful not to mix up liners. Mark each set top or bottom and place to one side in the original order in which they were inserted in the bearings. If the rings are found fast in grooves clean by washing in kerosene. Work them up and down in grooves until free. Now remove the first ring with the aid of three thin metal strips as illustrated. Insert these strips under the ring at the joint leaving two close to the joint. Work the other one to a position opposite the joint. The ring is now out of the groove and can easily be removed. Remove the others in like manner. Clean the rings and ring grooves in the piston thoroughly, using a knife to scrape them if necessary. When replacing the rings, put the inner ones in first, using the metal strips as before so as to slide the ring over the groove. After the rings are in position wash piston in gasoline or kerosene to remove all dirt and grit. Then oil the piston and rings thoroughly and place the piston in the cylinder. It is easier to do this with the piston upside down, as joints in the rings and the ring pins can be easier watched. Be sure that the rings are down in their grooves, and not on top of the piston ring pins, then push piston into cylinder.

This step is accomplished by the compression stroke of the piston, by means of which the charge is more completely mixed, its temperature is raised both by compression and by heat from the cylinder wall, and its pressure increased to a point which assists the quick ignition necessary for good economy and power.

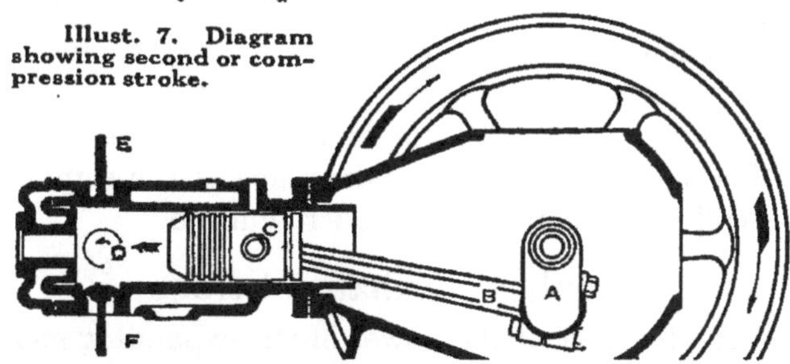

Illust. 7. Diagram showing second or compression stroke.

Points to be Watched During Compression Stroke

If the valves are leaky or gasket leaks, or the gases blow by the piston, compression will be partly reduced. See to it, therefore, that valves seat well, that piston fits accurately and rings are tight and well lubricated.[4] Low compression means loss of power, slow burning, dead or listless action.

Third or Power Stroke

When almost fully compressed the ignition or firing of the charge takes place. The quick burning of the fuel and air causes a great

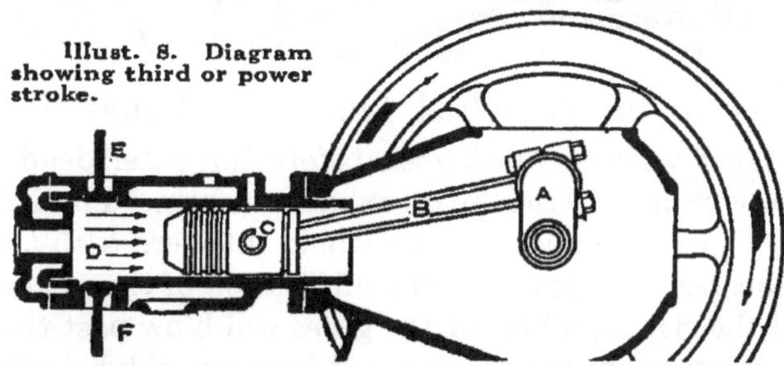

Illust. 8. Diagram showing third or power stroke.

If piston is put in upside down place a bar between the connecting rod bolts and turn piston over to its proper position. Now oil the crank pin, connect up. Be sure that all liners are replaced in original order, draw nuts tight, replace cotter pins and spread them at the ends.

Replace cylinder head and mixer.

See that engine turns over freely but that **bearings** are not **too loose,** or **too tight** for good lubrication.

NOTE 4—Well Fitted Piston Rings Essential

If piston rings are not well fitted, lubrication will not suffice to retain compression. Lubrication retains compression only when there is a proper fit between the piston and rings and the cylinder walls.

expansion of gas in the cylinder. This extra gas, along with the effect of the heat given off during combustion, causes a tremendous rise in pressure within the cylinder D, which pressure acting on the piston C, creates the turning impulse of the crankshaft A.

Points to be Watched During Power Stroke

Should the valves leak[1], or a gasket be leaky[2]; should the rings be loose[3] or the lubrication of the piston insufficient, it is evident that the full power of the expansion will not be as effective on the piston as it should be. The ignition also must take place at the right moment for the speed, as will be explained later under Ignition.

Fourth or Exhaust Stroke

After the greater part of the power of the expanding gases has been absorbed, it is necessary to get rid of them, and they should have a free outlet to the air through the exhaust valve F and muffler, if one is used.

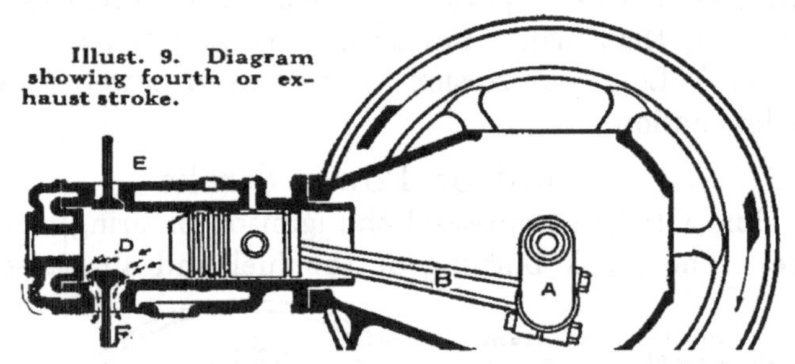

Illust. 9. Diagram showing fourth or exhaust stroke.

Points to be Watched During Exhaust Stroke

The exhaust valve F must open before the outer dead center and remain open throughout the entire exhaust stroke. The inlet valve E must be tight[1], or the exhaust gases would interfere with the incoming charge and decrease its power. The lubrication of the piston should be good and of the right quality, or the gases will blow past the rings[2] and cause carbonization, undue heating and burning of lubricating oil.

Internal Temperatures and Pressures

We are familiar with the reasonable changes of temperatures and pressures within the cylinder of a steam engine, but in the internal combustion engines we have a widely different set of conditions to deal with.

NOTE 1—See page 12, Note 1, Care of engine valves to insure compression.
NOTE 2—See page 14, Note 2, Tight gasket joint
NOTE 3—See page 15, Note 1, Leaky piston rings

As this engine is a "heat" engine, we must study it as such and give some time to the heat and pressure changes which take place within the cylinder. From a practical standpoint this understanding of what goes on inside of the cylinder is so helpful to anyone operating such an engine, that no one should fear the apparent technical difficulties. They are not hard to understand.

How Temperatures and Pressures are Determined

As the engine designer must know what is going on inside the cylinder, he devised a way of learning this by an instrument called the "Indicator," which draws on a paper what is termed a "card" or set of lines, telling just what is happening at every moment of the piston travel on each of the four strokes of the cycle. The pressure inside the cylinder pushes a pencil "up and down" against a spring, so that if the pressure is high the pencil moves high, and while this pressure line is being drawn, the movement of the piston "back and forth" causes the paper to move "back and forth" so we get a "card" or line drawn by the combined "up and down" and "back and forth" motions. When the fuel mixture is compressed, temperature rises in a definite relationship to pressure, so knowing the pressures by the indicator, we also learn the temperatures. This card shows a very accurate miniature of what really takes place out of sight in the cylinder. The card record of pressure height is kept down to about 2½ inches, and that of the stroke to about 3½ inches.

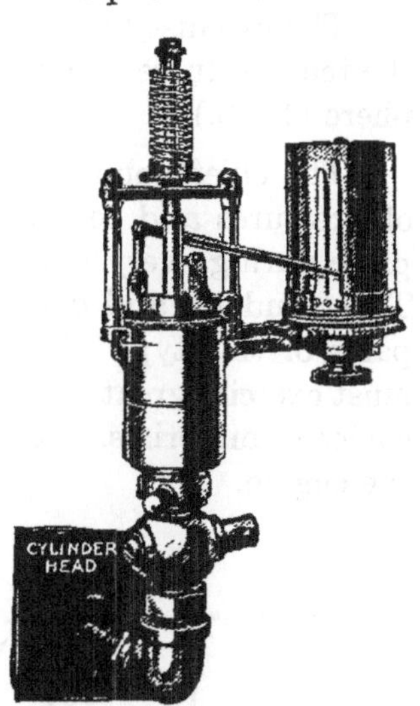

Illust. 10. An indicator attached to cylinder head.

Looking at the card, Illust. 11, we follow the arrow through the four strokes from bottom up—suction (1); compression (2); power (3); and exhaust (4).

The air mixture enters the engine on the suction stroke (1) at the surrounding temperature, which might be 70° Fahr. in a room—0° Fahr. in cold weather—100° Fahr. in hot weather—and at or just below the pressure of the atmosphere (14 lb. to the square inch). As the mixture gets within the cylinder it is heated to about 260° Fahr. by the piston and cylinder walls. The piston next starts on its compression (2) stroke, the intake valve and exhaust valve are closed, so the fuel mixture is trapped like air in an automobile tire pump. As the piston moves and the space between it and the cylinder head becomes smaller, the temperature and pressure rise, in the kerosene engine, from 800° to 900° Fahr., and to whatever pressure the designer has planned for, in this case from 75 lbs. to 85 lbs. to the square inch using water with fuel and 65 lbs. when not using water. Close to the end of the compression stroke (2), ignition takes place with a tremendous rise in pressure and temperature, 225 lbs. to 250 lbs. or more to the square inch and 2500° to 4000° Fahr. These temperatures and pressures decrease as the piston recedes from the head, but continue to push on the piston all the time until the exhaust valve is opened near the end of the stroke, when properly burned gases will escape through the exhaust valve at 40 lb. to 50 lb. pressure and 1000° Fahr.

The exhaust (4) continues to the end of the fourth stroke, lowering the temperatures and reducing the pressure to about that of the atmosphere (14 lb.).

The chief point of interest here is that great and violent changes of pressures and temperatures occur, and that these changes all take place during every two revolutions of the engine and in each cylinder. These sudden and extreme variations, to which in some measure all parts of this type of engine are subjected, indicate that the designer must exercise great care in determining every detail of design and in his choice of materials, in order to insure long and satisfactory operation of the engine.

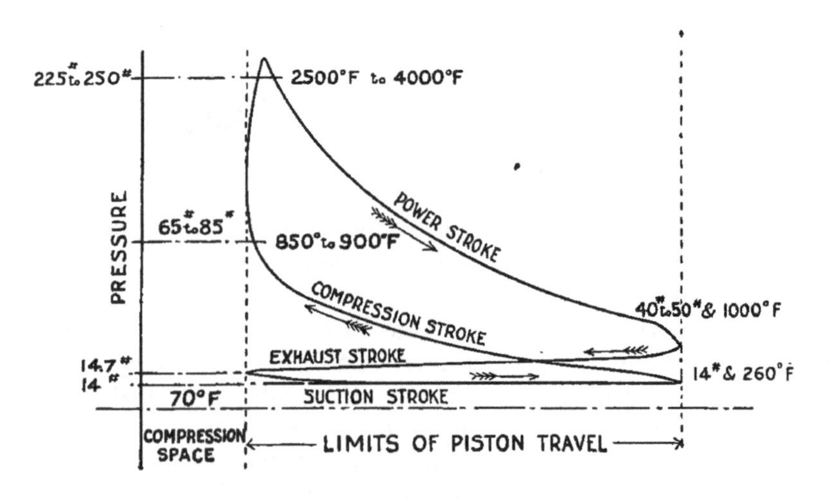

Illust. 11. Illustration of an indicator card. The diagram shows the limits of piston at both inner and outer points of travel and the temperatures and pressures at all points of piston travel in each cycle.

Chapter IV

Classification of Engine Parts by Functions—The Seven Systems

Understanding clearly what occurs within the engine cylinder, we are now ready to consider the design of the various engine parts affected, each according to its indicated needs. In all the different engine types on the market—whatever their purpose, design, number of cylinders, speeds, compression—we find certain groups of parts acting in common. The same parts are found in different groups according to the functions to be performed, so, for clearness, the different groups are termed systems under the following seven heads:

(1) The *Mechanical or Power System,* consisting of those mechanical parts which enable us to admit, hold and compress the fuel charge and which, after the combustion, take up this pressure and turn it into useful motion; also those parts which enable us to get rid of the burned gases and make ready for the new charge.

(2) The *Fuel and Carbureting System,* or those parts which have to deal with the storage, supply and preparation of the fuel and fuel mixture.

(3) The *Ignition System,* or those parts controlling the igniting or firing of the charge.

(4) The *Lubrication System,* or the means of reducing friction of all working parts to the smallest degree.

(5) The *Cooling System,* or the means of controlling cylinder temperature for fuel economy and proper lubrication.

(6) The *Governing System,* or the automatic means of maintaining steady engine speeds within the range of power of which the engine is capable and under variable loads.

(7) The *Air and Gas System,* or the means of permitting the entry into the engine of clean air, and exit from the engine of exhaust gases. Likewise control over the fresh mixture and the final gases.

Each of these systems must be thoroughly discussed and learned before the action of an engine can be properly understood, since the successful operation of the engine depends upon these seven systems working well together, like teams of horses. Each is necessary to the other, none can be eliminated. Further, each one has its special *Functions* to perform; its *Controls*—both human and automatic—which enable the operator to control time, quality or quantity, as the case may be; its *Adjustments* for proper functioning, providing for wear and tear; and its simple means of *Replacement* or *Repair.*

Chapter V
What Each of the Seven Systems Must Accomplish

Having classified or grouped all the parts of the engine into the various engine systems, let us now consider what function each system must accomplish.

The Mechanical or Power System

This system, which accomplishes the harnessing of the power generated and delivers it in useful form, must be so designed that it can perform each of its separate functions exactly on time. That is, it must receive the explosive mixture, completely trap and compress it, hold it following its explosion, and release the spent gases, all correctly on time.

Valve Design and Timing Important

The intake valve, then, must be large enough, must open and close at the right moment and open sufficiently to bring in this charge. As most engines take in the fuel and air mixture by the suction of the piston, the opening of this valve would be useless much before the piston begins to move away from the head, and it should still be open when the piston passes the outer dead center so as to give the incoming mixture every opportunity to fill the cylinder completely.

To set this valve, then, we arrange the parts which control it so that they will start the opening from 7° before to 10° after dead center for mechanical intakes and about 20° after dead center for automatic intakes[1].

NOTE 1—Intake Valve Control and Timing

Intake valves are operated automatically, i.e., under spring control only, or mechanically by cam, push rod and tappet. All International Harvester tractor intake valves are of the latter kind. In the timing diagram Illust. 12 the automatically operated intake valve opens about 20° after dead center, which is later than a mechanically operated valve, because the spring does not permit the valve to open until its tension has been overcome by atmospheric pressure against cylinder vacuum. Likewise the closing is earlier with automatically operated valves, because the spring tension is greater than the difference between pressures in the cylinder and outside; while mechanically operated valves are held open as long as desired regardless of pressure.

Titan 10-20 and 15-30..	Opens 10° after inner dead center
	Closes 25° after outer dead center
International 15-30.....	Opens 10° after inner dead center
	Closes 25° after outer dead center
Mogul 8-16 and 10-20...	Opens 20° after inner dead center
	Closes 20° after outer dead center

The time of opening and closing of the intake valve varies with the speed at which the engine is designed to run. In a slow speed engine the angle is less; in a high speed engine it is more, in order to allow the air full time to crowd into the cylinder. We all know it takes time for air to get in motion and also for it to slow down when it is once in motion, so we design the opening and closing of the intake valve to agree with this law of Nature.

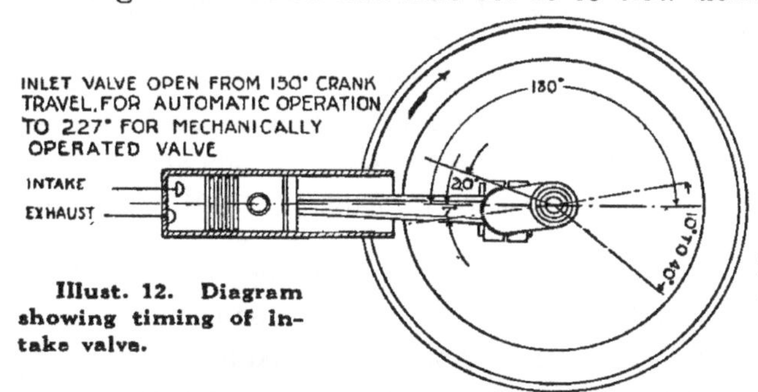

Illust. 12. Diagram showing timing of intake valve.

The exhaust valve must be open longer than during one complete stroke. To be sure all the exhaust gases get out within this time, the exhaust valve is opened before the outer dead center is reached, anywhere from 25 degrees to 45 degrees,[1] according to the speed of the engine, the lesser angle being used in slow speed, the greater angle in high speed. At the other end of the exhaust stroke, we again allow a small extra opening from 3 to 10 degrees, merely to be sure we do not shut this valve while there is still a chance to get rid of burned gases.

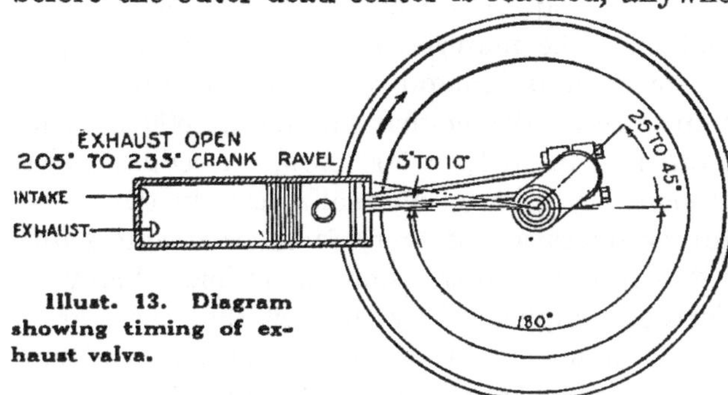

Illust. 13. Diagram showing timing of exhaust valve.

Adjustment screws and nuts are provided for setting these angles and they should be adjusted as occasion demands[2].

NOTE 1—Exhaust Valve Timing on I H C Tractors

Titan 10-20 and 15-30. } Opens 40° before dead center on power stroke
International 15-30.... } Closes at 5° after dead center on suction stroke
Mogul 8-16 and 10-20...Opens 40° before dead center on power stroke
Closes at 10° after dead center on suction stroke

NOTE 2—Valve Setting

If for any reason the valve setting has been disturbed or cam gears are to be replaced, care must be taken to restore setting to original position. On the Titan tractors turn the fly-wheel so that the marking Exh. O. on its rim is in the

Design Must Withstand Severe Shocks

Correct adjustment of the intake and exhaust valves enables us to explode a mixture under the most faborable conditions. The explosion affects all the other parts that go to make up the power system. These are the piston, the connecting rod with its two bearings, and the crankshaft with its bearings, flywheel, pulley, etc. A consideration of the conditions under which these parts do their work will show the immense value of the information we acquired while studying cylinder temperatures and pressures. Few people realize the heavy strains and stresses to which these parts are subjected in the every day work of a kerosene engine.

As an illustration, take a 20 H. P. 2-cylinder engine with 6.5 in. bore, 8 in. stroke and a speed of 500 r. p. m. Each piston has an area of 33.2 sq. in. We noted on page 19 an average explosion pressure on each square inch of about 250 lbs. It frequently goes well above this amount, but this explosion pressure is normal for the average engine.

Multiplying 250 lb. by 33.2 sq. in. we find that each piston head sustains a blow of 8,300 lb. The material and design to withstand one such blow of over 4 tons would demand serious consideration, but when one realizes that in a 2-cylinder engine running at 500 r. p. m. we get 500 such explosions in a minute, or 500 blows exceeding 4 tons each, taken by the pistons every minute, we realize clearly the necessity for the most careful consideration of every factor that enters into the design of the parts that receive and transmit such violent hammering. The problem is further complicated by the fact that these great and sudden pressures occur under conditions producing a piston temperature which has been found to be around 800° Fahr., or a temperature

---

highest vertical position. On the Mogul 8-16 and 10-20 the marking should be on the horizontal position toward rear of tractor.

After the fly-wheel has been placed in either of the positions mentioned above, turn the cam gear and shaft around until its two marked teeth mesh with the marked tooth on the small crankshaft pinion, and mesh gears in that position. With the cam shaft and gear in place and with the exhaust roller resting on the cam, adjust the valve rods so that the tappet arm will touch firmly the exhaust valve stem while valve is on its seat. To adjust intake valves, turn flywheel to same positions for the marking Int. O., and adjust valve rods in same manner as when adjusting exhaust valves.

In all cases remember, that it is more essential to have the exhaust valves close correctly than open correctly, although both are necessary.

Valves may be timed wrong because there is too much or no clearance between valve levers and valve stems. The correct clearance is not more than one thirty-second inch at point of greatest clearance between end of valve stem and that part of valve lever which comes in contact with valve stem.

high enough to show a dull cherry red in the dark. In an engine running with retarded spark this temperature may rise above 1000° Fahr. The importance of design, choice of material, treatment of material[1], to say nothing of high grade workmanship in the production of parts operating under such conditions as these, can hardly be overestimated. We begin to see now some of the reasons why there are so few successful kerosene engines on the market.

Good Bearings Essential

This 4-ton blow received by the piston is passed on to the connecting rod. The connecting rod transmits it to the crank pin, and the crank pin passes it on to the engine bearings and gears. The actual shock of the blow amounts to less and less as it is transmitted from part to part, being absorbed by the weight of the parts which take it up. Nevertheless, it is very evident that to absorb 500 such blows every minute requires a perfect fit of engine bearings, otherwise the blows will hammer out the bearing metal[2]. At the same time, the bearings must have a little play to allow for expansion by heat under load, and to permit a rolling film of oil. Well proportioned and well fitted bearings

NOTE 1—Heat Treatment

The method of heat treatment is discussed in connection with metals and processes on page 122.

NOTE 2—Testing and Adjusting Bearings

To determine if the connecting rod bearings are loose, remove the hand hole-plate on Mogul tractors or the crank case cover on Titan tractors, and turn fly-wheel until throw of crank is on top, place your hand on the connecting rod and crank and oscillate fly-wheel to determine lost motion. The connecting rod bearing should not be absolutely tight, but should have about $\frac{5}{1000}''$ to $\frac{8}{1000}''$ play in the bearings and from $\frac{1}{32}''$ to $\frac{1}{16}''$ side play.

If it is necessary to take up the connecting rod bearing, care should be taken not to remove too many liners, as this bearing must have a slight amount of play to operate properly. Be sure to replace the cap in its original position.

To determine if the main bearings are loose, place blocks under fly-wheel so that a lever can be applied on the under side of fly-wheel rim, and test by carefully bringing leverage enough to determine if crank shaft is loose in the bearings, by placing your hand on the fly-wheel hub and cap.

Great care should be taken not to spring the crank shaft out of line when testing the bearings.

To adjust a bearing remove a liner of the proper thickness from each side of the bearing. Replace the cap and bolt up tight. Now turn the fly-wheel and see that the engine turns as freely as before the adjustment was made. Extra liners are shipped with the engine. The liners in the bearings are of various thicknesses. When a liner is removed from a bearing save it. Whenever adjusting a bearing you may find it convenient to place one of these extra liners in the bearing joint and to remove one that is **slightly thicker;** in this manner very close adjustment can be made.

prevent the squeezing out of the oil film and the hammering out of the bearing metal, insuring maximum life for the engine parts.

Fuel and Carbureting System

The fuel supply for the engine, along with its controls, forms one of the most vital parts of the machine and is a source of satisfaction or dissatisfaction just in proportion as it is correctly designed for economical operation and to meet the requirements of the particular fuel used.

From a mechanical standpoint we must first have a supply tank, with necessary pipes leading to the mixer or carburetor.

The operator too often forgets that these parts need attention. All joints should be tight. Both tank and pipes require cleaning by the removal of slime, dirt, water and rust, which accumulate with time and cause serious trouble. Where pumps[1], check valves[2] or strainers[3] are a part of the system, they, too, should receive the care necessary for their proper operation.

What the Mixer Has To Do

The mixer or carburetor is, however, the device whose functions are of prime importance.

The mixer performs one of the most delicate functions of the entire engine; that of measuring out and preparing, almost instantly, a finely divided oil fuel—thoroughly mixed with sufficient air to make an explosive mixture. It must do it uniformly well, no matter what the variation in engine speed, no matter whether it requires a small or large quantity of fuel and under widely changing conditions of temperature and moisture in the surrounding air.

All this can be accomplished by a careful study of proportion of mixer parts and their arrangement. In engines of the type we are considering, air is drawn into the cylinder by the partial vacuum formed

NOTE 1—Care of Fuel Pump

Loose packing of fuel pump frequently causes leakage of fuel, which results in an insufficient supply to the mixer. Again, if the packing is too tight it will groove the pump plunger, causing leakage. Keep pump well packed, just tight enough to keep the mixer supplied with fuel. A good packing is made from asbestos string or cotton lamp wick covered with a mixture of flake graphite and lubricating oil.

NOTE 2—Pump Check Valves

A lack of fuel supply at the mixer may be caused by improper seating of the ball check valves in the fuel pump. Remove cap over the ball check so that the seats can be cleaned. If seats damaged reseat; if ball checks pitted or worn replace.

NOTE 3—Strainers

Somewhere in the fuel line is a strainer to remove foreign matter from fuel. On the Titan 10-20 there is also a strainer in the feed water line. Strainer should be taken apart frequently and cleaned, which can be accomplished by simply unscrewing the bottom from the strainer and shaking the dirt out of the strainer gauze.

when the piston recedes from the head. This inrush of air past the needle valve opening takes a certain amount of fuel with it. This amount is regulated by a needle valve which opens or closes the needle valve opening. The needle valve, therefore, regulates the quality of the mixture, and later we shall see that the governor regulates the quantity of the mixture.

For light and easily vaporized fuels such as gasoline the mixer or carburetor does not require the niceties of adjustment necessary in an apparatus designed to measure and divide the heavier, less easily vaporized kerosene.

Mixer Performs Delicate Functions

As an example of the delicate work required of a mixer, let us take a two-cylinder 20 h. p. engine running at 500 r. p. m., using kerosene and consuming at full load on the average .825 lb. for each delivered horse power.

Two cylinders, each developing 10 h. p. at a consumption of .825 lb. per h. p. require 8.25 lb. of kerosene per hour for each cylinder.

Good grade kerosene will weight 6.6 lb. per gallon. A gallon is equal to 231 cu. in., so 231 cu. in. of kerosene weigh 6.6 lb., or 35 cu. in. to each pound of fuel.

8.25 lb. of fuel would equal 288.75 cu. in. of kerosene. This amount of fuel must therefore be divided up each hour by the carburetor into as many equal parts as there are explosions.

With 500 revolutions we have 250 explosions each minute and 250 times 60 or 15,000 per hour in each cylinder.

8.25 lb. of fuel divided into 15,000 explosions means .0005 lb. for each explosion, and 288.75 cu. in. an hour makes .019 of a cu. in. taken into each cylinder every suction stroke, when the engine is developing rated h. p. Imagine a pound of kerosene divided into ten thousand equal parts. Six of those parts would be a little too much fuel for one charge in our engine. At smaller loads these proportions are correspondingly smaller.

If two carburetors feed to the two cylinders, each one must measure this quantity out carefully 250 times in a minute and if one carburetor has to furnish the fuel, this measuring is done 500 times in a minute.

It must be evident that the design of a carburetor to measure these minute quantities accurately, and at such a rate, requires thorough knowledge of all the qualities of the fuel to be handled, as well as ability to provide mechanical means for handling it under all conditions of engine operation.

Description and Operations of Titan 10-20 Mixer

Starting and Operation

Prime the engine with gasoline, using spring bottom oil can, inserting nozzle as shown in Illust. 14. One fuel needle valve handles both the kerosene and gasoline, and the switch from one fuel to the other is made by a switch lever. Set the fuel valve by this lever to admit gasoline if starting on gasoline, or kerosene if starting on kerosene. Turn air controlling damper with opening as required for the necessary air supply. Keep water supply turned off until engine is started and shows by pounding or bumping that water is needed. Turn flywheel until explosions occur, then fully open air damper for good running and set the needle valve at the proper point. When engine is warmed up (after about two or three minutes unless weather is very cold) turn the two-way valve so that engine operates on kerosene, and when pounding or bumping occurs, open water valve until just enough water is admitted to stop the pounding.

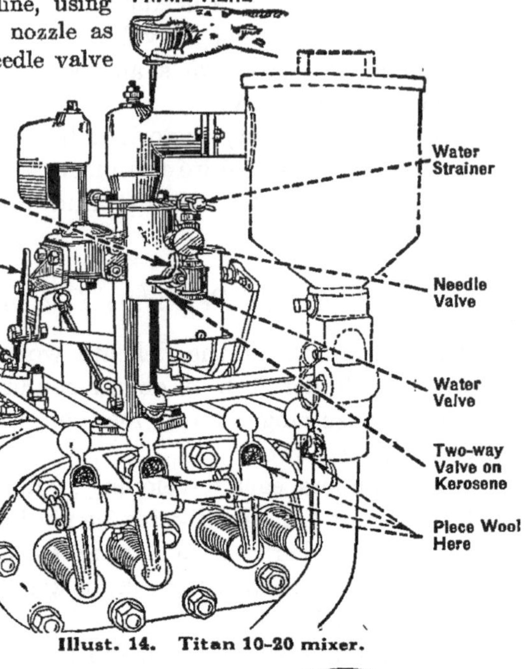

Illust. 14. Titan 10-20 mixer.

Description of Mixer

The mixer fuel cup, water connection and proportional air valve cage are shown in partial section in Illust. 15.

The fuel cup (B), water connection (C) and the proportional air valve cage (D) are shown as mounted on the mixer body, which is a straight passage casting at the lower end of which is fitted the throttle valve (E) on its shaft (F). (Illust. 15A.)

The governor adjusting lever connects at (G) and the spring (H) always tends to hold the valve open and takes up any lost motion of governor joints.

The travel of the throttle valve (E) is limited by the "OPENING" and "CLOSING" stop screws which are carefully adjusted at the factory.

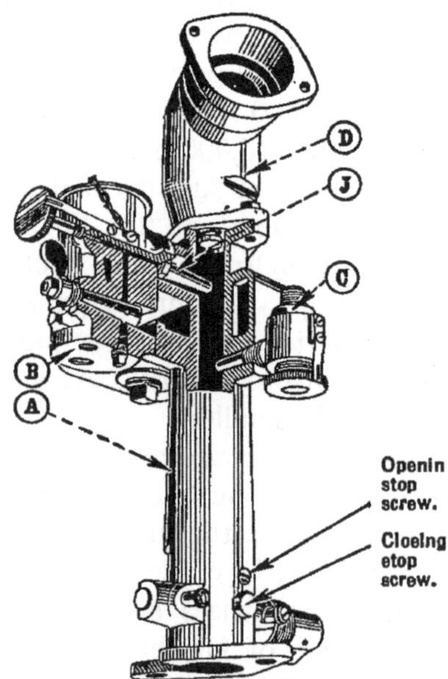

Illust. 15. Titan 10-20 mixer assembled with mixer fuel cup, water connection and proportional air valve cage in partial section.

Cast onto mixer body is a reservoir (I) to hold gasoline for starting the engine.

The fuel cup (B) bolts against the mixer body with its fuel nozzle (J) projecting through and to about the center of the mixer air passage.

The needle valve (K) when closed screws firmly against the seat of fuel nozzle (J) and is opened to admit the amount of fuel required for the load on the engine.

The fuel cup carries a two-way valve (L) controlled by handle (M) and which enables operator to use gasoline or kerosene. When handle (M) is vertical as shown in illustration, the fuel supply is from the gasoline reservoir; when turned to a horizontal position, gives kerosene connection. (O) shows cored holes and drilled ports for conducting fuel to nozzle (J).

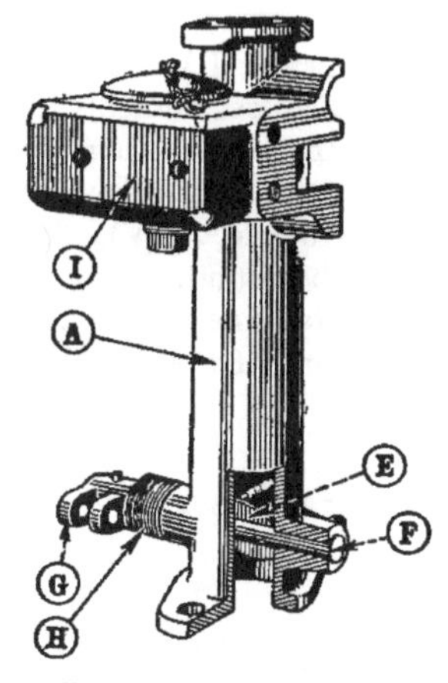

Illust. 15a. Titan 10-20 mixer body casting with throttle valve in section.

How Mixer Parts Work:

When air, by the suction of the moving piston, is drawn through the mixer passages it causes the proportional valve (T) Illust. 15D to move along the stem (W) until the air passage area at the throat of mixer is great enough to supply the required air to cylinder. The air required is determined by the position in which the governor holds the throttle valve (E) Illust. 15A. At the same time air is drawn past the proportional valve, a lesser quantity of air is drawn through the ports (P) Illust 15C in the water connection. When the quantity of air becomes great enough, it causes the disk (Q) to unseat the needle valve, and allows water to flow into the mixer. This flow of water is thus automatically made proportional to the air supply to engine cylinder. When the load is heavy the water supply is large, while on light load the water supply is cut off because enough air does not pass disk (Q) to cause it to move. By adjusting nut (P), the tension of spring (R) can be altered to allow valve and disk to move easily or hard. In this way the water supply is controlled by and mixed with the air exactly as the fuel is handled, except that on light load the water supply is cut off entirely.

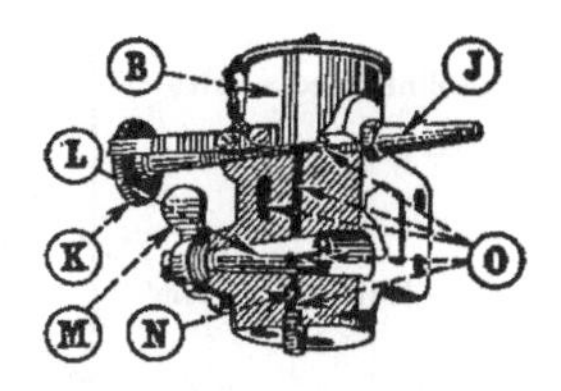

Illust. 15b. Titan 10-20 mixer fuel cup in section.

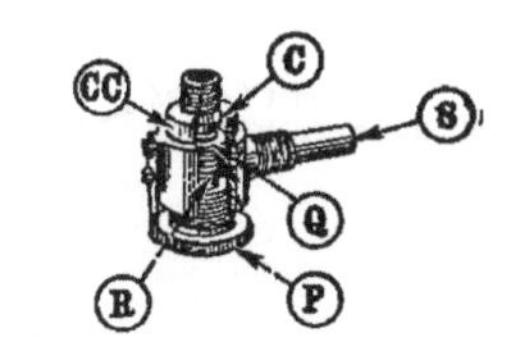

Illust 15c. Titan 10-20 water valve in section.

(C) Illust. 15C, is the water valve which screws into the mixer casing.

The water supply pipe connection is made at the top of this valve and the pipe is equipped with strainer and drain cock. (S) is the long nozzle which conveys water and air into mixer passage. Small air ports are cast into the water valve body at (CC). The water supply is cut off by a needle on which is carried the disk valve (Q). This needle valve is held to its seat by

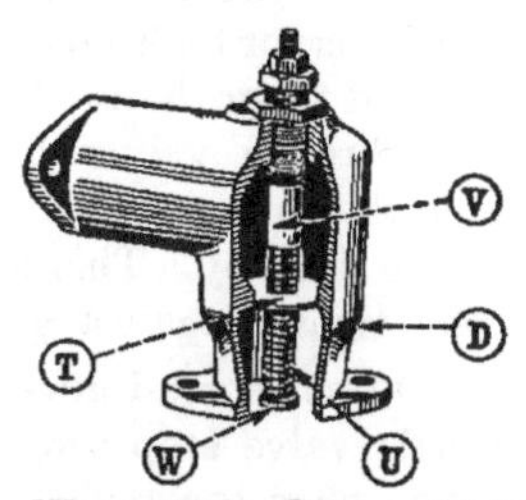

Illust. 15d. Titan 10-20 proportional air valve cage in section.

the spring (R). (P) is a regulating nut which adjusts tension of spring (R).

Damper controls the admission of hot and cold air or both, as desired.

In the main port leading down to mixer is a spring-sustained valve (T) which can be adjusted for position near the restricted neck of manifold by screw (W) and stop sleeve (V). By these two parts also the desired tension to the spring (U) may be found.

Gasoline enters two-way valve at end while kerosene enters valve at (N); only one of the passages is open at the same time.

Operation of Mixer on International and Titan 15-30 Tractor

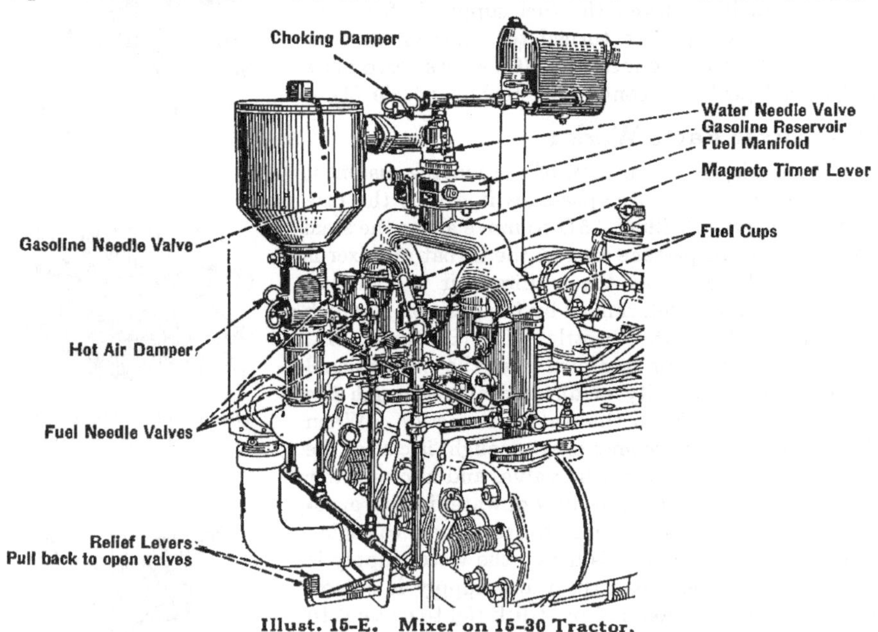

Illust. 15-E. Mixer on 15-30 Tractor.

The mixer consists of a manifold and four independent fuel cups and mixer bodies, each carrying its own throttle valve. These throttle valves must be adjusted to close at the same time so each has its independent governor rod. To adjust, push governor balls apart until governor collar is about 3/16" from the top of its travel and held them there. Back governor rod nuts away from throttle valve lever and close throttle valves firmly by hand, then adjust governor rod nut to just touch the cross rod in throttle lever and hold nut with cotter pin. Set each throttle lever in this way. This adjustment is very important. See that springs hold throttle levers tightly against governor rod nuts.

Do not spread governor balls so far apart while making this setting that the throttle valve stop screw will be subjected to the pressure of the governor ball springs when the engine is shut down. Governor collar should be from 1/8" to 3/16" from extreme top of its travel but throttle valves must open wide enough to ensure engine having full power.

The air cleaner is connected to the heating drum around exhaust pipe and can be used for hot or cold air as desired by turning damper at desired position.

As a general rule, use hot air as little as possible when pulling the load as heat reduces the power and efficiency of the engine.

How the Mogul 10-20 Mixer Does Its Work

Briefly speaking, this mixer consists of a vertical passage in which are located two dampers and into which protrude three needle valves. The principle on which it operates is the injecting of fuel, by the use of a nozzle, into a swift moving current of air. As this air passes the fuel nozzle, it sucks out the fuel and in doing so, the fuel is very finely atomized and partly vaporized. You will note that the mixer is located above the cylinder where gravity assists in carrying the atomized and vaporized mixture directly into the cylinder. There are no abrupt turns or long horizontal passages in which the fuel may become condensed before the mixture reaches the cylinder. The air passage is slightly cut down just above the kerosene mixer by what is called a choker. This choker increases the velocity of the air past the kerosene needle valve, which assists in breaking up the kerosene and results in more complete combustion. The choker is not necessary above the gasoline valve because gasoline is a lighter fuel.

The air is heated before it reaches the needle valves at the point (B), Illust. 15F. The heating of the air passage by the exhaust gases which circulate around the mixer at (B) is regulated by warm air damper (Illust. 15G). The heating of the air as it passes through the upper part of the mixer is not sufficient to materially affect its volume but just enough

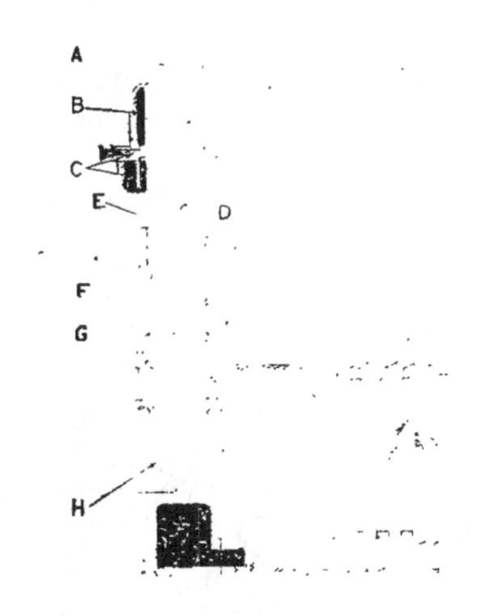

Illust. 15f. Sectional view of Mogul 10-20 mixer and cylinder.

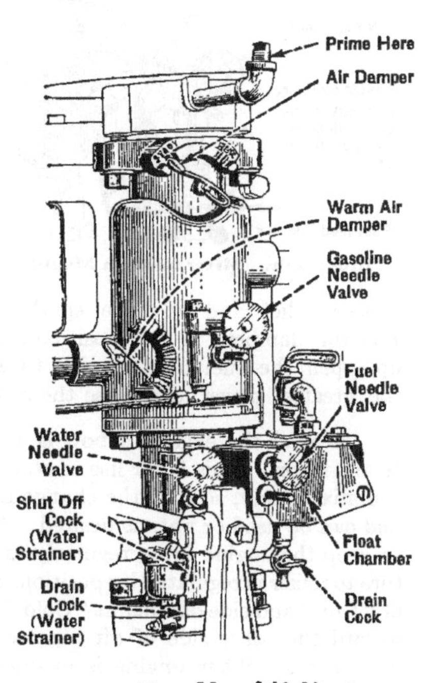

Illust. 15g. Mogul 10-20 mixer.

to assist in more effectively breaking up or vaporizing the lower grade of fuels.

The damper at (A) is used to restrict the passage and thus increase the velocity of air through the mixer when starting the tractor. The damper (F) is controlled by the governor. This damper regulates the charge in proportion to the load.

Operating Mogul 10-20 Mixer

Open the gasoline needle valve about three-quarters of a turn. A little gasoline used in priming the engine will insure quicker starting. Remove priming plug (Illust. 15C). Put air damper in position marked "Start." After engine is started, move air damper to position marked "Run." When the engine has been started on gasoline and the cylinder well warmed up, change over to kerosene or any other fuel by opening the fuel needle valve and closing the gasoline needle valve. Do not open the water needle valve until after the engine is running and you hear a bumping or knocking in the cylinder. Use only enough water to eliminate this pounding.

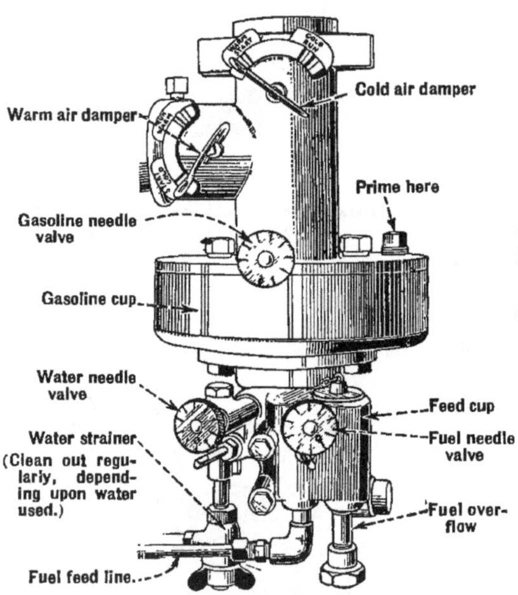

Illust. 15h. Mixer used on Mogul 8-16.

Operation and Starting of the Mixer on the Mogul 8-16

The principle of the Mogul 8-16 mixer is the same as that of the Mogul 10-20 mixer. (See page 30.)

Put the air dampers in position marked "Start" (Illust. 15H). Prime the air pipe with a small quantity of gasoline and open the gasoline needle valve. After adjusting relief and advance spark levers, turn flywheel until engine is started. Put the dampers in the position marked "Run." After the cylinder is warmed up, open the fuel needle valve to a point where the engine runs best and gives the greatest power, and close the gasoline needle valve.

Around the exhaust elbow is a jacket for the purpose of furnishing warm air to the mixer. This is for use in starting (in cold weather) to more quickly heat up the mixer body, so that the change from gasoline to other fuel can be made sooner and can be used or not, as desired. The correct amount of warm air is just enough to keep the engine firing regularly and is regulated by air dampers. Air temperature to mixer is regulated by positions of hot and cold air dampers. With top damper at "Run" and side damper at "Cold" all cold air is supplied. Moving these dampers toward the other side of air pipe will supply warm air in proportion to damper movements. When engine is in operation, adjust fuel needle valves until engine develops full power and operates properly.

The Ignition System

The function of the ignition system is to provide a controlled means of firing the charge of fuel and air mixture.

Various means have been used in the past for this purpose, yielding knowledge which, owing to its value in showing development and requirements, is here reviewed.

Must Withstand High Temperature

It is well to realize something of the exacting requirements of an ignition apparatus. First, the parts within the cylinder are subjected to the intense heats produced during ignition and burning of the charge —2000° to 4000° Fahr., and to sudden changes during each cycle, ranging from this exceedingly high temperature down to the cool temperature of the incoming charge of air.

Must Work Instantaneously

Next, consider the time required to complete this work. Take an engine running 600 r.p.m., and using spark plug ignition. It makes one revolution in 1/10th of a second. If we ignite the charge 30° ahead of center, there being 360° in each revolution, the time of ignition would be 30/360ths. This allows only 1/12th of the time required for one revolution or 1/120th of a second for the charge to burn and create its pressure within the cylinder—a very short time even for an engine of moderate speed. In that time the spark must jump between the points, the flame start and spread throughout the cylinder to all its corners, if best results are to be obtained. If the cylinder has irregular pockets, the flame must follow into them requiring more time than if there were no pockets. This accounts for the fact that L-head and T-head engines act either slower or with less power than valve-in-the-head types.

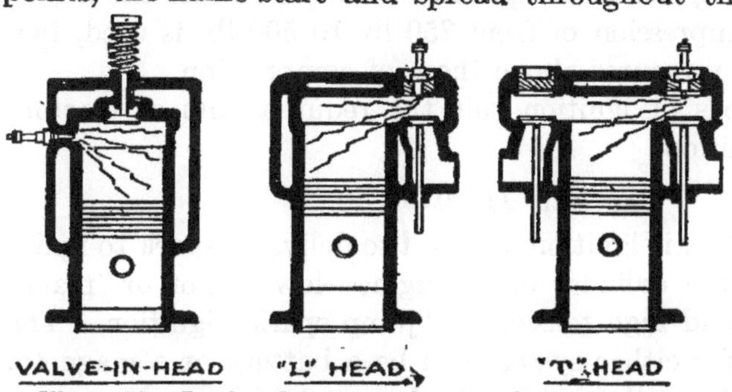

Illust. 16. Sectional diagram showing the construction of L-head, T-head, and valve-in-head types of motors.

Naked Flame Ignition

The first method of firing was by igniting the mixture with a naked flame. This flame was easily and often blown out, so the engine required constant attention from the operator. The uncertainty of action quickly put this system aside in favor of hot tube ignition.

Hot tube ignition consists of a piece of pipe closed at one end and screwed into the cylinder so that the inside of the tube can receive a part of the burnable mixture during compression. This tube was heated by means of a flame from the outside, thus producing the heat necessary to ignite the charge, but without the danger of blowing out the flame except in windy weather. The control had, therefore, been much improved but permanence and close regulation were still lacking.

Hot Bulb Ignition

Further refinement resulted in the design of the hot bulb ignition, which operates much the same as the hot tube. Its main weakness consisted in the time required to get the engine under way—from six to fifteen minutes to get up to speed without load and longer to get to the point of taking full load.

Operation necessitating the open flame of a gasoline torch to start and get under way is a distinctly undesirable system when frequent starts and stops are made, where widely varying loads are frequent, where fires are made possible, or where close regulation is desirable.

Ignition by Compression

Compression ignition was introduced with the Diesel and semi-Diesel types of engine and consists in a reduction of the compression space to a degree where sufficient pressure is produced and heat enough generated to cause complete burning of the fuel injected into the highly compressed air. Compression of from 250 lb. to 500 lb. is used, fuel being injected under pressures above those of compression.

None of the types of ignition suit the requirements of tractors as well as electric ignition.

Electric Ignition

Two systems of electric ignition are used to deliver a spark to ignite the fuel mixture in the cylinder of an engine—low tension or "make-and-break" ignition and high tension or "jump spark" ignition. The source of electricity for either system can be a battery or a magneto. Low tension means low voltage; high tension means high voltage.

Low Tension Ignition

The low tension system requires an ignitor which must have some mechanical means of opening or breaking apart the ignitor points to produce a spark gap. To get a hot spark at this gap requires a large volume of current and a low pressure or a low tension. This kind of current requires only a primary winding in the spark coil or magneto. Illust. 16A shows a low tension battery system with primary coil.

High Tension Ignition

The high tension or jump spark system always uses a spark plug which has a permanent spark gap that the spark must jump across. The current produced by a low tension system while of large volume does not have enough pressure to jump across this spark gap. To produce the high pressure necessary we add a secondary winding to the primary winding of the spark coil or magneto and thus induce in this secondary winding and circuit a voltage high enough to bridge the spark gap of a spark plug. This secondary winding makes a high tension or a high voltage system of a low tension system.

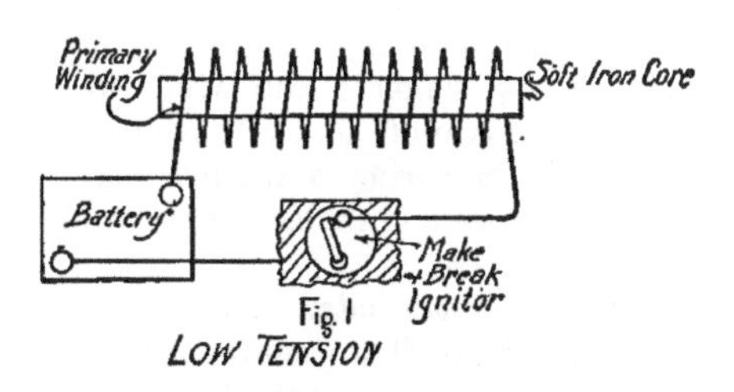

Illust. 16a. Low tension system. Note it has only a primary winding in tha circuit. In Illust. 16b by adding a secondary winding we secure a high tension system.

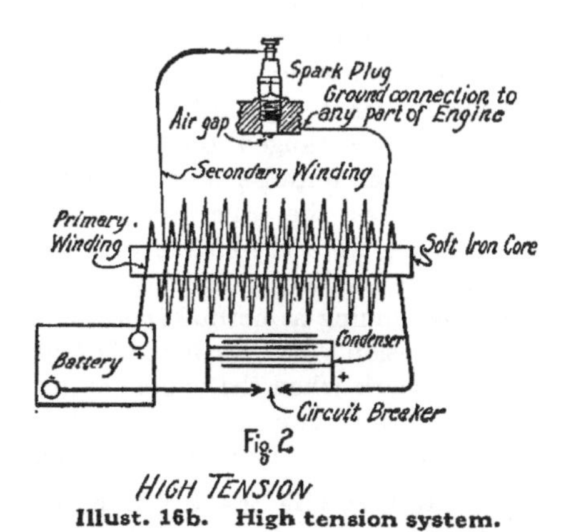

Illust. 16b. High tension system.

A "Good" Spark

By a "good" spark we ordinarily mean a large, hot spark. Igniting the charge in a cylinder may be likened to kindling a fire. By using plenty of kindling and a hot blow torch flame all over it at once, the fire would burn much quicker than if it were lighted with an ordinary match. Just so with lighting a fuel mixture in the engine cylinder. A big, hot, fat spark that will make the mixture burn as fast as possible is most desirable.

Why Early Ignition is Necessary

The only reason internal combustion engines must be operated with an early spark is in order to give the mixture time to thoroughly burn. We have not yet developed a spark so hot and so big within the cylinder that burning will be practically instantaneous. With present ignition sparks, flame propagation is so slow that unless the mixture is ignited a long way ahead of dead center it will still be burning when the exhaust valve opens, and a great deal of fuel will be thrown out of the exhaust valve unburned. Excessive heat and loss of power also result.

Care and Operation of Ignition Systems

Low Tension and High Tension Magnetos

Two types of magnetos for generating electrical energy to produce a spark are used, oscillating and rotary types. Oscillating magnetos are low tension; rotary can be either high or low tension. As a general rule high tension or jump spark ignition is used on the higher speed engines, and the low tension or make-and-break ignition is used on the slow speed engines. Formerly in all cases batteries were used for starting, and when the engine reached proper speed the magneto was switched in and then the engine ran on the magneto. Now some means is provided in the magneto itself, so that practically the same spark is given when the engine is turned over slowly as when it is running at normal or full speed. In the high tension rotary type of magneto this is taken care of by an impulse starter. In the oscillating type of magneto this is taken care of by retarding the spark.

The impulse starter on a high tension rotary magneto is a mechanical contrivance which temporarily locks the armature of the magneto and winds up a spring, and is arranged so that the impulse starter will trip off about 3° after dead center. When impulse starter is released or tripped, the spring is at such tension that it revolves the armature at practically the same speed as the armature would be revolving were the engine running at its normal speed.

On the oscillating magneto the time of tripping is made later than when the engine is running at normal speed, and by doing this the oscillator springs are at a greater tension when oscillator is tripped, so that the magneto actually produces a better spark when the engine is just turned over slowly for starting than when the engine is running at its normal speed with the spark advanced. Tripping of the oscillator for starting is about dead center of crankshaft.

Always Retard the Spark When Starting

It is necessary to use a late or retraded spark when starting, as the engine is moving very slowly, and if the mixture ignites before the piston comes to dead center, then the rotation of the engine will be reversed, as there is not enough momentum in the fly-wheel to carry it over dead center putting heavy strain on bearings and crank shaft. A retarded spark is also a hotter spark than spark in the advanced position. This hotter spark is necessary because, when starting the engine, the fuel mixture is not well balanced, as the speed is slow and the engine is cold.

Types of Magnetos Used on I H C Tractors

The high tension rotary magneto with impulse starter furnishes current for jump spark ignition on Titan 10-20 and 15-30, Mogul 10-20 and International 15-30 tractors. The oscillating low tension magneto supplies current for make-and-break ignition on the Mogul 8-16.

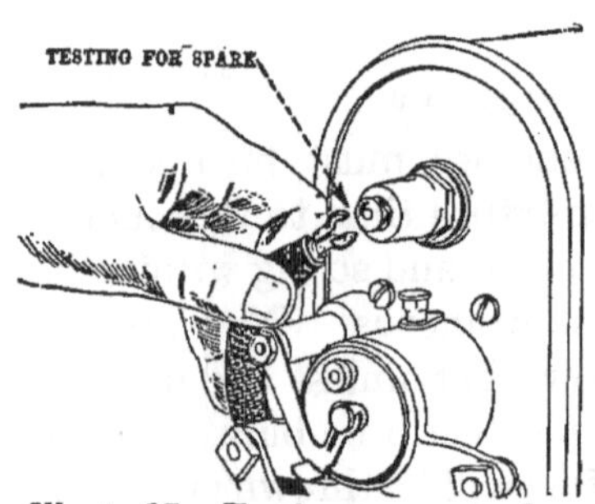

Illust. 17. Testing magneto for spark.

Testing for Spark

High tension magnetos may be tested for spark by removing cable and holding cable connection about $\frac{1}{32}$ inch from end of binding post; on turning the fly-wheel, a spark will result if magneto is in good condition. A good fat spark should result at all times if impulse starter operates.

Ignition System of the Titan 10-20 Tractor

High Tension Rotary Magneto with Impulse Starter

The magneto is driven clockwise (looking at it from impulse starter end) from the shaft through a heavy coil spring and runs as a rotary type.

Impulse Starter

For starting the engine, the armature of the magneto is prevented from rotating by the pawl B engaging the notch A when the lever C is released while the shaft revolves through a part of a revolution, increasing the tension in the coil spring.

When the point D strikes the lug on the side of the pawl B lifting it out of the notch A, the tension of the coil spring causes the armature to spring forward quickly and produces a spark.

This process is repeated until speed of shaft reaches such a point that the force of point D striking the pawl B throws it up far enough to permit the lever C to lock it.

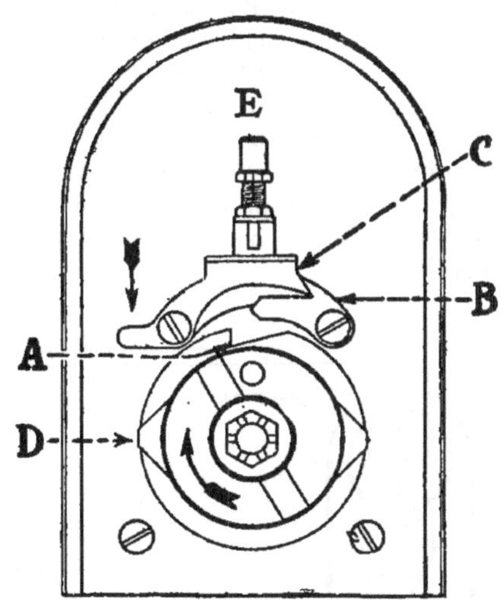

Illust. 18. Magneto diagram showing impulse starter hooked up or out of action and magneto operating as rotary.

Timing of Magneto

In case the magneto has been removed from its stand, or it is desired to check its timing, place magneto in its place on top of the engine crank case and fasten securely to bracket, but with coupling loose. Turn engine until crank pin for the left hand piston is a little above (about 3°) the dead center nearest the cylinder on the compression stroke. Dead center occurs when mark "center" across face of flywheel is at highest vertical position, but compression stroke must be carefully noted.

Set magneto lever A, Illust. 19, in retard position as illustrated.

(a) Unhook copper connector T 53 and turn up.

(b) Unscrew brass nut No. 79 until breaker box cover No. 95 can be pulled out and taken off.

(c) Turn the magneto until contact brush B in distributor touches segment on left hand side (this can be seen through the window in center of distributor block) and the platinum breaker points P are just being separated by the cam C and roller R.

(d) Connect magneto couplings securely together with cap screw, being careful to see that neither engine nor magneto is moved from the above settings.

(e) Replace breaker box and distributor cover and put back all connections, being sure that all parts are dry and clean.

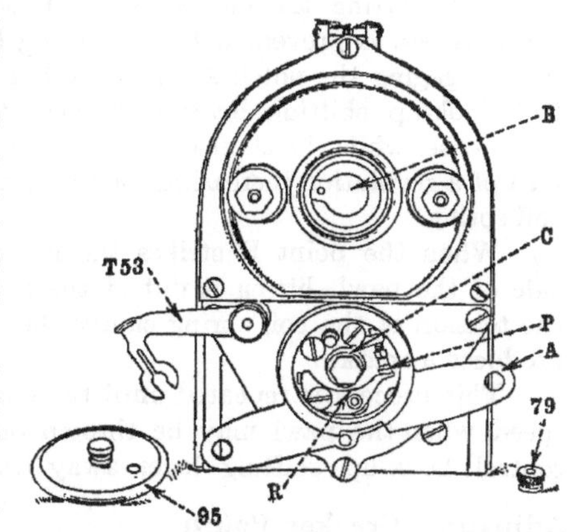

Illust. 19. Cover removed from distributor box and breaker box showing distributor brush and breaker points.

(f) Connect wires as shown in diagram (Illust. 20).

NOTE—Breaker points P Illust. 19, will wear slowly and should be adjusted so that maximum opening is not much over $\frac{1}{64}$ inch. Use guage furnished with magneto to make adjustment.

CAUTION—Impulse starting device should trip magneto when engine is from 0 to 3 degrees above compression stroke center. If the magneto does not trip at this point when above instructions are followed, it must be reset until tripping of point is correct.

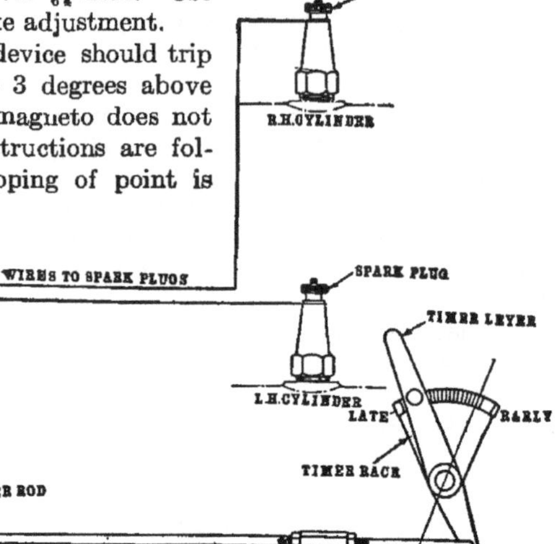

Illust. 20. Wiring diagram for Titan 10-20 tractor.

Ignition System of the Mogul 10-20 Tractor

High Tension Rotary Magneto with Impulse Starter

Description of Magneto (Illust. 22)

The magneto is driven counter clockwise (looking at it from impulse starter end) from the shaft C through a heavy coil spring and runs as a rotary type.

For starting the engine, the armature of the magneto is prevented from rotating by the pawl engaging the notch A when the hand control hook-up shifting lever is pushed toward crank case, while the shaft C revolves through a part of a revolution increasing the tension in the coil spring.

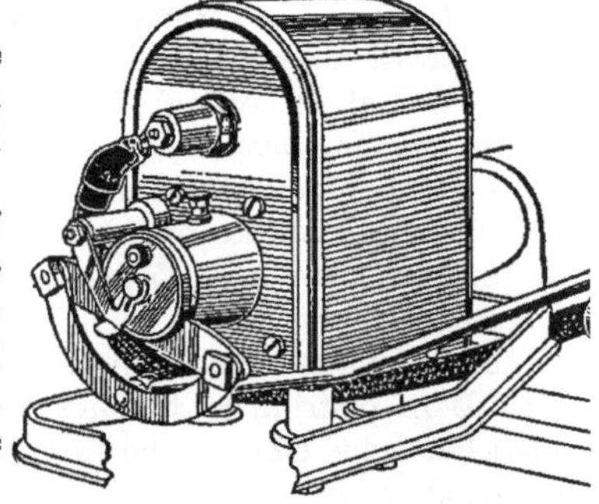

Illust. 21. Magneto in place on Mogul 10-20.

When the point B strikes the lug on the side of the pawl, lifting it out of the notch A, the tension of the coil spring causes the armature to spring forward quickly and produces a spark.

This process is repeated until the engine has attained at least half its regular speed, when the pawl may be thrown out of operation by pulling magneto hand control hook-up shifting lever away from crank case.

Adjusting Breaker Points

Breaker points E will wear slowly and should be adjusted so that maximum opening is not much over $\frac{1}{64}$ inch. Use gauge furnished with magneto to make adjustment.

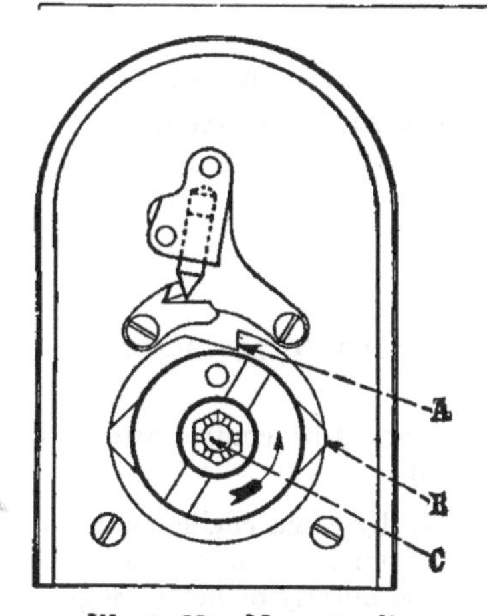

Illust. 22. Magneto diagram showing impulse starter hooked up or out of action.

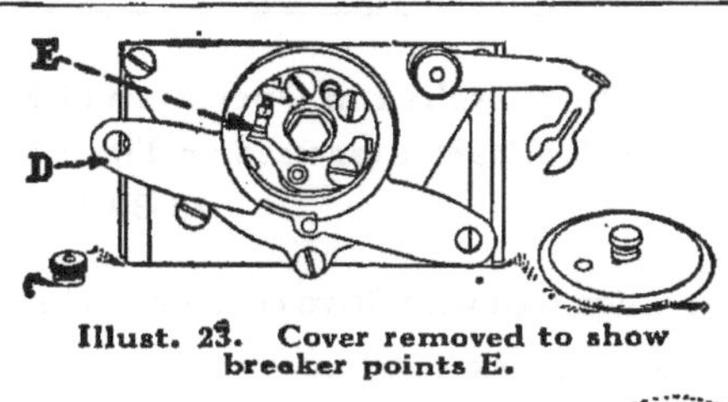

Illust. 23. Cover removed to show breaker points E.

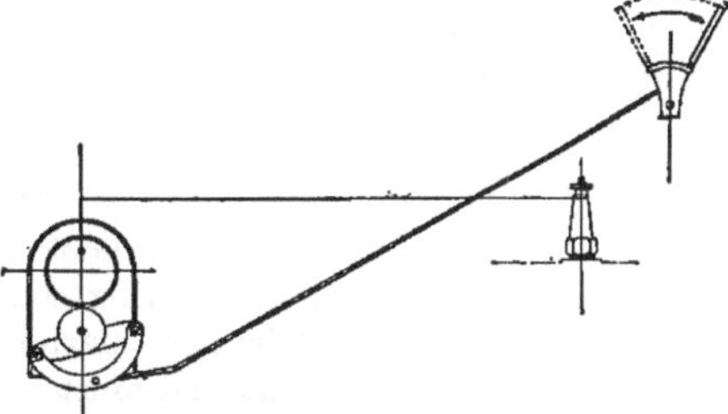
Illust. 24. Wiring diagram for Mogul 10-20.

CAUTION—Impulse starting device should trip magneto when engine is from *0 to 3 degrees above compression stroke center.* If magneto does not trip at this point it must be reset until it is correct.

Ignition System of the International 15-30 Tractor

High Tension Rotary Magneto with Impulse Starter

The magneto used on the I H C 15-30 is a high tension magneto with impulse starter, similar to the one used on the Titan 10-20 and Mogul 10-20, except that it has a four-cylinder distributor instead of a one or two-cylinder distributor. Like the Mogul 10-20, it operates counter-clockwise. The operation of the impulse starter, timing and all other points discussed under the ignition system of Mogul and Titan 10-20 tractors, apply also to this ignition system for the International 15-30.

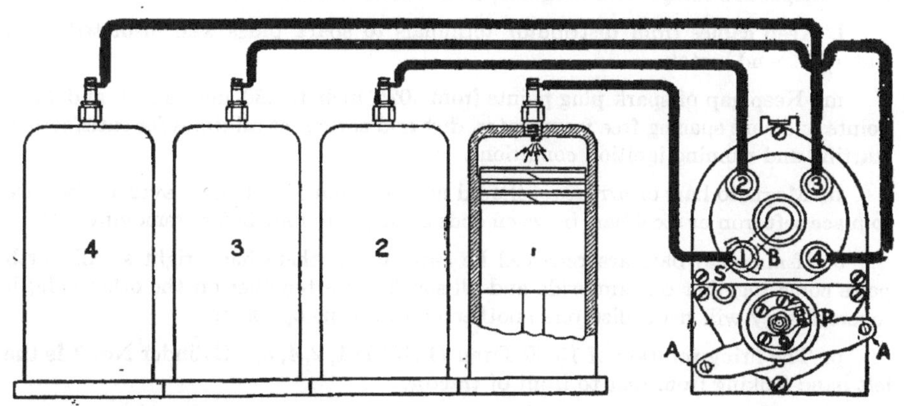

Illust. 26. Wiring diagram for Titan and International 15-30, — Firing rotation, cylinder 1, 2, 4, 3. Cylinder No. 1 is the left hand looking from rear to front of tractor.

Points to be Watched in Operation of High Tension Rotary Magneto with Impulse Starter (as used on Titan and Mogul 10-20, International 15-30 tractors)

a. Align well with drive coupling and shaft.

b. Keep bracket and magneto tight on engine.

c. Time so impulse starter will trip when crank is about 3° past inner dead center of compression stroke.

d. Then adjust spark advance connection between armature control arm and advance lever so full retard and advance can be obtained.

e. Impulse starter should always hook up automatically when engine is about up to speed, if it does not, then spring controlling hook-up is too stiff and must be adjusted. Then again, if impulse starter hooks up too quickly or before engine is under way, spring is too weak and must be adjusted to act as stated above.

f. In starting, trip impulse starter, put spark advance lever in retard position. This will prevent a kick back and reduce strains on engine that otherwise would occur with spark lever advanced. Engine speed is too slow at starting for advanced spark.

g. Distributor brush must be on or in good contact on distributor segment at both early and late spark positions.

h. Movable breaker arm action must be free, and stationary breaker arm must be well insulated and tight in housing so that the proper action is obtained to secure a good spark. The gap between breaker points should always be $\frac{1}{64}$ inch or not to exceed .016 to .018 inch.

i. Keep distributor brush and race free from carbon dust and dirt and keep breaker points clean, even and smooth.

j. Oil sparingly and keep clean to prevent short circuits. Use a light oil.

k. Don't allow tools or any hardened steel in contact with magnetos. Don't try to magnetize things from magneto, that will kill its life.

l. Keep cables from distributor terminals to spark plugs well insulated from water, oils and metals.

m. Keep gap of spark plug points from .025 inch to .30 inch apart and keep points and core spacing free from water, dirt and carbon at all times for satisfactory starting and running ignition conditions.

n. Magneto bars or armature should not be removed. If they ever are be sure to place soft iron or steel bars between ends of magneto bars before removing.

o. If magneto bars are removed be sure to put them back right so all north poles come together on same side and all south come together on the other side; if reversed they will neutralize one another and prevent operation.

p. The firing rotation of 15-30 Titan (1916) is 1, 2, 4, 3, Cylinder No. 1 is the left hand looking from rear to front of tractor.

15-30 International the same as above.

Testing Spark Plugs

To test a spark plug, remove plug from cylinder head and place in position on cylinder, as shown in Illust. 27, with a piece of paper the thickness of an ordinary business card between the points. Set trip on magneto for starting and crank engine over slowly. If the plug is in in good condition a spark will occur between the points and a small hole will be burned through the paper. Spark plug points should be set about .025″ or .030″ apart.

Caution.—Do not screw plugs in too tight or they will burn in so it will be impossible to remove them without ruining them.

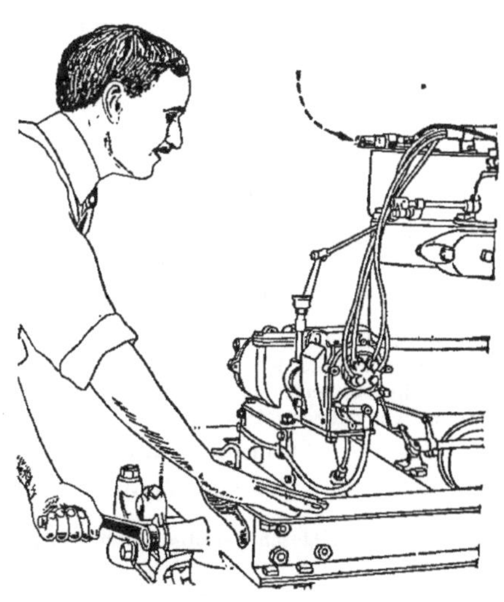

Illust. 27. Testing a spark plug.

Care of Spark Plugs

The gap should be from .025″ to .030″ or the thickness of gauge on screw driver sent with tools.

The plugs should be inspected from time to time and the pocket between the core and the outer shell should be kept free from carbon accumulation by use of wire brush. Only in extreme cases take plug apart.

Be sure all joints in plug are tight, as a leak in plug joints will cause plug to heat up and become damaged.

Ignition System of the Mogul 8-16 Tractor

Electrical Energy Furnished by Low Tension Oscillating Magneto

The oscillating magneto used on the Mogul 8-16 requires very little attention. It should be oiled sparingly with a good grade of sewing machine oil, not oftener than once a week and absolutely should not be tampered with.

Magneto may be tested for spark by taking cable from ignitor and holding in contact with side of ignitor movable electrode next to connection rod; on turning the fly-wheel, the lever will be pushed away from its position and, when this movement takes place, a spark will result if magneto is in good condition.

Wire Off—See that magneto connection cable is in proper contact and that clip holding cable to electrode is securely fastened to electrode. (See Illust. 28).

The ignitor trip rod should be so adjusted that there is $\frac{1}{16}$″ to $\frac{3}{32}$″ between head of rod and ignitor lever when magneto lever bar and ignitor trip are not in contact with each other. This is shown in Illust. 28.

The ignitor should be kept clean and in good condition. It will require least attention if fuel needle valves and cylinder lubricator are adjusted properly at all times.

Illust. 28. Magneto and Ignitor Mechanism.

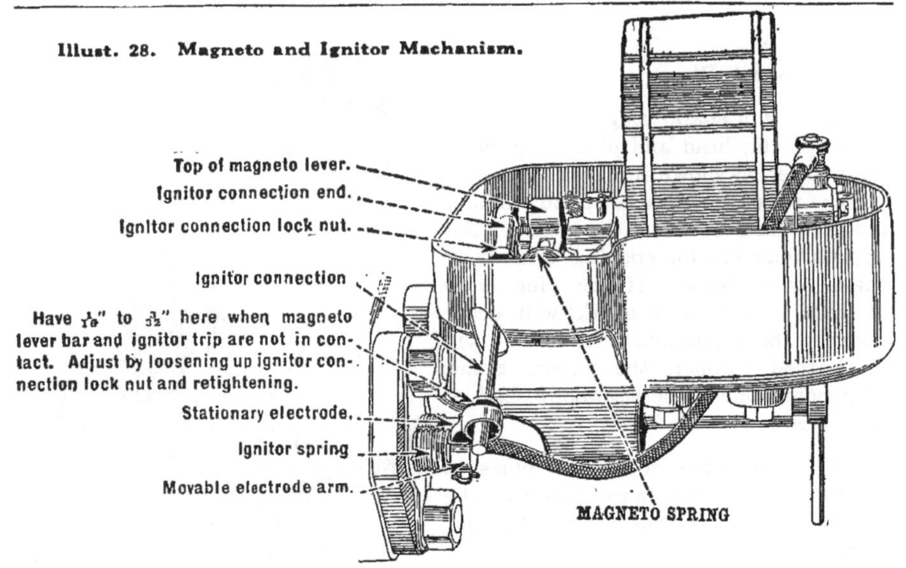

Points to be Watched in the Operation of Low Tension Oscillating Magneto (As used on the Mogul 8-16 Tractor)

(a) Attach and time so magneto will trip at starting (magneto tripping retarded) when crank is on or close to inner dead center of compression stroke.

(b) Oscillating magnetos, when tripping, do not produce spark in engine until trip finger returns after being released and strikes arm on movable electrode, opening ignitor points, so the time elapsing between tripping and the parting of ignitor points as on Webster-Horse Shoe and Accurate magnetos should be about 8° earlier, considering crank position, than the time desired to have spark occur in that particular engine, and with an oscillating Bosch magneto tripping must occur about 12° earlier, because springs on Bosch are longer, consequently slower acting.

(c) Although magneto trip timing may be adjusted right, the opening of ignitor points may not occur at right time, as indicated above, unless ignitor trip adjusting screw, rod or hook rod, as the case may be, are adjusted to open ignitor points as indicated in Sec. IV, a and b, page 44.

(d) To use batteries with oscillating magnetos, set ignitor trip adjusting screw, rod or hook rod to hold ignitor points apart not less than $\frac{1}{16}$ in., then when trip rod moves trip finger away from trip adjusting screw or rods, ignitor points will come together, setting up the circuit through battery and coil, filling the coil, making ready for spark, producing ignition conditions as satisfactory as with regular ignitor.

(e) For a good, hot spark trip rod must come in contact with magneto trip finger when crank has traveled in on compression stroke about 45° or 50°.

(f) Keep tight on bracket; keep clean; don't over-oil; keep contact and timing correct; one wire only from magneto terminal to stationary electrode; keep in good alignment; don't abuse by careless handling.

Miscellaneous Ignition Systems

There are so many International Harvester internal combustion engines and tractors in use everywhere that, as a matter of information, we give herewith suggestions for the care and operation of types of ignition systems other than used at present on International Harvester tractors.

I. Battery and Coil—Make-and-Break

1. Batteries

(a) Select dry cells of good strength.

(b) Keep dry and pack well for long life of cells.

(c) Keep cells insulated from one another. Never let zinc covering of one cell touch zinc covering of another cell; it will kill batteries.

(d) Cells are more active when warm than cold.

2. Wiring

(a) Always have wires tight at all terminals.

(b) Always wire from positive, carbon or center terminal of dry cells to spark coil, and from coil direct to ignitor for satisfactory results.

(c) Always wire from negative, zinc or outer terminal of dry cells to ground point or circuit breaker on engine. (See Illust. 29.)

(d) Always keep spark wires well insulated against water, oil and metals and from one another to insure satisfactory current and increased life of batteries

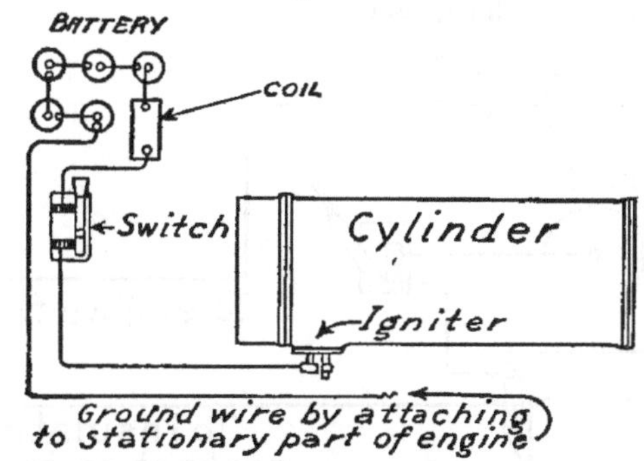

Illust. 29. Wiring diagram for make-and-break ignition with batteries and coil.

3. Spark Coil

(a) Always keep spark coil dry. If wet, will rust and destroy its efficiency.

(b) Keep free from vibration to prevent wires from breaking.

(c) Always keep wires tight at coil terminals for increased battery life.

4. Ignitor

(a) Stationary electrode must be well insulated against heat, pressures, fuel, oil and water penetration effects so that current can be carried to ignitor points when needed for spark.

(b) Be sure to have movable electrode free enough so ignitor points can part quickly, thereby producing a hot fat spark so necessary for good ignition. Ignitors should have a break gap from $\frac{1}{32}$ in. to $\frac{3}{32}$ in., depending on size of engine.

(c) Be sure of good clean tight contact between spark wire and stationary electrode at all times.

(d) Cleanliness in any ignition system aids in producing good results.

(e) Always keep ignition timing correct, from 5° to 7° ahead of inner center on compression stroke for every 100 r.p.m. of engines of low or medium speed.

(f) In order to fill coil completely with current, be sure to have ignitor points come in good contact when crank has traveled half way between outer and inner center of compression stroke.

(g) Ignition advance is directly related to engine speeds, kind of fuels used (quick or slow burning), engine design and altitude. High altitude gives rare air a slow burning mixture, consequently earlier ignition will be necessary.

II. Battery and Coil—Jump Spark

1. Wiring

(a) In addition to general points mentioned for make-and-break, and as this system carries a very much higher voltage current than in the make-and-break system, it becomes quite apparent that insulations in this system should be of the best in order to keep current in the right path. The tendency of an electric current is to seek the line of least resistance, so with poor insulation current would be lost on the way, and none or poor ignition will result.

(b) Wire from cells as per above to primary terminal of coil from the other primary coil terminal to commutator or contact terminal on engine, and from negative side of cell to engine ground, and high tension cable from induction terminal of coil to spark plugs. (See Illust. 29A.)

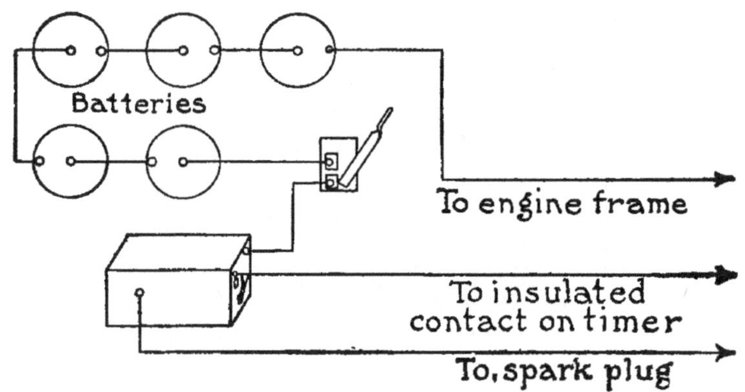

Illust. 29A. Wiring diagram for jump spark ignition with batteries and coil.

2. Spark Plug

(a) Keep spark plugs clean.

(b) Spark plug gaps should be from .025 to .030 of an inch apart. No. 24 gauge sheet steel will be right for measuring gap space in plugs. If gap space is too small or too great, it tends to destroy points and produce unsatisfactory ignition results.

(c) Indications point to better results with single than with multiple gap plugs.

3. Spark Coil

(a) Adjust induction coil vibrator to produce silvery toned, evenly spaced vibrations.

To save batteries, don't have vibrator points too close together.

III. Battery and Coil with Auto Sparker—Make-and-Break

(a) Battery used in starting, auto sparker for running, then wire up as follows: From battery as above stated to one side of 3-point switch, then from any one of armature terminals to other side of switch, then from primary coil to lower point of switch, then from coil terminal to stationary electrode of ignitor, then join wires from negative side of cells and wire from second armature terminal of auto sparker, then the spliced ground wire to ground point or circuit breaker on engine frame. (Illust 29B)

(b) Adjust auto sparker governor so speed does not exceed 1,000 r.p.m., and see that auto sparker is properly lined up on bracket.

(c) Keep armature, brushes and contact points clean.

(d) Never wire battery and auto sparker on same circuit.

(e) By changing field wires from one terminal to the other the rotation of armature must be changed correspondingly to deliver current to brushes.

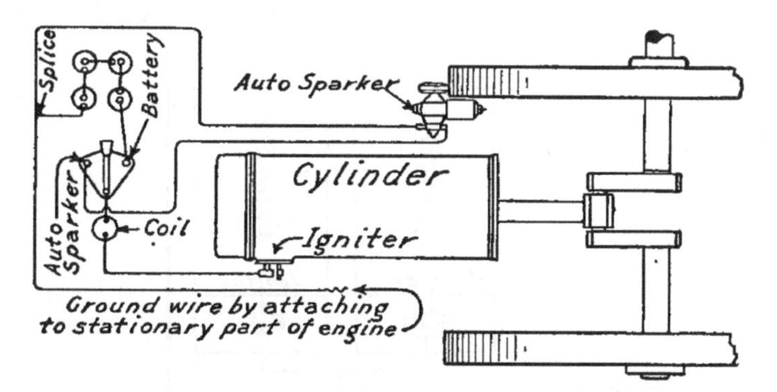

Illust. 29B. Wiring Diagram for Make-and-braak ignition with batteries, coil and auto-sperker.

IV. Battery and Coil with Rotary Low Tension Alternating Current Magneto—Make-and-Break

(a) Time engine correct for spark.

(b) Time magneto according to timing marks shown on armature shaft and hub so mark for either r. h. or l. h. rotation will be in line with one another when ignitor is tripping in correct time, as described above.

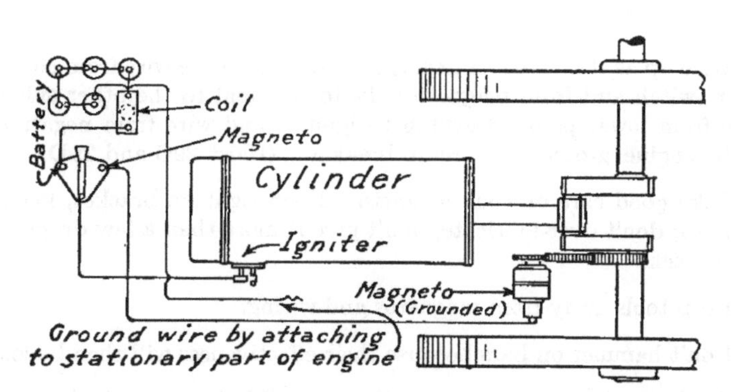

Illust. 29C. Wiring Diagram for Maka-and-braka ignition with batteries, coil and rotery magneto.

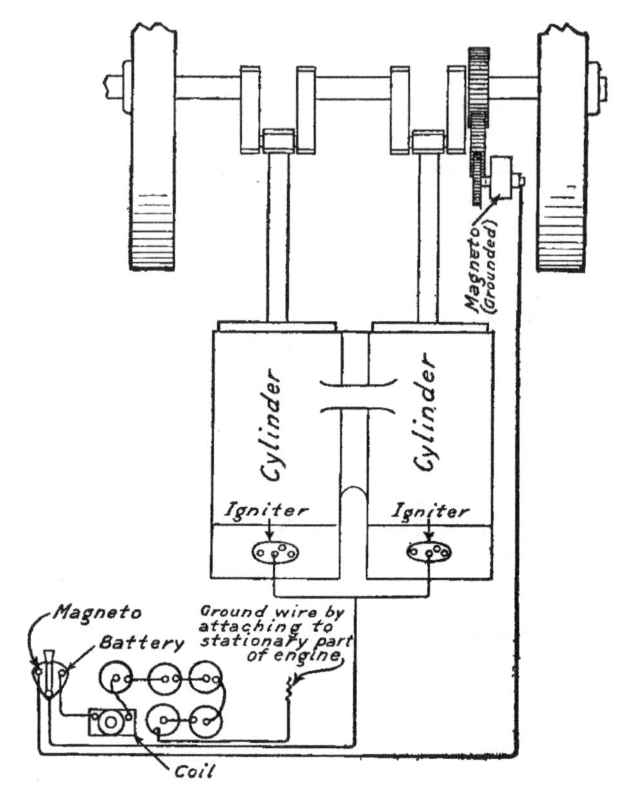

Illust. 29D. Wiring a 2-cylinder engine for make-and-break ignition with batteries, coil and rotary magneto.

(c) Wire up as described in Sec. I, 2-b and c, positive wire from coil to one side of 3-point switch and from magneto only to terminal to the other side of switch, then wire from lower point of switch to ignitor, and wire from negative terminal of cells to engine ground or circuit breaker. (Illust 29C and 29D.)

(d) Take good care of your magneto. Keep tight on bracket, keep race and brushes clean; don't over-lubricate, don't give it more than a few drops of oil once or twice a week.

(e) Keep tools away from magnetos and wiring.

(f) Don't hammer on bars because their effectiveness will then be lost.

(g) Don't try to magnetize everything possible by magneto bars. That will lower strength and shorten useful life of magneto.

(h) Don't wire coil nor battery and coil in magneto circuit, because it will kill battery and lower magneto life quickly and will also tend to prevent satisfactory starting and operation.

(i) Don't remove magneto bars nor armature, or they will lose about 15 per cent of their strength.

(j) If magneto bars or armature have to be removed, be sure to put a soft iron bar across from north to south poles of bars to prevent loss of magnetism.

V. Rotary Alternating Current Magnetos Only—Make-and-Break

(a) Keep in time with engine, Sec. IV, a and b, page 44.

(b) Don't wire up in circuit with battery and coil.

(c) No coil wanted or needed.

(d) Keep clean as described in Sec. III, c, page 43.

(e) Care for your magneto—Sec. IV, e, f, g, h, i, j, page 44.

(f) Don't over-oil—Sec. IV, d. page 44.

(g) Wire direct from magneto terminal to ignitor.

(h) In starting with rotary magnetos only, 2 revolutions fast is better than 100 revolutions slow.

(i) Care of ignitor—Sec. IV, a. b. c, page 44.

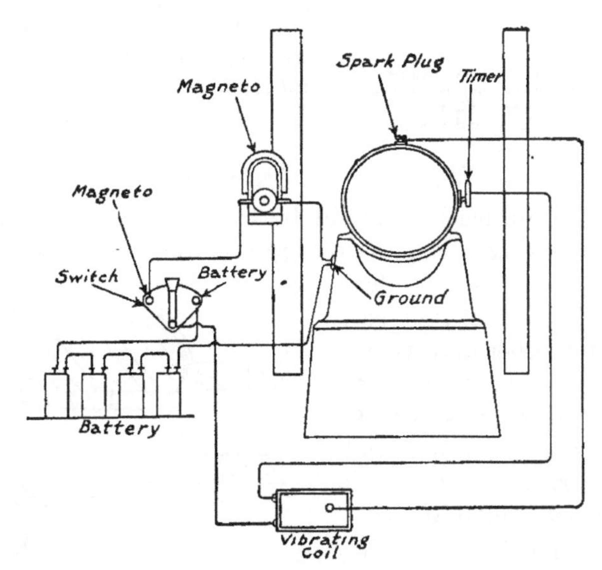

Illust. 29E. Wiring Diagram for jump spark ignition with batteries, coil and rotary magneto.

The Lubricating System

In working out this very important system of the engine, the designer endeavors to furnish a suitable means of lubricating every working or moving part. Friction losses are wasteful, hence each joint or part must be studied for its particular requirements. Some parts, like the piston, rings and valves, are subjected to the high heats noted, others, like the main bearings, crank pins and shaft bearings, get continuous grinding friction. Still others get only minor actions.

Methods of Lubricating

Lubrication for these groups should be ample and satisfactory for the needs. In some of the above cases, the oil is a cooling medium. Points under heat and pressure, such as the piston, rings, main bearings and crank pin, should receive it with the greatest certainty and regularity, so it should be fed by a force feed lubricator. Parts requiring less certainty can be fed by gravity oilers or grease cups, and the minor ones by careful use of an oil can.

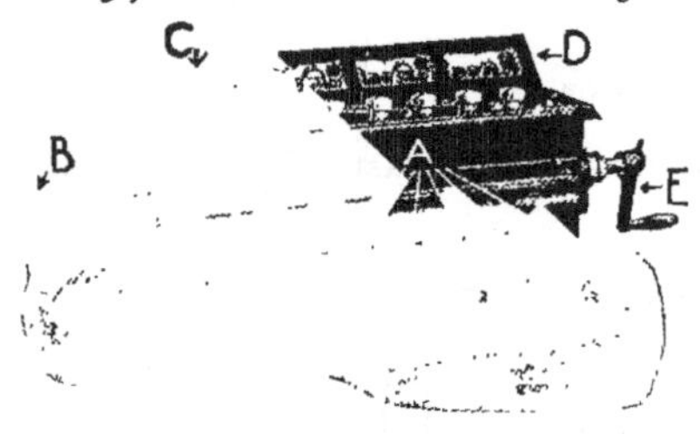

Illust. 30. Mechanically operated Force Feed Lubricator. A, oil tubes. B, force-feed drive lever. C, filler cap. D, sight feed hood. E, hand crank.

One of the chief functions of a force feed lubricator is to force to the cylinders and bearings fresh, clean, cool oil, which tends to cool the bearing surfaces and reduce friction more effectively than dirty, dead oil. This point is further discussed on page 53.

Purpose of Lubrication

The idea in lubrication should be to maintain a constant oil film between the working parts, an oil or grease roller or ball bearing, the oil globules being the balls or rollers. If the parts float on oil they cannot touch each other and wear is impossible. The designer therefore studies these pressures and regulates the sizes of parts, so that a film of lubricant will remain wherever needed if oil or grease is sufficiently supplied. The quality of the lubricant to be used will be discussed in Chapter VIII—Lubricants and Greases.

Illust. 31. How a film of lubricant between a bearing and a shaft looks through a microscope. Tha oil globules act just as ball bearings would.

CARE OF MECHANICAL LUBRICATOR

Illust. 30 shows the force-feed mechanical lubricator with which International Harvester tractors are equipped. From this lubricator the main bearings for the crankshaft, and connecting rods on the crankshaft, the pistons, with the connecting rod bearings inside the pistons are oiled. The responsibility of getting the oil to the bearings is partly taken from the operator's mind, but the responsibility of the operator, however, is to see that this lubricator is kept filled with the proper kind of oil and that it actually pumps and delivers oil regardless of weather or local conditions. See page 88 for list of suitable oils.

Filling

Remove filler cap at end of cover, pour in a recommended grade of lubricating oil (see page 88) until gauge glass is filled to within ¼ inch of top; replace filler cap securely and lubricator is ready for operation. Turn hand crank 40 to 50 times before starting engine.

Adjusted at the Factory

The mechanical lubricator is adjusted at the factory to supply the right amount of oil to the different bearings and to the cylinder. **It should not be tampered with unless you have a good reason to know that it is not working properly.** If the bearings or cylinder become overheated, they may not be getting sufficient oil. Examine the lubricator and see that it is working right.

Testing Amount of Oil Supplied

The right way to test the amount of oil supplied to the different parts is to count the number of drops or disconntect the ends of the pipes where they go into the bearings or cylinder, and measure the quantity each tube is feeding. The correct amount which should be supplied by each tube is listed in Tables on page 52. The table of oil proportions and quantities for the Mogul 8-16, 10-20 and Titan 10-20 is based on 200 revolutions of the hand crank, whereas the quantity for the International 15-30 is based on only 50 turns of the hand crank because of the larger number of feeds and the greater quantity of oil supplied. Please bear this point in mind when testing your oiler as to the quantity of oil it is feeding.

How to Measure the Oil

A small one-ounce bottle can be obtained at any drug store if you do not have one on hand. Use this as a check on the size of tablespoon—a tablespoonful is just half a liquid ounce.

In measuring with the average tablespoon, do not try to heap the oil up, but be sure that the spoon is just level full.

If the proportion supplied to the different tubes is correct but the total amount is not enough as shown by the total number of tablespoonfuls, an adjustment should be made on the lever as shown in Illust. 32.

Ordinarily when the oil drive rod is connected to hole 1, the ratchet on the inside of the lubricator moves one notch at a time (it cannot move less and operate the lubricator). When connected to hole 2, the ratchet moves two notches at a time, which will about double the oil supply. When connected to hole 3, the ratchet moves three notches, which gives about three times the quantity of oil as the first hole and about one and one-half times as much oil as the second hole. There may be variations from this due to adjustments on the oil drive rod and wear of joints. Because of this fact it will be safest to turn the flywheel over by hand and count the number of notches moved by the ratchet. For example, assuming that the oil drive rod is connected to hole 2 and that the ratchet moves two notches, also, when it is connected to hole 3 that the ratchet moves three notches. Now suppose that you find, on measuring, that the oil supplied by 200 turns of the hand crank is about 6½ tablespoonfuls, while it should be 10 tablespoonfuls. By changing the oil drive rod from hole 2 to hole 3, the quantity of oil supplied will be about 1½ times as much as in hole 2 which will be practically the required amount.

The Sight Feed Hood

The purpose of the sight feed hood is to enable you to see that oil is being supplied to the different tubes. By knowing that one-half the oil should go to the cylinder, one-third to the clutch side bearing, and one-sixth to the flywheel side bearing, and by carefully watching and estimating the amounts delivered by the different tubes, you can tell if the oiler is radically out of adjustment. It must be remembered that the size and number of drops of oil vary considerably, depending on the oil, on the temperature, etc. You cannot depend on counting the drops to determine the exact amount of oil supplied by the different tubes. You will notice that the drops run together in a chain and are very hard to count. The right way is to count the drops five or six different times of one minute each, then average the results. The number of drops supplied per minute should be used only as an approximate check on the total amount of oil going to the bearings.

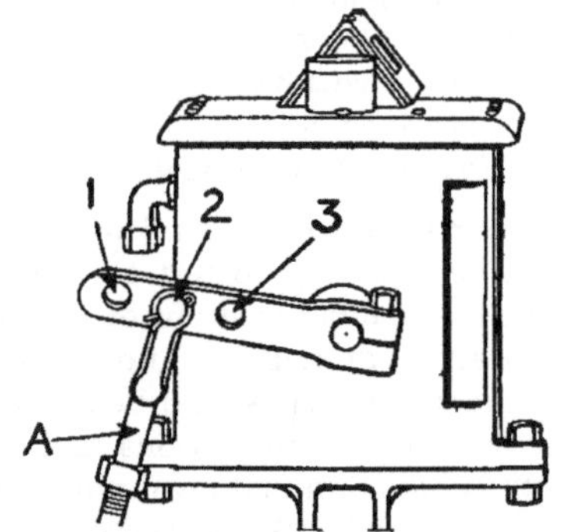

Illust. 32. End view of mechanical lubricator, A, the oil drive rod. To increase the supply of oil, use hold 3, to decrease it, use hold 1.

Knowing that, as near as can be determined, there should be from 45 to 50 drops of oil going to the cylinder per minute, 30 to 35 drops to the clutch side bearing per minute, and 15 to 20 drops to the flywheel side bearing per minute, you have a basis on which to judge whether the lubricator is supplying sufficient oil. If, for instance, only 15 or 20 drops are being supplied to the cylinder per minute, you will know that the lubricator is out of adjustment and should be fixed promptly. Do not try to adjust the lubricator until you have disconnected the tubes and made the tests as described above.

How to Make Inside Adjustments on 8-16 Mogul Lubricator

Let us again caution you not to make any adjustment inside the lubricator unless absolutely necessary. It perhaps will be better if you can have one of our experts assist you in making the inside adjustments of the lubricator. In making inside adjustments proceed as follows: Remove the cover of the lubricator. A feed regulator will be found in front of each sight feed. Use a screw driver and turn the screw **clockwise,** or to the right, to supply more oil, and **anti-clockwise,** or to the left, to reduce the supply. Disconnect the pipes where they enter the bearings or cylinder. Place a clean bottle under each tube, give the hand crank 200 turns and then measure the oil that comes from each tube. (See page 52 for quantities). When properly adjusted, connect the tubes and turn hand crank 40 to 50 times before starting engine. **Be sure that the quantity of oil supplied is large enough—better to have a little too much instead of not enough oil.**

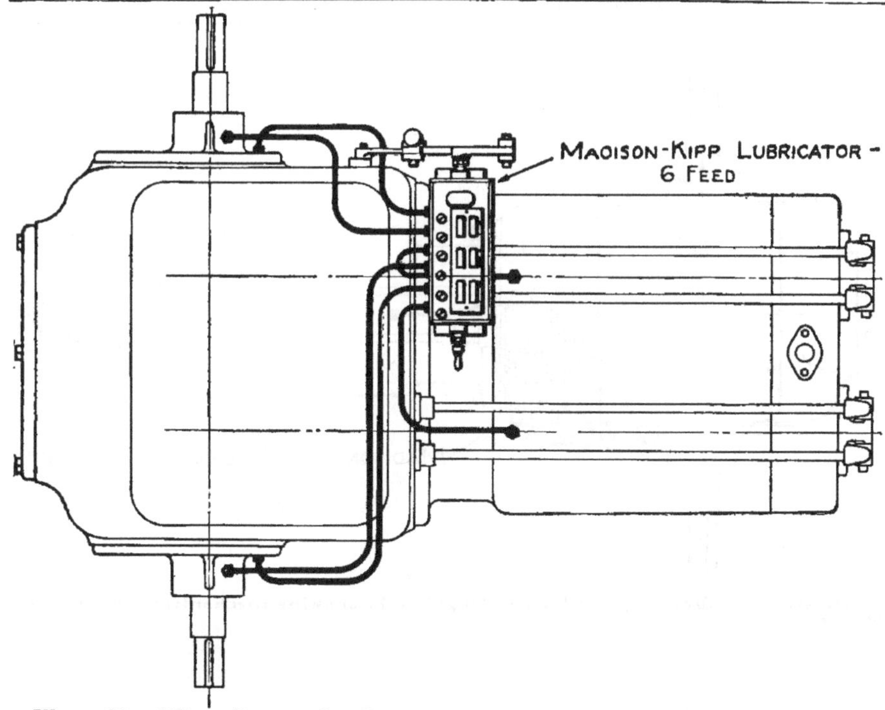

Illust. 33. Oiling diagram for the Titan 10-20 showing installation of mechanical lubricator and oil tubes.

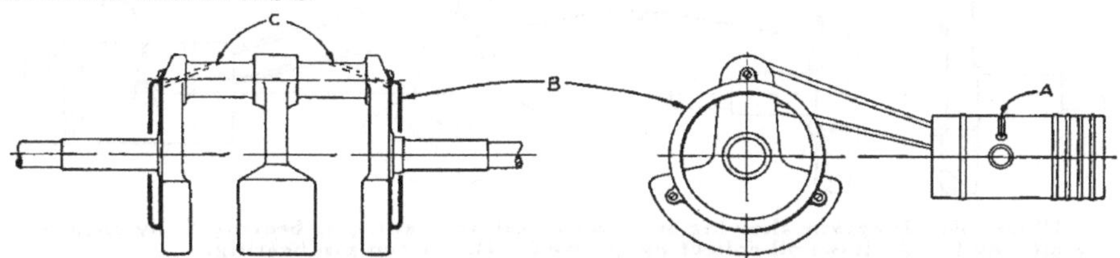

Illust. 34. This shows the method of oiling crank pin bearings C by means of the oil rings B. A shows the oil collecting groove for the piston pin bearing.

Adjusting Lubricator Pumps on the Mogul 10-20, Titan 10-20, Titan and International 15-30 Tractors

The lubricators used on these tractors have a feed regulator screw on top in front of each sight feed (see Illust. 30), therefore it is not necessary to remove the cover as on the lubricator used on the Mogul 8-16, because the adjustments are made from the outside and not from the inside. Use a screw driver and turn the screw clockwise or to the right to supply less oil, and anti-clockwise or to the left to supply more oil, then to test the amount of oil being supplied by each tube, proceed as outlined in the previous paragraph.

Cleaning Lubricator

As there is apt to be some sediment and water collect in the bottom of the lubricator, it should be cleaned occasionally. In the back of the lubricator near the bottom a ¼-inch pipe plug will be found. Remove it and drain out all the sediment and water that has collected. Rinse the lubricator out well with kerosene.

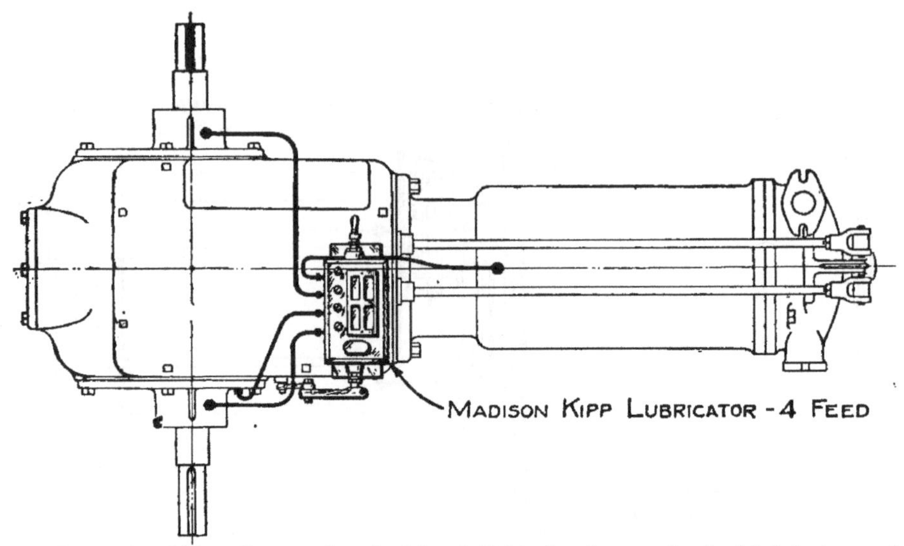

Illust. 35. Oiling diagram for the Mogul 10-20 showing mechanical lubricator and oil tubes.

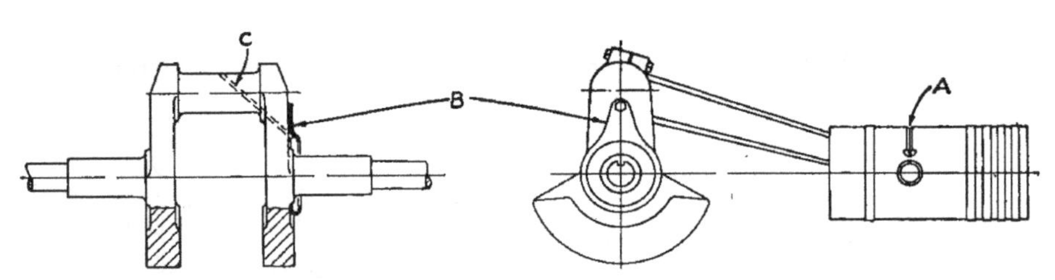

Illust. 36. Diagram showing method of oiling crank pin bearing C by means of the oil ring B. A shows oil collecting groove for the piston pin bearing.

After the kerosene has drained out, replace the pipe plug, refill the lubricator with oil and turn the hand crank to make sure the pipes leading to the cylinder and bearings are full, which will insure a sufficient quantity of oil being supplied to the bearings and to the cylinder, before starting the engine.

Connecting Pipes

A little shellac on the joint of the lubricator cover will prevent any leakage of oil.

Measurements

1 Teaspoonful equals approximately 6.3 cubic centimeters.

1 Teaspoonful is approximately 180 drops as delivered from pipes in good condition.

30 Cubic centimeters equal 1 fluid ounce.

2 Tablespoonfuls equal 1 fluid ounce.

1 Tablespoonful equals 4 fluid drams.

Do not try to economize on oil—oil is cheaper than repairs.

TABLE I

Indicating Proportions and Quantities of Oil Which Should Be Delivered By Each Tube of the Various Lubricators Used on International Harvester Tractors

Tube No. From Hand Crank End	Parts Oiled	Proportion of Total Oiled	Delivered by 200 Turns of Crank	No of Drops per Revolution
1	Cylinder........	About ½ of total amount.........	About 3.3 to 4.4 teaspoonfuls.....	3 to 4 drops
2	Main bearing on transmission side.	About ⅓ of total amount.........	About 2.2 to 3.3 teaspoonfuls.....	2 to 3 drops
3	Main bearing on fly wheel side..	About ⅙ of total amount.........	About 1.1 to 2.2 teaspoonfuls.....	1 to 2 drops
	TOTAL.........	....	6.7 to 10 teaspoonfuls............	6 to 9 drops

TABLE II

Tube No. From Hand Crank End	Parts Oiled	Proportion of Total Oil	Delivered by 200 Turns of Crank	No. of Drops per Revolution
1	Cylinder........	About ½ of total amount.........	About 3.3 to 4.4 teaspoonfuls.....	3 to 4 drops
2	Main Bearing on transmission side.	About ⅙ of total amount.........	About 1.1 to 2.2 teaspoonfuls.....	1 to 2 drops
3	Main bearing on fly-wheel side..	About ⅙ of total amount.........	About 1.1 to 2.2 teaspoonfuls.....	1 to 2 drops
4	Crank shaft connecting rod bearing.......	About ⅙ of total amount.........	About 1.1 to 2.2 teaspoonfuls.....	1 to 2 drops
	TOTAL	....	6.6 to 11.1 teaspoonfuls.......	6 to 10 drops

TABLE III

Tube No. From Hand Crank End	Parts Oiled	Proportion of Total Oil	Delivered by 200 Turns of Crank	No. of Drops per Revolution
1	Left cylinder....	Slightly less than ¼ of total amount.	About 4⅔ teaspoonfuls to 5.5 teaspoonfuls.......	About 5 drops
2	Left crank pin . .	Slightly more than ⅛ of total amount	About 2.2 to 3.3 teaspoonfuls.....	2 to 3 drops
3	Left main bearing	Slightly more than ⅛ of total amount	About 2.2 to 3.3 teaspoonfuls.....	2 to 3 drops....
4	Right cylinder...	Slightly less than ¼ of total amount..	About 5.5 teaspoonfuls............	About 5 drops
5	Right main bearing...........	Slightly more than ⅛ of total amount	About 2.2 to 3.3 teaspoonfuls.....	2 to 3 drops
6	Right crank pin..	Slightly more than ⅛ of total amount	About 2.2 to 3.3 teaspoonfuls.....	2 to 3 drops
	TOTAL	....	20 to 24.4 teaspoonfuls	18 to 22 drops

TABLE IV

Indicating Proportions and Quantities of Oil Which Should Be Delivered By Each Tube of the Various Oilers Used on International Harvester Tractors

Tube No. From Hand Crank End	Parts Oiled	Proportion of Total Oil	Delivered by 50 Turns of Crank	No. of Drops per Revolution
1	Right main bearing..........	About 1/16 of total amount	About 1.1 teaspoonfuls...........	About 4 drops
2	No. 1 crank pin box..........	About 1/16 of total amount	About 1.1 teaspoonfuls...........	About 4 drops
3	No. 2 crank pin box..........	About 1/16 of total amount..........	About 1.1 teaspoonfuls...........	About 4 drops
4	Center main bearing..........	About 1/16 of total amount.........	About 1.1 teaspoonfuls...........	About 4 drops
5	No. 1 cylinder and piston.........	Slightly less than 1/8 of total amount..	About 1.9 to 2.2 teaspoonfuls.....	7 to 8 drops
6	No. 2 cylinder and piston........	Slightly less than 1/8 of total amount....	About 1.9 to 2.2 teaspoonfuls.....	7 to 8 drops
7	Center cam shaft box..........	About 1/32 of total amount.........	About .55 teaspoonful.............	About 2 drops
8	No. 3 cynlider and piston.........	Slightly less than 1/8 of total amount..	About 1.9 to 2.2 teaspoonfuls.....	7 to 8 drops
9	No. 4 cylinder and piston........	Slightly less than 1/8 of total amount..	About 1.9 to 2.2 teaspoonfuls.....	7 to 8 drops
10	No. 3 crank pin box..........	About 1/16 of total amount.........	About 1.1 teaspoonfuls...........	About 4 drops
11	No. 4 crank pin box..........	About 1/16 of total amount.........	About 1.1 teaspoonfuls...........	About 4 drops
12	Left main bearing	About 1/16 of total amount.........	About 1.1 teaspoonfuls...........	About 4 drops
	TOTAL.........	....	15.9 to 17.3 teaspoonfuls	58 to 62 drops

FRESH OIL IS NECESSARY TO BEARING SURFACES

The force-feed lubricator is used in preference to crank case systems of lubrica-
n in International Harvester tractors. Its purpose is to supply **fresh** "live" oil
'ays to cylinders and bearings. Good, fresh oil has proved itself to be from two
three times as durable as the "dead" oil that is used in the crank case of some
es of engines.

The advantages to the tractor in having fresh oil are much longer life, freedom
n repairs, and continuous rated power.

A tractor which has the crank case system of lubrication uses oil over and over
in. After a few hours' run, sediment and condensed fuel collect in the crank
e, mixing with the lubricating oil. The result is invariably that tremendous
r and loss of power occur from the action of this mixture of grinding sediment
l "dead" oil.

The longer life of International Harvester tractors is partly due to the force-
d lubricator. **Fresh** oil is furnished to all bearing surfaces in just the proper
ntities to maintain a perfect oil film.

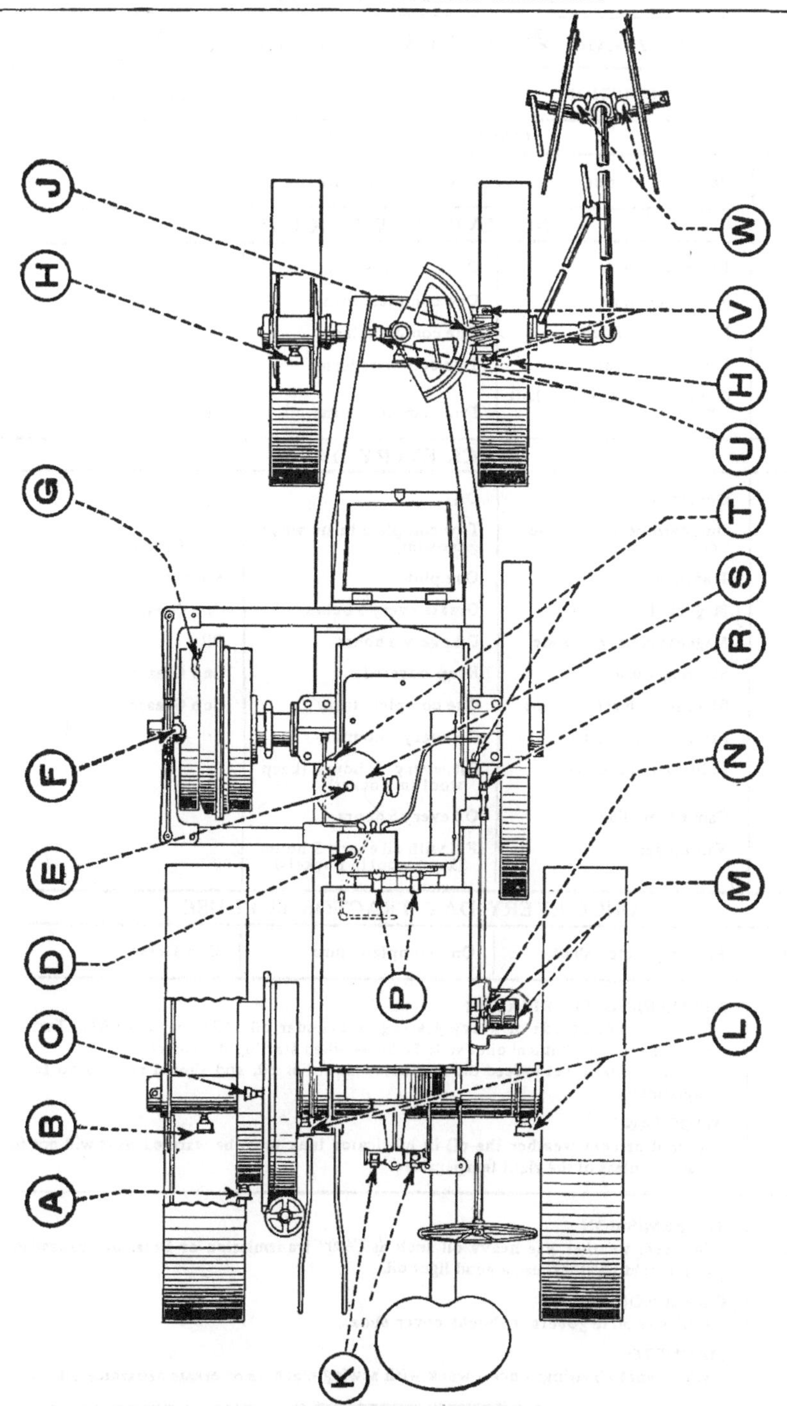

Illust. 37. Diagram showing where to oil the Mogul 8-16-H. P. tractor.

How and When to Oil the Mogul 8-16

KEY	DESCRIPTION	QUANTITY	LUBRICATION
	ONCE EVERY HOUR		
L	Rear axle bearing	Two complete turns	Cup Grease
	ONCE EVERY TWO HOURS		
A	Differential hub	One complete turn	Cup Grease
B	Rear wheel hub	One complete turn	Cup Grease
C	Differential pinion	One complete turn	Cup Grease
H	Front wheel hub	Two complete turns	Cup Grease
T	Governor and cam shaft bearing	Two complete turns	Cup Grease
	TWICE EVERY DAY		
E	Governor	Oil	Cylinder oil
F	Outboard bearing grease cups	Two complete turns when plowing	Cup Grease
G	Transmission	One pint	See note below
N	Magneto trip	Grease every 5 hours	Cup Grease
N	Magneto roller and slide	Oil every 5 hours	Oil
J	Steering worm	Keep covered	Cup Grease,
W	Steering hub grease cups	One complete turn	Cup Grease
V	Steering worm shaft	Oil every 5 hours	
R	Lubricator eccentric	Oil every 5 hours (keep wool in pocket)	
P	Cam roller slide	Oil every 5 hours	
K	Valve levers	Fill with oil every 5 hours (keep wool in pockets)	
	ONCE EVERY DAY TRACTOR IS IN USE		
U	Steering sector shaft	One complete turn	Cup Grease

D — MECHANICAL LUBRICATOR

Fill with a good grade of heavy gas engine cylinder oil. (See list page 88). Turn the crank on the mechanical oiler 40 to 50 times when starting the engine

☞ This oiler is set to feed the requisite amount of oil, and should require no further adjustment.

IMPORTANT

In cool or cold weather the oil in lubricator tank must be warmed, as it will not flow readily unless of the right temperature.

G — TRANSMISSION

In warm weather, use heavy oil such as "600" transmission or Polarine transmission oil; in cold weather, use a good light oil.

S — GOVERNOR

Cylinder oil in governor should cover shoe.

M — MAGNETO

Oil magneto bearings once a week with sewing machine or cream separator oil

Caution. Use only recommended oils and greases as listed on pages 88, 89 and 90.

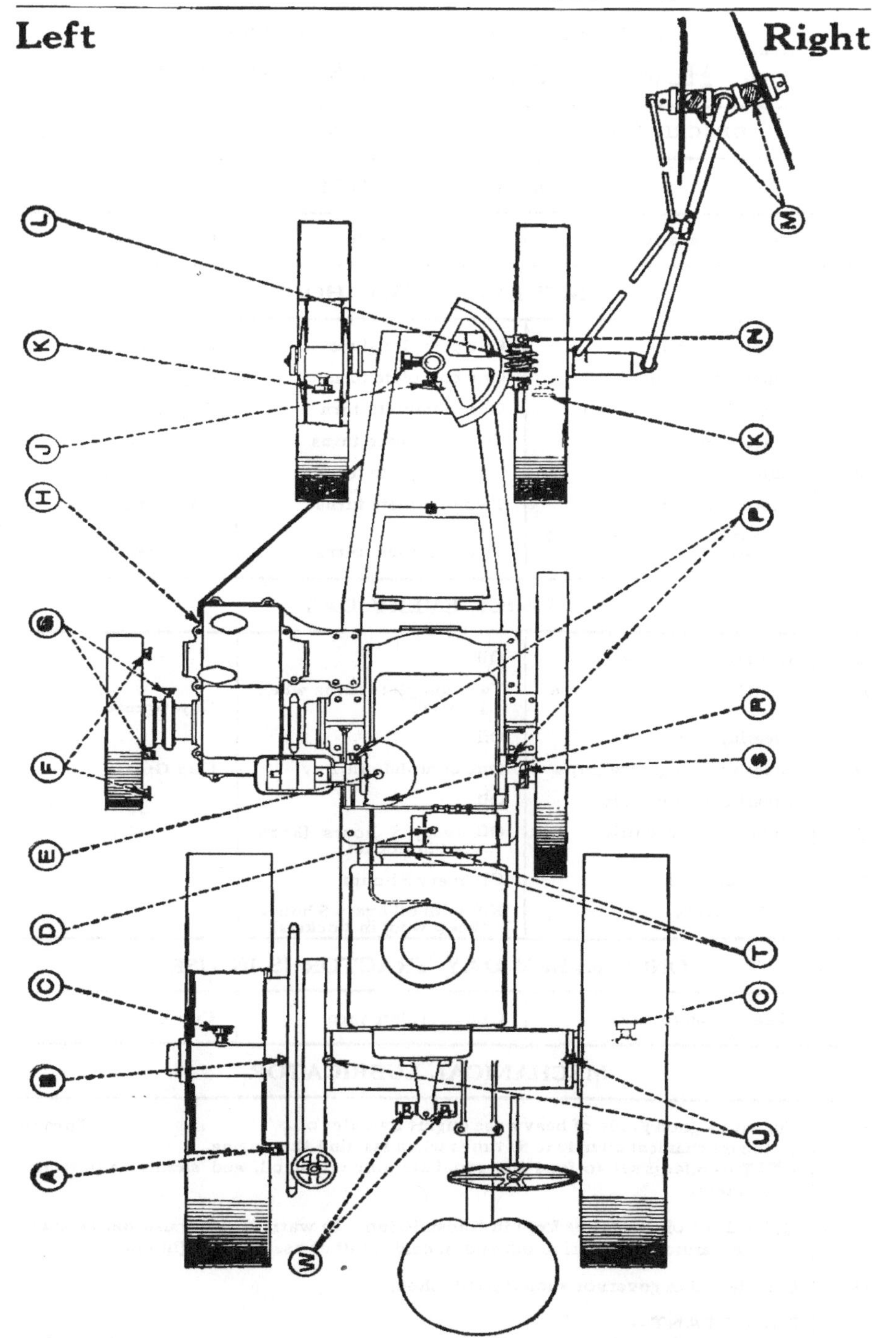

Illust. 38. Diagram, showing where to oil the Mogul 10-20-H. P. tractor.

How and When to Oil Mogul 10-20

EY	DESCRIPTION	QUANTITY	LUBRICATION
ONCE EVERY HOUR			
U	Rear axle bearing	Two complete turns	Cup Grease
ONCE EVERY TWO HOURS			
A	Differential hub	One complete turn	Cup Grease
B	Differential pinion	One complete turn	Cup Grease
C	Rear wheel hub	One complete turn	Cup Grease
G	Clutch spider	Two complete turns	Cup Grease
G	Clutch shifter ring	Two complete turns	Cup Grease
K	Front wheel hub	Two complete turns	Cup Grease
P	Governor and cam shaft bearing	Two complete turns	Cup Grease
TWICE EVERY DAY			
E	Governor	Oil	
F	Clutch spider grease cups	Two complete turns when plowing	Cup Grease
L	Steering worm	Oil	
M	Steering hub grease cups	One complete turn	Cup Grease
N	Steering worm shaft	Oil	
S	Lubricator eccentric	Oil every 5 hours (keep wool in pocket)	
T	Cam roller slide	Oil every 5 hours	
W	Valve levers	Fill with oil every 5 hours (keep wool in pockets)	
ONCE EVERY DAY TRACTOR IS IN USE			
J	Steering sector shaft	One complete turn	Cup Grease

MECHANICAL LUBRICATOR

D — Fill with a good grade of heavy gas engine cylinder oil. Turn th on the mechanical oiler 40 to 50 times when starting the engine.
☞ This oiler is set to feed the requisite amount of oil, and should require no adjustment.

H — 1½" to 2" of oil should be kept in transmission. In warm weather use heavy trans oil or Polarine transmission oil, and in cold weather use a good light oil.

R — Cylinder oil in governor should cover shoe.

IMPORTANT—
In cool or cold weather the oil in lubricator tank must be warmed, as it will not flow unless of the right temperature.

Caution. Use only recommended oils and greases listed on pages 88, 89 and 90

Lefft **Right**

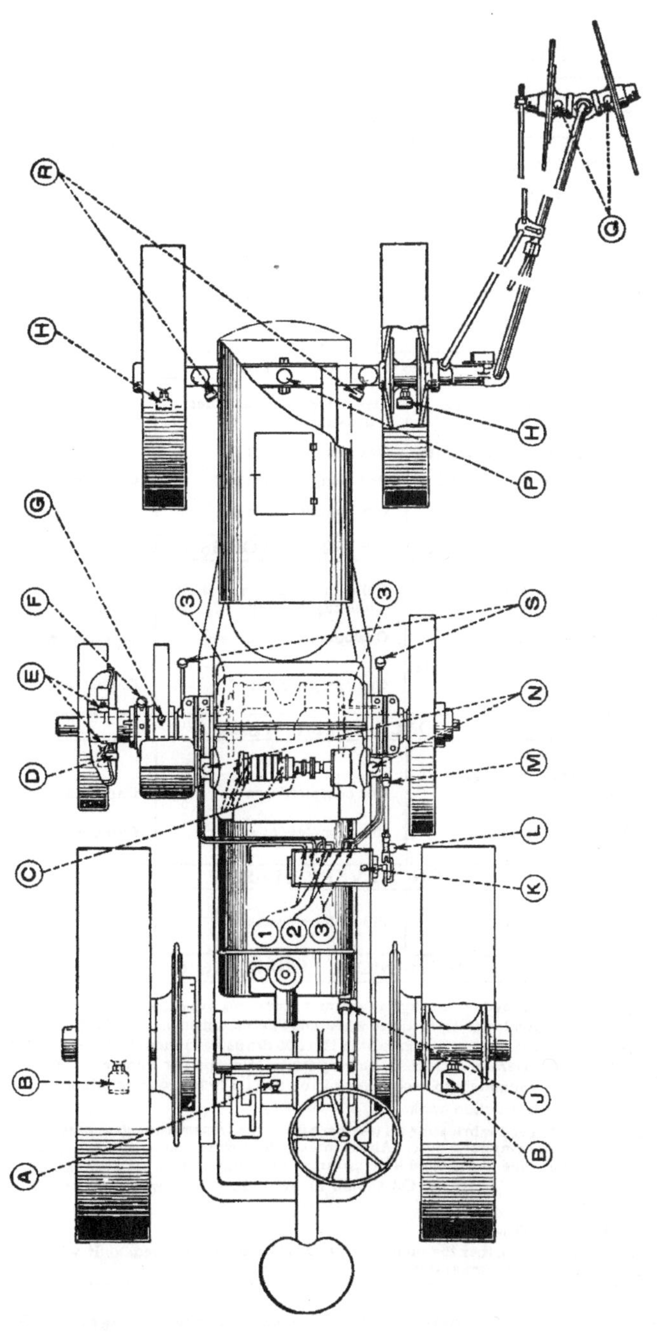

Illust. 39. Diagram, showing where to oil the Titan 10-20-H. P. tractor.

How and When to Oil Titan 10-20

KEY	DESCRIPTION	QUANTITY	LUBRICATION
	ONCE EVERY TWO HOURS		
B	Rear wheel hub grease cups	Two complete turns	Cup Grease
E	Clutch spider grease cup	One complete turn when running in belt	Cup Grease
F	Clutch shifter ring grease cup	Two complete turns	Cup Grease
H	Front wheel hub grease cups	One complete turn	Cup Grease
N	Cam shaft bearing grease cups	One complete turn	Cup Grease
S	Countershaft bearing grease cups	Two complete turns	Cup Grease
	TWICE EVERY DAY		
E	Clutch spider grease cups	Two complete turns when plowing	Cup Grease
R	Steering knuckle grease cups	One complete turn	Cup Grease
M	Eccentric strap grease cup	One complete turn	Cup Grease
Q	Steering hub grease cup	One complete turn	Cup Grease
	ONCE EVERY DAY TRACTOR IS IN USE		
G	Crank shaft gear sight feed oil cup	Fill with a good grade of oil; one cup per day	See list
L	Bell crank grease cup	One complete turn	Cup Grease
P	Front axle king bolt grease cup	One complete turn	Cup Grease
	ONCE EVERY WEEK		
A	Gear shifter sleeve grease cup	One complete turn	Cup Grease
D	Clutch arm grease cup	One complete turn	Cup Grease
	ONCE EVERY SEASON		
J	Steering gear case	Fill with cup grease	
	MECHANICAL LUBRICATOR		
K	Fill with a good grade of heavy gas engine cylinder oil. (See list page 88.) Turn the crank on the mechanical oiler 40 to 50 times when starting the engine. "1"—Adjust to feed not less than 7 cubic centimeters to each piston (25 to 30 drops per minute). "2"—Feed not less than 4 cubic centimeters to each main bearing (12 to 14 drops per minute) "3"—Feed not less than 4 cubic centimeters to each crank pin oil ring (12 to 14 drops per minute).		
C	See magneto instruction book.		
	Keep enough good lubricating oil (see page 88) in the transmission gear case to cover the teeth of the smaller compound gear. About three gallons will be sufficient, and it may be poured in through filler pipe in the hand hole cover at the front end of the gear casing. Oil should be kept about even with the edge of the hand hole opening.		
	IMPORTANT— In cool or cold weather the oil in lubricator tank must be warmed, as it will not flow readily unless of the right temperature.		

Caution. Use only recommended oils and greases listed on pages 88, 89 and 90.

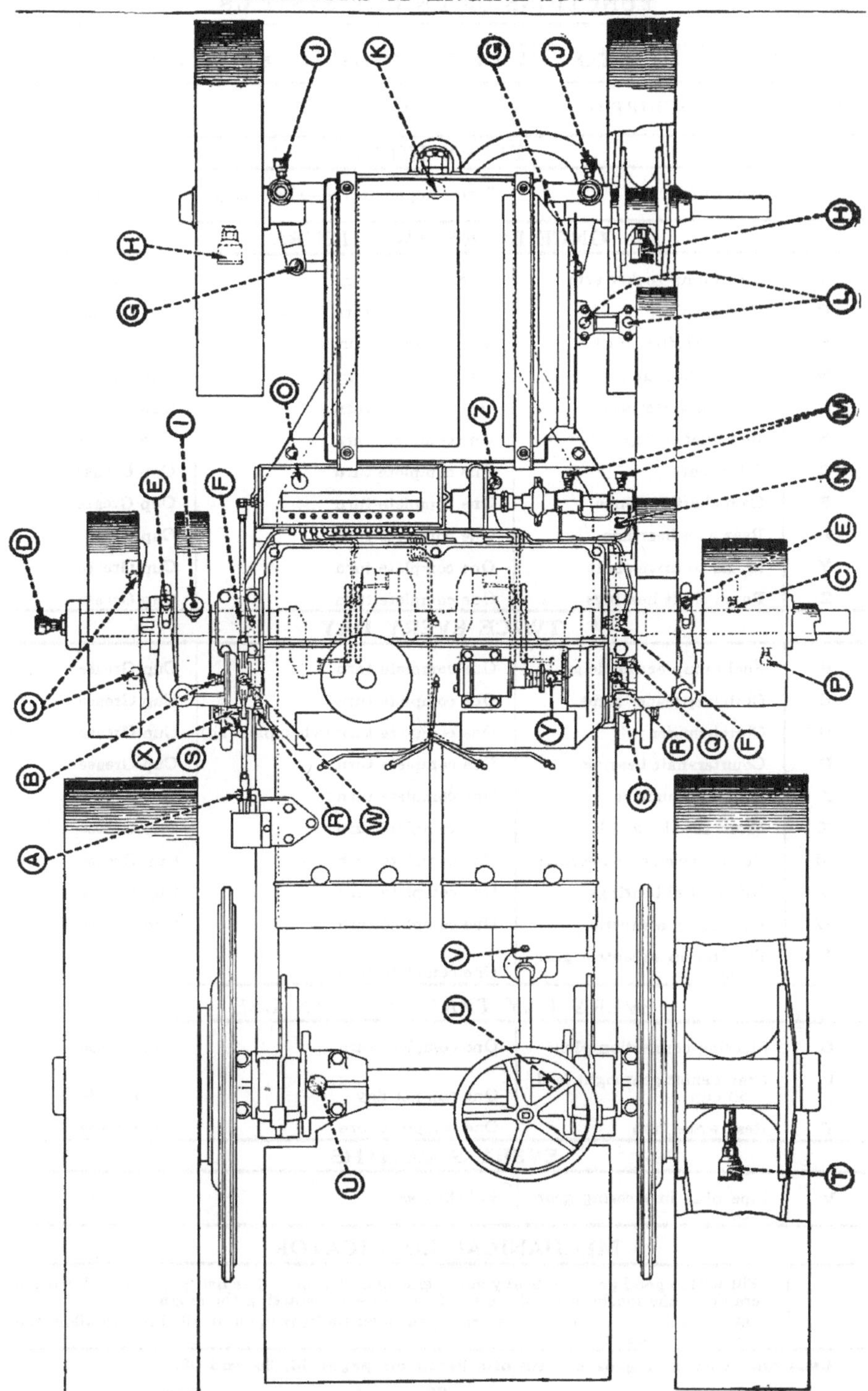

Illust. 40. Diagram, showing where to oil the Titan and International 15-30 H. P. tractor.

How and When to Oil Titan and International 15-30

KEY	DESCRIPTION	QUANTITY	LUBRICATION
		EVERY HOUR	
P	Belt Pulley	Two complete turns (when using belt)	Cup Grease
		ONCE EVERY TWO HOURS	
A	Fuel pump rocker arm	One complete turn	Cup Grease
D	Clutch spider	One complete turn (when in belt)	Cup Grease
E	Clutch shifter rings	Two complete turns	Cup Grease
H	Front wheel hubs	Two complete turns	Cup Grease
L	Fan shaft bearings	One complete turn	Cup Grease
N	Belt idler pulley	One complete turn	Cup Grease
Q	Idler gear	One complete turn	Cup Grease
R	Cam shaft bearings	One complete turn	Cup Grease
U	Rear axle bearings	One complete turn	Cup Grease
Y	Magneto drive shaft	One complete turn	Cup Grease
Z	Pump shaft bearings	One complete turn	Cup Grease
		TWICE EVERY DAY	
B	Fuel pump eccentric gear	One complete turn	Cup Grease
C	Clutch spreader arms	One complete turn	Cup Grease
D	Clutch spider	One complete turn (when plowing)	Cup Grease
F	Countershaft bearings	One complete turn	Cup Grease
J	Steering knuckles	One complete turn	Cup Grease
K	Front axle king bolt	One complete turn	Cup Grease
M	Pump drive shaft bearings	One complete turn	Cup Grease
S	Differential bearings	One complete turn	Cup Grease
W	Fuel pump eccentric	One complete turn	Cup Grease
X	Fuel pump eccentric gear shaft	One complete turn	Cup Grease
		EVERY DAY TRACTOR IS IN USE	
G	Steering connection pins	One complete turn	Cup Grease
I	Crank shaft gear sight feed oil cup	One cup per day	Good grade of oil
T	Rear wheel hub	One complete turn	Cup Grease
		EVERY 6 MONTHS	
V	Pipe plug in steering gear case	Fill the case	Cup Grease

MECHANICAL LUBRICATOR

Fill with a good grade of heavy gas engine cylinder oil. (See list, page 88.) Turn the crank on the mechanical oiler 40 to 50 times when starting the engine.

☛ The drain at rear of crank case pan must be kept open at all times to allow the used oil to pass off.

Caution. Use only greases and oils listed on pages 88, 89 and 90.

Care and Use of Grease Cups

Hard oil is used in bearings where the pressure is too great for thin oils and in other places where only a small amount of oil is needed. In any event, even though the grease cup is simple, it must be given some real attention. A very

Illust. 41. Grease cup not properly filled. The first few turns will not send grease into the bearing—but will compress it in the cup.

Illust. 42. Another careless way of using a grease cup—entire bearing is not lubricated.

Illust. 43. The proper way to lubricate with a grease cup. Note grease full length of bearing and oozing out at ends.

common mistake is made in filling by not squeezing the grease down in the top of the cup. When the cup is not properly filled, the first few turns down do not force the grease into the bearings but simply compact it in the grease cup (Illust. 41). Because of this fact a man may think he has done his part and greased the bearings when he really hasn't. Illust. 42 shows another thing that happens when the grease cup is carelessly used. This bearing is only partly supplied with grease. Illust. 43 shows the right way to handle the grease cup. Screw the top down until the bearing is well filled or until it can be plainly seen that the grease is oozing out at both ends of the bearing.

Keep Grease Free From Dust

The can containing your supply of grease should not be allowed to stand open so that dust can get into it. Dust is gritty and if carried into the bearings with the grease will cut the bearings rapidly and often cause them to heat excessively.

When filling the grease cups it is important to wipe the dust from the cup and especially out of the threads on the cup before filling. Dust accumulates on the cup and in the threads, and when the top is unscrewed this dust is carried up to the edge. When grease is put in, the dust gets in with it and bad results are very likely to follow.

Oilers—Oil Holes

See that all oil holes, oil or grease passages, are open and that the oil or grease actually reaches the bearings. Frequent inspection and cleaning of all oil holes, oil and grease passages, may save a bearing from being seriously damaged. It often happens that the oil passages get clogged right at the bearing so it is best to completely clean the oil passage all the way to the shaft.

Oil Bath

Several parts of Mogul and Titan tractors operate in an oil bath. Because of the very nature of this system of oiling it is sometimes neglected. A man may think that because he has supplied a certain amount of oil at a certain time that the bearings are properly lubricated. It is always best to inspect these parts frequently and be sure that they are supplied with a sufficient amount of oil. By doing this you take no chances. Too much oil is not as harmful as too little oil. At any rate, oil is cheaper and better than delays and repair parts.

The Cooling System

The cooling system of an engine is provided to maintain such temperatures within the cylinder as will permit of proper lubrication.

The necessity for cooling applies of course mainly to the parts affected by the heat generated during the explosions—to the cylinder walls, piston, rings, valves, and piston pin. We noticed how the natural temperatures within the cylinder would heat the engine parts up to a red heat, unless we cooled them. This is the condition that makes cooling necessary. Red hot parts cannot be lubricated. The oils would be destroyed before they could perform their function[1].

The cooling system is therefore a decisive factor in the efficiency of the engine.

Some idea of the different methods of engine cooling may be useful in determining which is most desirable for tractor use.

Air Cooling System—By furnishing the cylinder and head with fins or projecting ribs of iron, we are able to create a large radiating surface to carry away the heat.

If a sufficient supply of air reaches these ribs, by fan or rotation of the engine itself, continuous operation of this kind of engine is possible. This system of cooling is used on small engines intended for short or intermittent work, on flying machines and often on cheap engines.

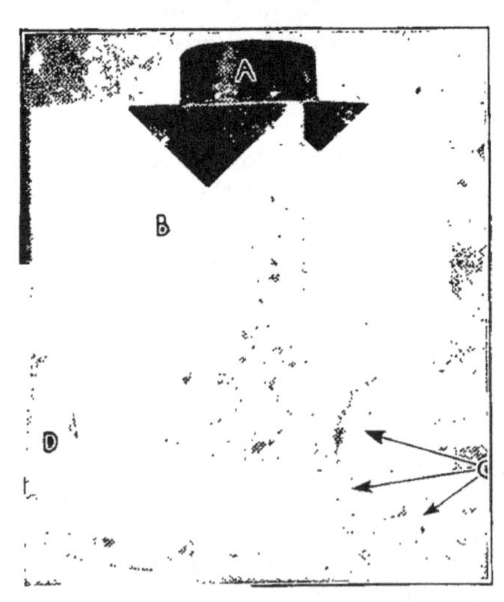

Illust. 44. The hopper-cooling system as used on Mogul tractors. There is no pump in this system. A and B, hopper; C, water jacket; D, point of attachment to crank case.

Hopper Cooling System[2]—In this method a quantity of water standing in a hopper which surrounds the cylinder is depended upon to carry away the surplus heat by evaporation, so as to maintain satisfactory lubrication within the cylinder. The hopper requires replenishing at intervals depending upon its size. Care is necessary never to expose any part of the cylinder wall above the water, and also when refilling to pour in the cool water slowly, in order not to strain

NOTE 1—Special Lubricating Oils

The higher temperatures under which the kerosene engine operates requires special quality of lubricating oils and greases. See Note 1, pages 88 and 90, for list of suitable oils and greases.

NOTE 2—Hopper-cooling system used on Mogul 8-16 and 10-20 tractors.

the cylinder by rapid chilling. An outside continuous water supply fed to the hopper, which will maintain a constant level, is preferable where available.

The hopper cooling system is very useful in climates where freezing is likely to occur, as by proper shaping of the hopper, any ice which may form can be given a chance to expand without injury to the engine.

Thermo-Syphon Cooling System[1]—This method is extensively used as it enables the cylinder temperature to rise rapidly to the desired or boiling point and automatically starts the water circulating through the cooling system.

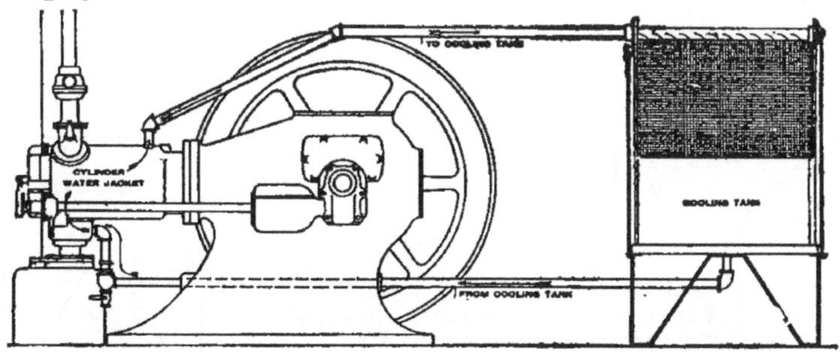

Illust. 45. Diagram showing a stationary engine cooled by the thermo-syphon system.

The basic idea of this system is the fact that hot water weighs less per gallon than cold water. For example, water about to freeze at 34° Fahr. weighs 62.4 lb. per cubic foot. Water at 212° Fahr. or just ready to boil weighs 59.8 lb. per cubic foot This difference in weight causes the heavy cold water to push up the lighter hot water. The regulation of the desired temperature is obtained by the height of the pipe above the cylinder. For low cylinder temperatures, this height is low. For high temperatures the height is greater. The height of the pipe above the cylinder should never be more than will permit water to flow when the jacket water reaches boiling temperature, otherwise steam only will come off. In any case, the water from the tank must keep the water level above the top of the cylinder.

The chilling effect of a rapid supply of extra water is not as immediate with the thermo-syphon system as with the hopper. This system is very simple and effective.

Controllable Temperature Cooling System—Under certain circumstances it may be desirable to have a control over the temperature surrounding the cylinder. For example, an engine operating on gasoline will work well at cylinder temperatures ranging from 160° to 180°

NOTE 1—Thermo-Syphon Cooling

This system is used on Titan 10-20 tractors.

Fahr.—while kerosene requires for best results a higher range, say from 200° to 212° Fahr.

By an arrangement similar to that shown below,the water from the pump can go through the short path, through the valve when open or around and through the cylinder to the tank. As the path through

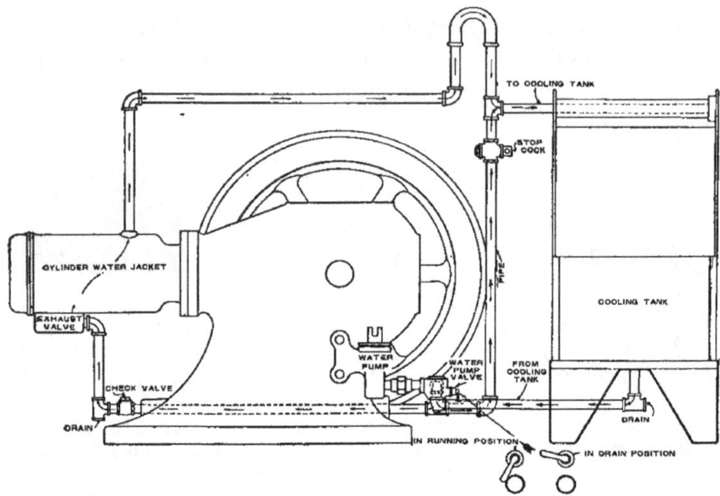

Illust. 46. Diagram, showing a stationary engine cooled by the controllable temperature system.

the valve is shorter and with less friction, most of the water will circulate this way, unless diverted by partly closing the valve.

By regulating this valve any proportion of the flow can be circulated through this short line on around the cylinders with a corresponding change of temperature in the cylinder water jacket, which becomes cooler as more of the water goes around the cylinder.

Impulse System of Cooling[1]—With the increasing use of the lower grades of fuels, the maintenance of uniform high jacket temperature became more necessary. The impulse system of cooling which achieves this result—is the most satisfactory system of any for kerosene engines.

By this device the pump keeps up a constant circulation from and into the tank. A large part takes the short circuit. The long circuit through the cylinders is fed by a small pipe. This small pipe is under the pump pressure, as is the large pipe, but the resistance through the cylinder and the loop at the top adds enough friction to the line, so that no water flows in this direction until the cylinder heats up the water to a boiling temperature. When the water tries to rise above

NOTE 1—Impulse Cooling

By removal of stop cock in vertical line shown in Illust. 46, the controllable temperature system becomes an impulse cooling system.

this temperature, steam is formed, which ejects on impulses a quantity of water over the loop and permits the entry of a supply through the small pipe. If the engine works under a light load, few impulses are made; if it works under a heavy load, many are made—hence we have an automatic constant regulation of the temperature to or about the boiling point of water. This uniformity works for a high efficiency in fuel consumption.

Pump, Fan and Radiator System—This system carries the water from the radiator through the pump and into the engine and back to the radiator for cooling.

Combined Pump, Fan, Radiator and Thermo-syphon[1]—The thermo-syphon system is used entirely for the cooling of the cylinder, maintaining a constant temperature of the cylinder wall. The pump, fan and radiator is an independent system. The pump draws the water from the tank into the radiator, where it is cooled by the fan, and returns it through the tank where it is subject to the thermo-syphon action for cooling the engine.

Selecting Water Supply

In all water cooling systems, use clean rain or soft water, because hard waters deposit lime and similar sediments, which incrust metal surfaces and prevent the heat from coming through to the water. When dirty water must be used, strain it. Hard waters are those which usually come from some depth and have absorbed certain mineral products, just as sugar is taken up by water[2]. These substances are usually soluble in cold water, but are set free when the water is heated.

Boiler compounds satisfactorily used with local waters may be used to remove the scale. Better however by far, prevent its formation by arranging for a supply of soft water[3].

NOTE 1—Combined Pump and Thermo-Syphon Cooling

This system of cooling is used on the International 15-30 tractor.

NOTE 2—Preventing Lime Deposits

One way of preventing deposits is to add one-half teacup of kerosene to each tank or hopper filling of water. Kerosene adheres to the metal surface of the cylinder walls and piping and prevents scale formation or incrustation.

NOTE 3—Removing Scale from Cooling System

The use of water containing salt, gypsum, sulphur or other impurities will cause deposit to form on exhaust valve and in the water jacket and interfere with the working of the engine, will destroy lubrication and cause the cylinders to wear.

Should a deposit of lime form in the cylinder water jacket it can be removed with a solution of seven parts of rain water to one part of muriatic acid, which may be obtained at any drug store. (Ask for commercial muriatic or hydrochloric acid. It costs less and will serve the purpose just as well as the higher grades.) Allow this to remain in the water jacket about 36 hours and the deposit can be easily removed by flushing or scraping where possible.

Oil Cooling

Fluids other than water are seldom used in the cooling system, but oil has been used to some extent. If a light oil be used, such as kerosene or distillate, there is danger of fire; if heavy oils are used, such as fuel oil, they tend to congeal or solidify at low temperatures. In warm weather there is the disadvantage that oil can carry away only 45 per cent as much heat as water, so the cooling system must circulate the oil more than twice as fast around the cylinder to carry away the same amount of heat in a given time, and the cooling surface must be correspondingly larger to give up the heat to the air.

As weight is an important factor, and easy, quick starting desirable, the disadvantages of oil cooling are considered greater than its advantages for tractors and even for stationary work.

The Governing System

Every engine is designed to operate best at one definite speed, which rated speed is indicated on the nameplate. The function of the governing system is to give us a means of adjusting that speed and then permitting the mechanism to control the speed automatically.

For stationary engines and tractor engines it is desirable to have the engine designed for a fixed speed. It may under certain conditions be run above or below this speed with good results, though better at lower than at higher speeds. Five per cent may be said to be the safe maximum increase; the minimum may be as low as the engine will run idle.

Regular Engine Speed Best

The rated speed should not generally be exceeded, because the entire machine is balanced for that speed. Speeds above normal cause vibrations, which, especially in a tractor engine, set, as it is, upon a frame and wheels resting on soft ground, may be very destructive to the entire outfit. The vibration due to change of speed is not so noticeable in stationary engines bolted down to a solid base.

The prevailing idea is that an operator can increase the power of the engine by speeding it up. This is true to a certain extent, but it is also possible to speed the engine up so high that it takes all of its power to keep itself going. The operator must recognize the fact that speeding should be used only in an emergency—and that the designer, when he fixed a definite speed, must have indicated the one best suited for the engine to give full, constant and satisfactory power.

Hit-and-Miss Governor

Two systems of governing prevail in engines today—the hit-and-miss type and the throttling or volume type.

The hit-and-miss type develops power very economically. It consists of a device which enables the engine to take in a full charge of explosive mixture in proportion to the load on the engine, storing the power in a flywheel and then transforming it into work until the speed drops below normal, when a new charge is taken in and exploded. The heavier the load, the more frequent the charge.

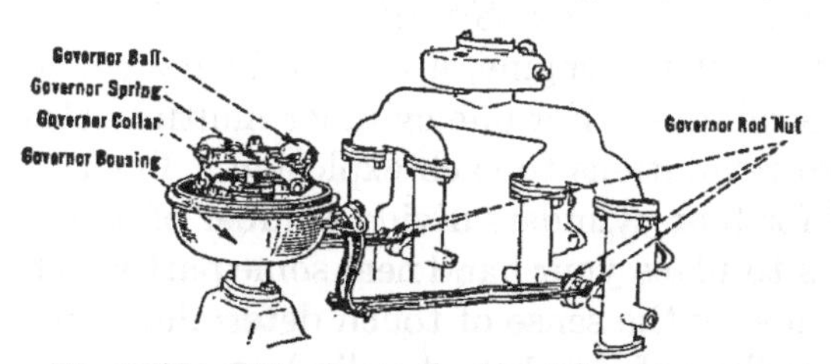

Illust. 47. This shows the throttle governor on the International 15-30 tractor. The upper part of the governor housing has been removed to show the governor balls, springs and collar. Note governor rods between governor and throttle valve whereby governor is enabled to control the quantity of fuel supplied to the engine. A hit-and-miss governor permits either a full charge of fuel or none to reach the cylinder, while the throttle governor permits any quantity of fuel needed to be delivered for each explosion.

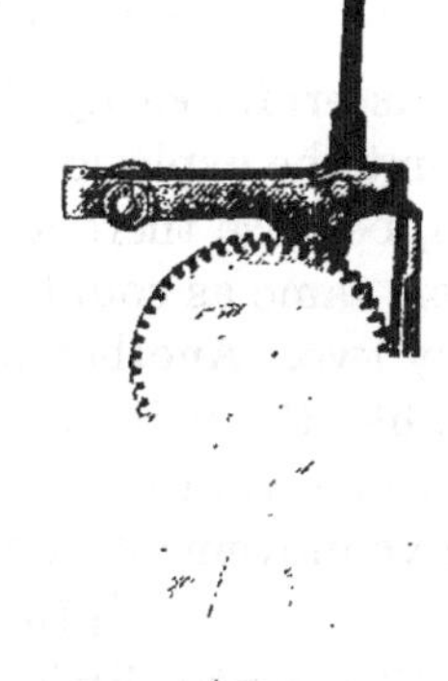

Illust. 48. A hit-and-miss type of governor.

While this system has the advantage of economy, especially for stationary engine practice, it is not as suitable for tractor purposes as the throttling system of governing. First, because of vibration due to the irregular impulses, and second, because it does not work well with the lower grades of fuels, since the cylinder chill, whenever a miss-stroke takes place, will cause difficulty in operation with these fuels except on constant full load.

Throttling Governor

The throttling system of governing is now extensively used and consists of a control in the intake pipe determining the quantity or volume of the mixture. Different engines use variations of the quantity, or a variation of the quality or a combination of these, in accordance with the intention to get an engine that will operate well or economically at low speeds or light loads.

For satisfactory operation on lower grades of fuel than gasoline, this system is very necessary, as the engine remains quite uniformly hot, causing an explosion in each cylinder every other revolution.

The operator should check up the engine speed now and then, and all parts and joints of the governing device should be kept well oiled and free from cramping[1].

These parts function so delicately that a tight joint or loose joint takes the control away from the governor and results in racing or irregular operation[2]. Likewise, when more cylinders than one are controlled separately from the governor, care must be taken to see that all throttles are adjusted alike so that one cylinder will not do more work than the other.

To Determine Engine Speed

To ascertain easily the speed of the engine, use an ordinary watch and count the explosions for a minute. For one cylinder multiply this by two, because there are two revolutions to each explosion. For two cylinders same as count, and for four cylinders divide number of explosions by two. Another way is to place your hand near some part which moves, like the valve lever, thus by the sense of touch determining the number of revolutions. Regardless of number of cylinders count any one valve movement and multiply by two.

The Air and Gas System

Until recently little attention was given to this very important system, which enables the air to get into the cylinder, and the exhaust gases to get away from the cylinder and engine.

Until the tractor became a special machine the value of clean air was not given much thought, but it is now recognized that many of the early troubles within the engine were attributable to quantities of fine, earthy and sandy dust drawn into the cylinder through the intake.

Air Cleaners Necessary

An example will show that this feature is very important. A 2-cylinder engine with 6.5-in. bore and 8-in. stroke, making 500 r. p. m.,

NOTE 1—Governor Control of Engine Speed

In addition to this, it may be well to mention that the speed of engines can be changed by either tightening or loosening the governor springs. In no case is it advisable, due to increased possibilities of vibration, to increase the speed of any engine over and above that stated on the engine.

On the volume governed engines provision is made between the governor and the butterfly valve for the proper speed control through volume admission. If the engine should race, which is found at times due to wear, showing that the butterfly does not close in time when the engine speed is up to normal, the necessary adjustment can be made to bring the engine back to proper speed. If engine speed is too low, we lose power; if it is too high, the engine is injured and economy is lost; therefore, always maintain the proper speed.

NOTE 2—Loose Governor Gear

Irregular operation may be due to a loose gear either on cam shaft or on governor shaft.

takes in about 46,000 cu. ft. of air in operating 10 hours or one day. The fine dust which surrounds any tractor operating in dry weather during plowing, disking, or harrowing, naturally is drawn in with the air, and this fine dust, combining with the fuel and lubricating oil, makes a most effective cylinder, ring and valve destroyer.

Air strainers now on the market remove from 96 to 98 per cent of these impurities from the air, thus prolonging materially the life of the tractors on which they are used. Straining through carded long fibre wool[1], through a suitable cloth[2] or using centrifugal force to take out these particles are the means now utilized.

NOTE 1—Air Cleaner on Titan 10-20—I H C 15-30

The air cleaner consists of a large metallic drum containing carefully carded sheep wool, through which the air supplied to mixer must pass. Below this metallic drum is a casting containing a 2-way damper controlled by shifter handle. When the shifter handle is in the position shown, hot air is taken through the air cleaner. The shifter handle can be thrown about 90° in a counter-clockwise direction which cuts off the hot air and supplies cold air through the wool. Intermediate positions may be obtained as desired.

The purpose of the wool is to screen out all fine dust particles, sand, grit, etc., which, if drawn into the engine cylinder, would cause it to wear excessively. It will depend upon operative conditions how often it is necessary to clean the wool, but it is safe to say that when disking, drilling or plowing in dry conditions, the wool should be cleaned every day. This will be very easily done provided the wool is **thoroughly** dry. It will be cleaned by compressing wool into a close ball and then shaking it out two or three times. When replacing the wool be careful to see that it is spread uniformly and has not become matted into chunks, as either the matted condition or the irregular spreading of the wool will allow the air to force unobstructed passages through which dust and finer dirt may pass.

Illust. 49. Air cleaner used on Titan tractors.

CAUTION. When operating tractor, the cover for air cleaner must be kept tightly in place.

NOTE 2—Air Cleaner Used on Mogul Tractors

This air strainer consists of a large metallic drum perforated and covered with two thicknesses of muslin or cotton cloth, through which the air supplied to mixer must pass. It depends upon operative conditions how often it is necessary to clean the cloth, but it is safe to say that when disking, drilling or plowing in dry conditions, this should be cleaned every day.

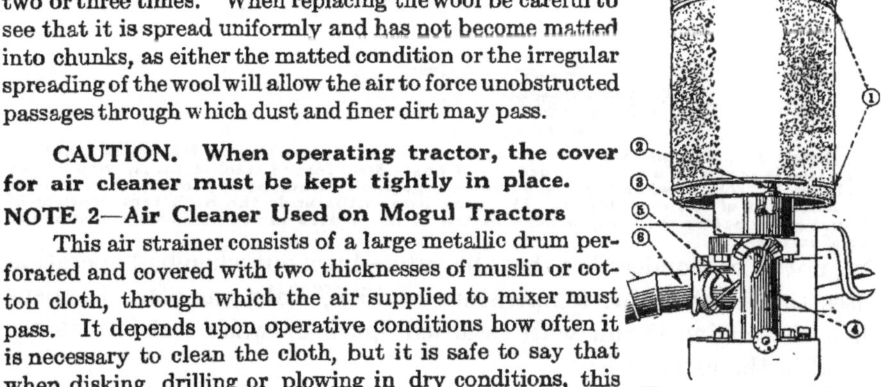

Illust. 50. Air cleaner used on Mogul tractors.

The smaller and lower down the tractor engine is, and the closer to the ground the intake is, the more necessary it is to give attention to this point.

Short, free, direct air passages into the engines are now demanded. In the multiple air intake types of engines, not in the class here discussed, we see the effect of this air system idea extended to the use of multiple air intake valves, to enable fast-running engines to get quicker and freer opening into the cylinder.

Give the engine plenty of good, cool, clear air along with the fuel and it will deliver results. Frequently engines are installed in hot, dark, damp corners, or are boxed in, so as not to be able to secure a sufficient quantity of necessary air. An engine will not do well where a healthy man would not live.

Quick, Complete Exhaust Desirable

When the explosive mixture has been burned within the cylinder it is desirable to get rid of the exhaust gases as quickly and completely as possible, and by the shortest unrestricted way. Mufflers must, therefore, be carefully designed so as to minimize resistance or back pressure. Likewise, stationary engines should not be installed with long exhaust pipes, because the back pressure created cuts down power, destroys crank pin bearings, and burns out exhaust valves.

From our previous illustration, we find the exhaust gases leave the cylinder usually at about 1000° Fahr., which means that the exhaust valve is punished 250 times a minute in our 500-revolution engine by the passage of quantities of hot gas at this temperature. It is, there-

Illust. 51. Exhaust valve construction used on International Harvester tractors. This valve is made by a special process. It has a drop forged steel stem, A, with a grey iron head, B. The steel and iron are walded together by a scientific process which makes a perfect joint of the two metals. The grey iron withstands the high temperature of exhaust gases better than any other construction. Valves such as this are expensive to manufacture.

fore, not to be wondered at that the valves burn out when bad operation raises this 1000° Fahr. temperature to 1500° Fahr., as often happens when the engine is run with retarded spark or when restrictions are placed in the exhaust line.

Give the exhaust a short clear path with as little obstruction as possible, and the result will be appreciated.

Chapter VI
Liquid Fuel for Internal Combustion Engines

The fuel usable in internal combustion engines may be classed as gaseous, liquid and pulverized (coal or other dusts). The ones most suitable for stationary and tractor purposes are the liquid fuels, so we shall devote our attention mainly to them.

Liquid fuels are obtained from a number of sources, the largest and most important of which is petroleum, which is pumped or flows from wells widely distributed over the world. The principal wells so far developed to the point of commercial profit are those of the United States, Mexico, Russia, Austria and Roumania.

Composition of Fuels

In analyzing petroleum or crude oil as it is pumped from the well we find a long series of different chemical substances mixed together into one fluid. These substances appear in the gaseous, liquid and solid state, soaked and mixed together. The gases are trapped like air in water, the solids and semi-solids are soaked in the lighter liquids. However, all of these gases, liquids and solids are definite relationships of carbon (C) and hydrogen (H). In nature we recognize the element hydrogen as a part of many substances—particularly of water. Carbon forms the main part of coal, of the diamond and of graphite.

Nature takes very minute parts of these substances in different proportions and from them forms the oils we are discussing. By analyzing these oils we find the hydrogen and carbon united together in a peculiar definite relationship.

Paraffin Series of Hydrocarbons

The relationship most commonly found in crude petroleums is one part of carbon and twice as many parts of hydrogen plus 2. This relationship C_nH_{2n+2} designates the paraffin series of hydrocarbons. The simplest compound in the paraffin series is one part of carbon with four parts of hydrogen which is a gas. The next simpler compound is two parts of carbon and six parts of hydrogen, and so on down the list, remembering always that every time we add one carbon atom we add two hydrogen atoms.

The gases, liquids and solids in the paraffin series, are as given in Table V.

Table V—Paraffin Series of Hydrocarbons

Character	Chemical Formula	Boiling Point of the Liquid	Approximate Grouping	Baume
	CH_4	−329° fahr.		
Gases	C_2H_6	−199° fahr.		
	C_3H_8	− 49° fahr.	Petro. Ether	108°–80°
	C_4H_{10}	+ 34° fahr.		
	C_5H_{12}	+ 93° fahr.		
	C_6H_{14}	+156° fahr.		
	C_7H_{16}	+210° fahr.	Light Gasoline	50°–90°
	C_8H_{18}	+250° fahr.		
	C_9H_{20}	+302° fahr.	Heavy Gasoline	
Liquids	$C_{10}H_{22}$	+351° fahr.	Illuminating Oil	44°
	$C_{11}H_{24}$	+383° fahr.		
	$C_{12}H_{26}$	+419° fahr.		
	$C_{13}H_{28}$	+454° fahr.	Kerosene	40°–47°
	$C_{14}H_{30}$	+486° fahr.	Distillate	28°–39°
Viscous	$C_{15}H_{32}$	+518° fahr.		
Liquids	$C_{16}H_{34}$	+549° fahr.		
	$C_{17}H_{36}$	+577° fahr.		
	$C_{18}H_{38}$	+604° fahr.	Gas Oils	34°–42°
		Melting Point		
	$C_{19}H_{40}$	92° fahr.		
	$C_{20}H_{42}$	99° fahr.	Fuel Oils	25°–30°
	$C_{21}H_{44}$	106° fahr.	Spindle Oils	26°–35°
Semi-Solids	$C_{22}H_{46}$	113° fahr.	Vaselines-$C_{18}H_{34}$ to $C_{32}H_{66}$ and other series	
	$C_{23}H_{48}$	120° fahr.	Cylinder Oils	20°–27°
	$C_{24}H_{60}$	125° fahr.	Paraffin Waxes	
	$C_{25}H_{52}$	130° fahr.	Dust Lng. Oils	24°–34°
Solids	$C_{26}H_{54}$	134° fahr.	Road Binders	34°–35°
	$C_{28}H_{58}$	140° fahr.		
	$C_{29}H_{60}$	145° fahr.		
	$C_{31}H_{64}$	155° fahr.		
	$C_{32}H_{66}$	158° fahr.		
	$C_{34}H_{68}$	162° fahr.		
	$C_{60}H_{122}$		Pitch	

The Process of Refining

The fuels we buy on the market are separate parts of the long series given in the table and are obtained by refining the crude oil. To the right of the table are some familiar commercial names—petroleum ether, gasoline, kerosene, distillate, gas oil, fuel oil, spindle oil, lubricating oil, vaseline, cylinder lubricating oil, paraffin wax, dust laying oils, road binders, pitch. They are placed about opposite the substances known to have the properties we recognize by these names.

Note that the simpler substances at the top of the list appear as gases, then we find liquids, semi-solids and at the bottom solids. The change is not sudden, but gradual all the way down.

These groups can be most easily separated from one another by taking note of their boiling points, and this forms the basis of the great distilling industries which supply these products.

The mass of crude oil is put into vats and subjected to a constant heat up to a definite point; the vapor which passes off, being then cooled, is called a fraction. This explains the term "fractional distillation."

For instance, in Table V, under the Column "Boiling Point," is indicated the temperature which must be reached before the liquid begins to evaporate. By noting these boiling points it will be seen that if a temperature of 300° is reached all the lighter gases will pass off and all the gasolines will evaporate. Therefore, when the temperature of 300° Fahr. is reached, the condensed liquid produced by this boiling is set aside as Fraction 1 and could be termed the gasoline fraction. Continued heating causes exactly the same action, so that when 575 to 600° fahr. is reached, the burning oils, that is, those containing kerosene, have all been evaporated and condensed, and these are set aside as Fraction 2. Upon further heating the lubricating oils begin to evaporate, are condensed, and these produce Fraction 3. There then remains in the still the residue, which includes the road binders and pitch.

The important point to remember is that it takes more heat to vaporize each succeeding chemical compound as we go from the simple to the complex, and that kerosene is lower down in the list than gasoline, therefore more heat is required to vaporize or gasify it.

Weight of Distillation Products

Were we to have equal quantities of each of the several separate chemical compounds in the paraffin series, and were we to weigh them, we would find that the first or simpler ones are lighter than the next succeeding ones respectively. This rule holds true all the way down the list, so that while a gallon of the lightest gasoline weighs 5¾ lb., fuels at the heavy end weigh about 7½ lb. per gal. Should we take common gasoline as weighing 6 lb. per gal. and kerosene 6.6 lb. per gal. it is easy to see that kerosene weighs 10 per cent more and therefore this factor must come up in the design of the carburetor, for it requires 10 per cent more power to lift the fuel to the needle. *We noted the required niceties of the measuring done by the carburetor in the discussion of the Fuel and Carbureting System, so the effect of this difference must indicate that the same carburetor, unless specially designed, cannot handle both gasoline and kerosene equally well.*

Heat Value or British Thermal Units in Fuels (B. t. u.)[1]

Wherever any substance burns heat is given off, the amount of which depends upon the composition of the substance. There is no known common material which has available more concentrated heat power in a given quantity, than the hydrocarbons or petroleum oils. These can be burned completely.

This burning is very interesting and should be understood. The carbon and the hydrogen in the fuel separately unite with a portion of the air to form new substances. Air is composed of a number of gases—one of which, nitrogen, is a peculiar gas which refuses to combine chemically with other substances, except under very extreme conditions. Oxygen, another of the gases in air, however, is very active, and unites easily with many substances.

If we measure the gases contained in the air by weight, we find 23 per cent is oxygen and 77 per cent is nitrogen. By volume 21 per cent is oxygen and 79 per cent is nitrogen. Very small quantities of other substances are present. The air and fuel, then, in an engine presents four important substances—hydrogen, carbon, oxygen and nitrogen. When the carbon and oxygen come together under proper conditions, they unite chemically and form new gases, CO, carbon monoxide[2], or CO_2, carbon dioxide. The first gas is combustible, the second one is not. When the engine is in operation the presence of the first gas is noticeable by an odor and by the fact that it gives us a headache. The odor indicates that the engine is not getting enough air or it is getting too much fuel, which causes the formation of CO or carbon monoxide. In other words, there is not sufficient oxygen for the volume of carbon.

NOTE 1—British Thermal Heat Unit

One B. t. u. is the amount of heat required to raise the temperature of 1 pound of distilled water from 62° to 63° Fahr. Water at 62° is selected because that is the point of greatest condensation. One B. t. u. will do 746 foot pounds of work, or it requires 42.42 B. t. u. to produce one h. p.

NOTE 2—Carbon Monoxide Dangerous

A gas engine running under the conditions of throttling and low speed may throw off over 13 per cent of the exhaust as carbon monoxide gas. It is not a suffocating gas like carbon dioxide, but instead it is an extremely poisonous one. The air we breathe should never contain more than 1/10 per cent even for very short intervals, and the average of carbon monoxide should always be below 5/100 per cent. Carbon monoxide gas poisons and destroys the lungs. Engines operating under full load when overfed with fuel throw off even more carbon monoxide than when running on light load. If the tractor is operated indoors for any purpose, take special care to ventilate the place where any exhaust gases might accumulate.

Oxygen and one pound of carbon burned completely liberates 14,650 British thermal units.

Oxygen and one pound of hydrogen burned completely liberates 62,000 British thermal units.

Combinations of carbon and hydrogen liberate relatively quantities of heat units depending on the above facts.

Table VI
Heat Value in Fuels

	Baume	Specific Gravity	Heat Units per Lb.	Lb. per Gallon	Heat Units per Gallon
Gasoline	70	.700 lbs.	21,050B.t.u.	5.83 lb.	122,721 B.t.u.
Gasoline	63	.725 lbs.	20,770B.t.u.	6.04 lb.	125,450 B.t.u.
Kerosene	42	.813 lbs.	19,930B.t.u.	6.82 lb.	135,922 B.t.u.

Table VI. illustrates the points of decreasing heat units per pound and increasing heat units for each gallon of liquid. As we buy our fuels by the gallon, we are interested in this feature: that there are more heat units per gallon in kerosene than in gasoline.

It is evident, then, that we should be able to do as much or more work with a gallon of kerosene as we can with a gallon of gasoline, provided that all points relating to design and operation of the engine are properly cared for. For us this is the important fact. If we analyze the design of an engine from this standpoint, that is, the larger number of heat units in kerosene, we find that many features of the engine will have to be designed especially to care for the excessive heat units passing through the engine. The higher temperature caused by the larger number of heat units in kerosene affects the power system, the fuel system, the ignition system, the cooling system, the lubricating system, and the air and gas system. This will probably explain why so many engines are not successful kerosene burners. They were designed for gasoline, and the designers forgot that *six of the seven systems designed for gasoline require special attention if the engine is to burn kerosene, owing to the larger number of heat units passing through the engine.*

Viscosity of Kerosene Affects Mixer Design

The resistance to free flow of a liquid is called viscosity. We recognize this feature when we try to pour molasses from a pitcher, or heavy lubricating oil from one vessel to another. The little particles of the substance hang together or stick to the container.

This characteristic of the hydrocarbons is found in every substance in the paraffin series to a lesser or greater degree. It is less pronounced in the lighter substances but very decided when we proceed into the kerosene and the substances beyond. This characteristic becomes valuable enough in the heavier compounds to enable us to use them as lubricating oils. We have first the light lubricants, then the medium lubricants in which the viscosity is greater, and then the heavy lubricants with the greatest viscosity. The point to remember in this connection is that kerosene being lower down in the series than gasoline, it must have greater viscosity.

In our discussion of the fuel and carbureting system we found how delicate the work of the carburetor really is. It must measure out and prepare almost instantly a finely divided fuel thoroughly mixed with air, hundreds of times each minute, depending on the r. p. m. The quantity of fuel it handles is almost too small to be measured. It is evident that a carburetor designed for gasoline will not successfully handle kerosene owing to the fact that kerosene has greater viscosity. The drops of kerosene are held together more firmly, hence the carburetor or mixer for handling kerosene must be made to give more help in tearing up these drops. The greater viscosity of kerosene therefore vitally affects the fuel and carbureting system of the engine, and the designer who would design a successful kerosene-burning engine must take this fact into consideration.

This greater viscosity of kerosene also affects the lubricating system. In the kerosene-burning engine, which operates at a higher temperature than a gasoline engine, proper lubrication implies the use of an oil which will remain viscous under the high internal heats as well as one which will not burn up at these high temperatures.

Flash and Burning Point of Oils Affect Design

The apparatus to determine the flash and burning point is a simple one, in which the oil tested is slowly heated, using a thermometer to record the temperature. At frequent intervals a flame is passed over the surface to determine if the slight vapor coming off will flash. The temperature recorded when this occurs is the flash point. The operation is continued until the flame remains and burns the liquid continuously, which gives us the burning point.

The flashing and burning of both fuel and lubricating oils is very important because it explains to us the necessity of having a hotter spark to ignite a kerosene mixture than gasoline mixture, owing to the higher flash and burning points, and also explains, in another way why it is desirable to run a kerosene engine hotter than when using gasoline.

Globulation, Minutization, Reglobulation and Their Effect on Mixer Design

Each fuel has a peculiar sized drop which it will form if given a chance to drop from a point. The size of this drop is affected by the viscosity of the fluid and the temperature of the liquid. In engines, the rule holds true that when we feed drops of fuel into the engine, it is certain that under the same temperature, drops of gasoline will be smaller than the drops of kerosene. We must, therefore, take these drops and still further tear them up or minutize them, for unless we do, they cannot easily change into the vapor state when the heat gets at them. This minutization should be one of the principal functions of the carbüretor.

When the fuel is once minutized, it should be almost immediately burned, otherwise the natural tendency is for the vapor to reglobulate or go back into large drops. This feature has a great deal to do with the success or failure of an engine designed to handle kerosene or other fuels heavier than gasoline[1].

Mixtures and Flame Propagation

We know that it is essential in a good engine to have a thorough and proper mixture of the fuel vapor and the air. Nature demands a definite weight of air present to furnish the fuel with sufficient oxygen to completely burn the mixture. If the mixture is too weak or too strong, slower burning takes place than when mixture is just right. We figure on giving the engine an excess of air rather than too little,

NOTE 1—Location of the Mixer

The tendency of heavier fuels to reglobulate has an important bearing on the location of the mixer. The kerosene mixer should be placed higher than the cylinder, so that there is a direct downward passage for the air and fuel into the cylinder. This will not give the kerosene vapor an opportunity to condense on the walls between the needle valve and the cylinder. Not only should the mixer be close to the cylinder, but there should be no abrupt turns or right angle elbows in the fuel passage to the cylinder. The passage should be short, direct and unobstructed. Long, horizontal manifolds or passages give the fuel a chance to reglobulate.

When a carburetor is used this location above the cylinder is not so essential.

for it is better to have some oxygen leaving through the exhaust than to have unburned or incompletely burned fuel leaving the engine.

Under any circumstances we must recognize Nature's law that in burning gasoline the flame burns or propagates through the mixture at a certain speed, and under similar conditions a flame will not burn as fast through a mixture of kerosene vapor and air. This factor is all important in designing engines to operate on lower grade fuels, for if the governor controls the engine to a speed too slow or too fast for the flame, the energy resulting from the explosion is only partly utilized. This is illustrated by a man helping to push a wagon. He cannot help much if the wagon is traveling as fast or faster than he does. Only when he is able to travel faster than the wagon, can he exert his force to advantage. It is just so with a kerosene mixture in an engine governed to permit the piston to travel near to or faster than the push of expansion.

Compression and its Effects on Fuels and Engine Designs

It has long been known that in any internal combustion engine, the cycle is aided very much by compressing the new charges so as to promote economy and smooth operation. The main effects we are aiming at are first, the thorough mixing and mingling of the fuel particles with the air and second, the raising of the temperature and pressure near to the ignition point so that little time is lost in exploding the mixture.

To illustrate this point, let us review an engine running on gasoline and in which the compression is gradually raised and note the effect on its horse power.

Table VII

Relation Between Compression and H. P. Developed

Compression	Horse Power Developed
45 lb.	1.00
60 lb.	1.21
75 lb.	1.34
90 lb.	1.46
105 lb.	1.55

This must emphasize the value of compression to the operator who wishes to get the best out of the engine and who must see to it that the engine maintains its proper operating conditions. Another example will still further emphasize this.

Table VIII

Relation Between Compression and Fuel Consumption

Compression	Kerosene Consumed in Lb. per H. P.	
60 lb.	.950 lb.	Sp. Gravity .813 Baume—42
70 lb.	.800 lb.	
80 lb.	.730 lb.	
90 lb.	.700 lb.	
100 lb.	.680 lb.	
110 lb.	.670 lb.	

A similar relationship exists between temperature and pov veloped and temperature and fuel consumption.

In other words, there is every reason why we should utilize bo highest sensible compression, and the highest sensible temperatu the engine in order to get the highest economy from the fuel a r engine. The only limit for each is the practical satisfactory ope n of the engine.

The factors which operate against this end are two. A pr e too high causes the well known knocking indicated by pre-igniti the cylinder, and a temperature too high interferes with prop orication.

Pre-ignition means that the fuel self-ignites or ignites ahead of t ment where it is mechanically intended to ignite because the su unding temperature and pressure combined are above the point ich the fuel vapor will remain unignited[1].

Since this pre-ignition, if excessive, makes the engine practica controlled, we must see to it that we maintain conditions wh able us to control it.

Use of Water with Kerosene

One means of enabling us to control this pre-ignition is by supp water along with the fuel in small quantities. This water regula me propagation and gives us all the desirable features of high co ession and the highest temperature with good economy. Anot thod is to lower compression to the point where it will not cause p ition.

TE 1—Other Causes of Pre-ignition

Pre-ignition may also be caused by
ep sand holes in the exhaust valve disk, head, or cylinder
wing carbon or metal points in cylinder
egular ignition
ck of water with heavy fuels under high compression.

Water Aids Combustion

The injection of water with heavy fuels in engines with compression of 75 to 85 lbs. helps to render the mixture homogeneous so that it burns uniformly when ignited. We have also found that without the use of water we had to return part of the exhaust gases to deaden the mixture, or decrease the compression, or run the engine too cold, or retard the spark in order to keep the engine running. All these difficulties have been overcome through the injection of a little water. Compression, temperature and spark advance can be maintained at the point which will insure the utmost economy in fuel consumption and the delivery of the greatest possible amount of power.

Water Prevents Pre-Ignition

The use of water also helps to prevent pre-ignition when 75 lbs. to 85 lbs. compression is used. Pre-ignition is prevented by the water injection because the water in the mixture prevents the breaking up of the fuel which would result in chemical pre-ignition as explained on page 83.

Water Keeps Cylinder Clean

Another reason for injecting water is to aid in keeping the cylinder clean. Water prevents, to a certain extent, the formation of carbon deposits in the cylinder, because it keeps the carbon, if present, broken up to such an extent that it passes out through the exhaust passage.

Compression for Various Fuels

Different fuels require different compressions. For best results the following are generally accepted.

Table IX

Fuel	Compression	
Gasoline	75 lb.	These values depend on factors of speed and type of engine.
Kerosene (with water)	85 lb.	
Illuminating Gas	85 lb.	
Producer Gas	130 lb.	
Alcohol[1]	200 lb.	
Crude Oil	350 lb.	

NOTE 1—Using Alcohol in I H C Engines

Extensive experiments indicate that by raising compression in I H C engines up to 135 or 150 pounds per square inch, we secure as low fuel consumption per H. P. hour on alcohol as we can possibly obtain with a good grade of gasoline.

Table X

Temperatures of Ignition of Various Fuels

In air at atmospheric pressure the following are standard:

Benzine	780°
Gasoline Vapor	950°
Alcohol Vapor C_2H_6	950°
Illuminating Gas Mixture	1100°

Here we have some valuable data which helps to explain an important factor in igniting different fuels. It is plain that if by temperature and pressure we develop heat greater than the ignition points of various fuels our engine will pre-ignite and we lose control over it. The temperature, then, within any engine previous to the proper ignition time, must be below the ignition temperature set by Nature's law.

We now have seen some of the influencing factors in the characteristics of the fuels of one series, the paraffin series. Other fuels, like the napthenes, have similar characteristics, but there are still many liquid fuels available.

Alcohol or Vegetable Fuels

Among the vegetable fuels there is a great field ahead for the alcohols, as these fuels can be made from all kinds of vegetable matter. Three different alcohols are available in quantity: wood alcohol CH_4, but this is not suitable for use in engines; grain alcohol C_2H_6, and so-called denatured alcohol, consisting of a mixture of 100 volumes of grain alcohol, 10 volumes of wood alcohol and ½ volume of benzine. This compound has a heat unit rating of 11,800 B. t. u. per lb. Alcohols work well in engines designed for gasoline and kerosene but for real economy require the compression noted in Table IX—200 lb. per sq. in. There is a good future for the alcohol engine, if the manufacturing and tax cost can be reduced, but the present prices are beyond the point of making the fuel acceptable.

Cracked Fuels

Tremendous demands for easily handled fuels like the gasolines, and the constantly rising price for these have set the engineering and chemical world working to devise substitutes, or aid in the increased production of the gasolines. Among the resulting patented processes which have been successful, are many which make use of the so-called "Cracking Process." The cracking of oils is based on the discovery that if the complex lubricating oils are overheated and put under pressure, the chemical composition is broken up and the atoms re-unite on a different basis to form the lighter fuel oils. The general temperature at which this overheating takes place is a temperature around 650° Fahr., to 850° Fahr., and under a pressure of 60 lb. to 75 lb. A commercial process using this idea is the Burton process.

A similar process is known as the Rittman process. Improvement in these processes enables us to convert a large percentage of fuel oils into gasoline of first quality.

Chemical Pre-Ignition

It is this same "cracking" of fuels, which is used to increase the available supplies of the lighter fuels, which sometimes takes place within the cylinder of an engine and causes pre-ignition[1]. This pre-ignition, which results when the engine is too hot, might be termed chemical pre-ignition in order to distinguish it from other kinds of pre-ignition, which may be caused by some foreign substance within the cylinder retaining heat enough to ignite the new charge before the desired time, or a pre-ignition due to careless operation of the engine.

Chemical pre-ignition is a duplication of the "cracking" process within the cylinder. It results because the kerosene is subjected to a high pressure and temperature, which breaks up the chemical combinations of carbon and hydrogen and permits them to reunite in the form of simpler gasolines which are more volatile and hence ignite before the desired time or the time at which the heavier fuel, had it not been broken up, would have ignited.[2]

CORRECTIONS

Page 82—Formula for wood alcohol should read.............. CH_3OH
Formula for grain alcohol should read............ C_2H_5OH

Page 83—Note 2—7th line from bottom.......... $C_{13}H_{28}=C_6H_{14}+H$
should read—...................... $C_{13}H_{28}=2\times C_6H_{14}+C$

$C_{13}H_{28}=C_6H_{14}+H$. The simpler gases like C_5H_{12} and C_6H_{14} are much more volatile than $C_{12}H_{26}$ or $C_{13}H_{28}$, with the result that they pre-ignite in the cylinder.

When kerosene is subjected to 75 lbs. to 85 lbs. compression, chemical pre-ignition, or breaking up into lighter fuels, is prevented, as previously explained, by the use of water. Water is fed into the cylinder when pounding indicates that chemical pre-ignition is occurring. As soon as water is injected, pounding stops, which indicates that breaking up of fuel is being prevented.

Table X

Temperatures of Ignition of Various Fuels

In air at atmospheric pressure the following are standard:

Benzine	780°
Gasoline Vapor	950°
Alcohol Vapor C_2H_6	950°
Illuminating Gas Mixture	1100°

Here we have some valuable data which helps to explain an important factor in igniting different fuels. It is plain that if by temperature and pressure we develop heat greater than the ignition points of various fuels our engine will pre-ignite and we lose control over it. The temperature, then, within any engine previous to the proper ignition time, must be below the ignition temperature set by Nature's law.

We now have seen some of the influencing factors in the characteristics of the fuels of one series, the paraffin series. Other fuels, like the napthenes, have similar characteristics, but there are still many liquid fuels available.

Alcohol or Vegetable Fuels

Among the vegetable fuels there is a great field ahead for the alcohols, as these fuels can be made from all kinds of vegetable matter. Three different alcohols are available in quantity: wood alcohol CH_4, but this is not suitable for use in engines; grain alcohol C_2H_6, and so-called denatured alcohol, consisting of a mixture of 100 volumes of grain alcohol, 10 volumes of wood alcohol and ½ volume of benzine. This cor

wel

req

a g

car

the

and the constantly rising price for these have set the engineering and chemical world working to devise substitutes, or aid in the increased production of the gasolines. Among the resulting patented processes which have been successful, are many which make use of the so-called "Cracking Process." The cracking of oils is based on the discovery that if the complex lubricating oils are overheated and put under pressure, the chemical composition is broken up and the atoms re-unite on a different basis to form the lighter fuel oils. The general temperature at which this overheating takes place is a temperature around 650° Fahr., to 850° Fahr., and under a pressure of 60 lb. to 75 lb. A commercial process using this idea is the Burton process.

A similar process is known as the Rittman process. Improvement in these processes enables us to convert a large percentage of fuel oils into gasoline of first quality.

Chemical Pre-Ignition

It is this same "cracking" of fuels, which is used to increase the available supplies of the lighter fuels, which sometimes takes place within the cylinder of an engine and causes pre-ignition[1]. This pre-ignition, which results when the engine is too hot, might be termed chemical pre-ignition in order to distinguish it from other kinds of pre-ignition, which may be caused by some foreign substance within the cylinder retaining heat enough to ignite the new charge before the desired time, or a pre-ignition due to careless operation of the engine.

Chemical pre-ignition is a duplication of the "cracking" process within the cylinder. It results because the kerosene is subjected to a high pressure and temperature, which breaks up the chemical combinations of carbon and hydrogen and permits them to reunite in the form of simpler gasolines which are more volatile and hence ignite before the desired time or the time at which the heavier fuel, had it not been broken up, would have ignited.[2]

NOTE 1—Pre-ignition

See Note 1, page 80, for other causes of pre-ignition.

NOTE 2.—Action of chemical pre-ignition

We know that kerosene is made up of several compounds, and we shall take two or three of these to explain the point. In kerosene we find $C_{12}H_{26}$ and $C_{13}H_{28}$. When pre-ignition occurs it indicates that these two combinations have been broken down. $C_{12}H_{26}$ tries to form itself into two parts of a simpler hydrocarbon or light gasoline C_5H_{12}, which leaves as free atoms two carbon particles and two hydrogen particles. When $C_{13}H_{28}$ breaks down we have two parts of light gasoline C_6H_{14} with one carbon part set free. $C_{12}H_{26}=C_5H_{12}+C_6H_{12}+2H$. $C_{13}H_{28}=C_6H_{14}+H$. The simpler gases like C_5H_{12} and C_6H_{14} are much more volatile than $C_{12}H_{26}$ or $C_{13}H_{28}$, with the result that they pre-ignite in the cylinder.

When kerosene is subjected to 75 lbs. to 85 lbs. compression, chemical pre-ignition, or breaking up into lighter fuels, is prevented, as previously explained, by the use of water. Water is fed into the cylinder when pounding indicates that chemical pre-ignition is occurring. As soon as water is injected, pounding stops, which indicates that breaking up of fuel is being prevented.

Effects of Pre-Ignition

The free carbon particles which are left over after the breaking down of the heavier fuels into the lighter fuels explain the deposits in the cylinder and smoke in the exhaust.

The carbon that thus comes out in the exhaust is lost. In $C_{12}H_{26}$ we saw that two parts were set free. This means a loss of 2/12 or 16 per cent of the total heat value of the carbon. Likewise two parts of hydrogen were set free, so that we lose 2/26 or 8 per cent of the heat value of the hydrogen. In the case of $C_{13}H_{28}$ we lose 8 per cent of the carbon value as the fuel breaks down. This indicates that we should by every means possible prevent chemical pre-ignition, because when it occurs we lose a large percentage of the heat value of the fuel through the carbon and hydrogen that are set free. Again, pre-ignition exerts pressure on the piston much too early to be turned into useful work. This effort is all lost. Sometimes pre-ignition takes place in engines which have no water control because of an obstruction in the cooling system which prevents its satisfactory operation.

Sooting Up or Carbonizing in the Cylinders

Several causes can be mentioned for carbonizing within the cylinders. The first is undoubtedly due to poor carburetion where the fuel is not sufficiently broken up. If a globule of fuel comes into the cylinder not properly vaporized it is not in a condition to be completely burned in the time allowed and only the outer shell of it can be burned off, the center is heated up and ejected through the exhaust as smoke or is deposited as soot within the cylinder[1].

Often much of the so-called soot or carbon is not carbon at all, but the remains of the minute particles of dirt drawn in through the intake with the air. This mixed with oil or fuel settles around in different pockets or beneath the rings, causing trouble.

A cold engine, poor lubricating oils and excessive feeding of lubricating oils also cause carbon deposits.

NOTE 1—Prevention and Removal of Carbon Deposit

When carbon has deposited, there is only one safe way to remove it—scrape the cylinder and head, piston, rings and grooves. Do not rely upon patented carbon removers—they are ineffective in most cases. U. S. government experts report good results in removing carbon through the injection of alcohol into the compression chamber and then igniting the charge.

When it is necessary to remove the cylinder head, piston and rings, follow carefully the instructions given on page 15 for the removal and replacement of these parts.

Chapter VII
Getting the Most Power Out of Fuel

Fuel fed into an engine has the possibilities of 100 per cent of power, and were none of it lost, we should be able to get all of this at the crank-shaft. This, of course, cannot be done, but we can so operate the engine that we shall get the largest possible part of this 100 per cent turned into useful work.

There are four main channels through which this power or the available heat units are used up:

Friction Losses of Engine Itself

1. This is the power taken to operate the mechanism and to keep it going; the friction of bearings and energy taken to store momentum in the parts. These losses are both heat and power losses.

Exhaust Losses

2. There is a great deal of heat carried away by the exhaust gases. Roughly speaking, three-fourths of the air taken in is nitrogen which passes through the engine unaffected, except for a rise from room temperature to around 1000° fahr. This heat is all lost along with that carried away by the combusted gases.

Cooling and Radiation Losses

3. These losses are caused by the necessity of keeping a temperature of internal working engine parts low enough to permit ample lubrication at all times. Hence we must lose much of this heat through the cooling medium and by radiation to the air.

Power

4. The important thing in engine operation is to convert the largest per cent of heat into available power.

To illustrate, and at the same time to give typical values of the distribution of these heat unit losses for an engine operating at rated speed and of the type we are discussing, the following is offered:

	Average Percentages	Favorable Percentages	Excellent Percentages
1. Friction losses used up....	15%	13%	10%
2. Exhaust losses carry away.	33%	30%	29%
3. Cooling and radiation losses	40%	40%	39%
4. Power available..........	12%	17%	22%
	100%	100%	100%

If, due to a defective, poor or unsuitable lubricant, or poor mechanical adjustment of the moving parts, friction losses should rise 3 points, it must of necessity rob the power (4) of the 3 points, thus reducing the effectiveness of the engine 25 per cent. That is big interest to pay for poor oil and poor care.

If, due to care in the mechanical timing of all parts, together with care in adjusting for early ignition, thereby giving the mixture every chance of being thoroughly burned and the power transformed, we would be able to reduce the heat losses to the exhaust by even 3 points, and by adding these to the 12 points useful power, our efficiency would be improved 25 per cent.

It is not uncommon for a poor operator, working his engine with late spark, to have his losses through the exhaust rise from 33 per cent to 55 per cent. Such an engine will show a red hot exhaust pipe.

Careful Operation Gets Best Results

A little thought along these lines and an understanding of their effects, good and bad, must make any operator realize that to get good results much depends on how he handles the engine.

Man is given five senses—hearing, seeing, smelling, feeling, and tasting. He has use for most of them when operating an engine.

He can *hear* the exhaust—a too short crack instead of smooth operation indicates a loss. His ear will tell him the correct point of ignition—let him advance his spark until he hears a slight ping. A squeak or rattle indicates something is wrong[1].

He can *watch* the exhaust and see smoke, white, blue, or black, which tells him much relating to lubrication and carburetion.

He can *smell* the exhaust and realize when something is wrong with the outfit's mechanism or operation.

NOTE 1—Keep Nuts and Bolts Tight

The operation of the tractor tends to loosen nuts and rivets. The vibration, even though it may not be excessive, in fact, hardly noticeable, will have a tendency in time to loosen nuts and cause squeaks and rattles with ultimate breakdowns unless given attention. See that lock washers are in place. Make a systematic examination of your machine at stated times, and tighten all cap screws, nuts, bolts and rivets. The first and most important of these are the bearing nuts and bolts. Go over these first. Then go over the transmission nuts and bolts, then the cylinder and head nuts and bolts, then the magneto nuts and bolts, and after that all others not included in the above. All rivets should be inspected occasionally and if loose, tightened. Tighten by holding heavy sledge or weight solidly against rivet head and hammering rivet on other end. See Note 1 page 98 for care of wheel rivets. The principal thing in this connection to remember is to make the examination systematic and thorough, and always in the same order, going over most important bolts first.

He can *see* an overheated exhaust pipe and *feel* the vibration of the engine, or the overheating of a bearing.

Be awake and let the engine speak to you, learn the engine's language. When the engine wants more fuel it pops up the intake or explodes in the exhaust; when it has too much, black smoke issues from the exhaust[1]; when it wants water, it pounds; when it labors hard, it may want less load or a better adjustment of the spark; if it operates in a dull, listless, weary way, perhaps the lubrication is bad or the compression poor.[2]

The best automobile driver, aeroplane man, engine or tractor operator, is the one who makes use of these senses or points, because it is he who must get the last ounce of power from the fuel.

Comparison of Economy of Steam and Kerosene Engines

From this discussion the idea must not be gotten that kerosene or similar engines are not efficient, for they are the most efficient types of present day power plants. Even a poorly operated and poorly designed internal combustion engine of small power may be more efficient than a high grade, high powered steam engine using every facility towards economy, when both are compared as engines transforming heat into power.

If a common high speed, simple, small-powered steam engine and boiler transforms 5 per cent of the available heat units in the coal, it is considered to be a fair engine, whereas a small internal combustion engine will transform 15 per cent of the available heat units if given reasonable operating conditions. Excellent results with a high grade steam engine show 17 per cent of the available heat units transformed, while results of very high grade Diesel type internal combustion engines of large power gives 39 per cent efficiency.

NOTE 1—Mixture too rich, causes black smoke; too much lubricating oil, blue smoke; too much water with kerosene, white smoke.

NOTE 2—Learning the Engine's Language

On pages 135 to 145, inclusive, are listed the troubles which are ordinarily met with in the operation of an engine. These troubles are classified as starting troubles, loss of power, poor speed, etc. A very careful study of these pages will give anyone an excellent knowledge of what various symptoms indicate. In other words, the language of the engine will be readily intelligible. It is only by thoroughly understanding your engine that it will be possible to get from it the economy explained on page 85.

Chapter VIII
Lubricating Oils and Greases

From the table of the paraffin series we see the origin of lubricating oils. The natural crude oils from some fields are not as well supplied with these hydrocarbons as are others. Those which are best suited[1] for our purposes come largely as mineral oils. They are treated especially

NOTE 1—List of Suitable Lubricating Oils

If every tractor operator fully realized the difference between tractor operation and motor truck operation, he would quickly appreciate the great importance of continuous and sufficient lubrication for all tractor parts. The average automobile motor carries a relatively light load with many periods of recuperation, such as coasting down hills or idling at the curb. In contrast with this the tractor motor is delivering its full rated power with wide open throttle practically all the time that it is at work. It pulls a dead load all day with no chance to rest. As a result of high full-load explosion pressures and temperatures, the average operating temperatures of the tractor motor are considerably higher than those in the automobile engine, and a heavier and more substantial oil must be used to reduce wear and heavy repair bills, and to secure economy and satisfactory operation.

Every owner of an International Harvester tractor is strongly urged to use one or another of the oils recommended by the Company and listed below, as these oils have been proved by test to be adapted to tractor lubrication. If none of the listed oils are available, a suitable oil may be obtained from the Harvester Company through your dealer.

If in any territory there is an oil not listed herewith which can be procured more easily, have your dealer write the nearest branch of the International Harvester Company of America and arrange for a test of this oil before using it in International Harvester tractors, even though this oil may be recommended by agents.

Amoco Kerosene Tractor Oil	American Oil Co., Baltimore, Md.
Analie No. 2 Special Tractor Oil	Sonaborn Bros., Dallas, Texas
Aristo Motor Oil No. 1	Union Oil Co. of California
Aristo Motor Oil No. 4	Union Oil Co. of California
Atlantic Tractor Engine Oil	Atlantic Refining Co., Philadelphia, Pa.
Barber Heavy Tractor Oil	W. H. Barber Agency Co., Minneapolis, Minn.
Baton Tractor "B" Oil	Baton Oil Co., Iola, Kans.
Baton Tractor "C Oil	Baton Oil Co., Iola, Kans.
"B" Tractor Oil	Balso Oil Co., Council Bluffs, Iowa
Challenge BMO No. 8 Oil	Balso Oil Co., Council Bluffs, Iowa
Champion Motor Oil, Heavy	Independent Refining Co., Oil City, Pa.
Diamond "A" Gas Engine Oil	Pierce-Fordyce Oil Ass'n, Dallas, Texas
Eagle Gas Engine Tractor Oil	Standard Oil Co. of New Jersey
Faultless Tractor Oil	Hawkeye Oil Co., Waterloo, Iowa
Gamut Oil	Utah Refining Co., Salt Lake City, Utah
Gem Tractor Oil	Moore Oil Co., Cincinnati, Ohio
Grange Tractor Oil	Paragon Refining Co., Toledo, Ohio
Havoline Kerosene Tractor Oil	Indian Refining Co., New York
Havoline Tractor "B" Oil	Indian Refining Co., New York
Heavy Atlas Tractor Oil	Atlas Oil Co., Cleveland, Ohio
Heavy En-Ar-Co. Motor Oil	National Refining Co., Cleveland, Ohio
Heavy Lubro Tractor Oil	Hutchinson Oil Co., Hutchinson, Kans.
Heavy Velvet Tractor Engine Oil	Nourse Oil Co., Kansas City, Mo.
Hercules Tractor Oil	Moore Oil Co., Cincinnati, Ohio
Imperial Gas Engine Tractor Oil	Imperial Oil Co., Ltd., Toronto, Ont., Canada
Int'l Gas Engine Cylinder Oil	British American Oil Co., Toronto, Ont., Canada
Ivalene Kerosene Tractor Oil	Winona Oil Co., Winona, Minn.
IXL Tractor Oil	Petroleum Oil Co., Spartanburg, S. C.
Knox Auto Tractor Oil	Noble Refining Co., Cleveland, Ohio
Magnolene Tractor Oil	Magnolia Petroleum Co., Dallas, Texas

to free them from acid and improve suitability for special purposes.

Characteristics of Good Oil

An oil for a specific purpose, in order to properly serve as a lubricant, must have four characteristics:

1. It must be capable of forming a thin film of oil between the two bearing surfaces.

2. It must be able to withstand the heat, to which the working parts it is meant to lubricate are subjected, without burning, decomposing or thinning down too much for lubrication. (This applies particularly to cylinder lubrication where the pressure from the explosions in the cylinder has a tendency to drive out the oil.)

3. It must be able to resist being squeezed out from between the moving parts, especially crank shaft and piston pin bearings.

4. It must have low internal frictional qualities. By this is meant that the molecules of oil in the film which is under pressure should not generate heat by their rubbing together.

The flash and burning points must be high for cylinder oils, ranging about 421° Fahr. for the flash and 450° for the burning point.

The viscosity factor is very important. Kerosene or gasoline will

Medium Tractor Oil..........Crew-Levick Co., Philadelphia, Pa.
Mobiloil "A" Oil..........Vacuum Oil Co., Rochester, N. Y.
Mobiloil "BB" Oil..........Vacuum Oil Co., Rochester, N. Y.
Mobiloil Zeta Heavy..........Vacuum Oil Co., Rochester, N. Y.
Moco Tractor Oil No. 1..........Marshall Oil Co., Marshalltown, Iowa
Moco Tractor Oil No. 2..........Marshall Oil Co., Marshalltown, Iowa
Molco Gas Engine "Heavy" Oil
Manhattan Oil & Linseed Co., Minneapolis-St. Paul, Minn.
Monalene Tractor Oil
Monarch Mfg. Co., Council Bluffs, Ia., Toledo, O., and San Francisco, Cal.
Monoline Oil..........Montana Oil Co., Helena, Mont.
Motor "B" Tractor Oil
Monarch Mfg. Co., Council Bluffs, Ia., Toledo, O., and San Francisco, Cal.
Mutual "C" Oil..........Mutual Oil Co., Kansas City, Mo.
Mutual "E" Oil..........Mutual Oil Co., Kansas City, Mo.
Parker Anti-Carbon Auto Oil No. 4..........Parker Refining Co., Cleveland, Ohio
Pennant Tractor Oil, Heavy..........Pierce Oil Corp., St. Louis, Mo.
Quality Tractor Oil..........Nourse Oil Co., Kansas City, Mo.
Sample "A" Oil..........Sinclair Refining Co., Chicago, Ill.
Shell Tractor Oil..........Shell Co. of California, Seattle, Wash.
Socony Gas Engine and Tractor Oil..........Standard Oil Co., New York
Special Tractor Oil..........Crew-Levick Co., Philadelphia, Pa.
Stanocola Gas Engine Tractor Oil..........Standard Oil Co. of Louisiana
Stanolind Gas Engine Tractor Oil..........Standard Oil Co. of Indiana
Superior Gas Engine Oil..........Magnola Petroleum Co., Dallas, Texas
Superior Soo Brand No. 1235..........Superior Oil & Supply Co., Chicago, Ill.
Tiolene Heavy "A" Oil..........Tiona Oil Co., Warren, Pa.
Topaz Gas Engine Oil No. 1..........Cudahy Refining Co., Chicago, Ill.
Tractor Gas Engine Oil..........Standard Oil Co. of Ohio
Trop Artic "E" Oil..........Manhattan Oil & Linseed Co., Minneapolis-St. Paul, Minn.
Uncle Sam Tractor Oil..........Uncle Sam Oil Co., Kansas City, Kas.
Union Tractor Oil..........Independent Oil Co., DeKalb, Ill.
Valvoline Tractor Oil..........Valvoline Oil Co., Chicago, Ill.
Velvet Tractor Oil..........Pure Oil Co., Minneapolis, Minn.
Zerolene Heavy Lubricating Oil..........Standard Oil Co. of California

dilute lubricating oil rapidly, rendering it unsuitable for lubrication purposes unless redistilled. This point is important because many persons believe that by simply straining a lubricating oil it can be re-used. No oil can be brought back to its normal state except through heat distillation.

A splash system of lubrication for kerosene engines is, therefore, unreliable.[1]

Select Greases with Care

Reliable greases[2] can generally be secured, the only caution necessary being to get those consisting largely of mineral fats or petroleum jellies. These are more likely to retain their good qualities than those containing much vegetable or animal fat. Vegetable and animal fats tend to become rancid or acid, causing injurious effects.

Adulterants of various kinds are added to thicken some greases or to preserve and harden them. Rosin, soap, tar, or mineral graphite each have their value under certain conditions, but in general anything but pure stock should be avoided. Even graphite which is added to make a graphite grease must be used with care for graphite, while excellent in helping to cool a hot bearing, in time tends to choke up oil passages or fill extended oil grooves and thus in the end bring on the troubles it temporarily cures.

Cheap greases should be carefully watched, for great quantities of them are sold in which considerable water has been beaten, thus giving weight without lubricating quality. Such greases, while cheaper per pound to buy are dearer in the end because a larger quantity must be used to do the lubricating properly.

NOTE 1—Testing Oils

A simple way to test both the quality and viscosity of a lubricant is to place a small piece of glass at an angle of 60° and drop an equal quantity of each lubricant on the upper edge so that it flows down over the glass. The one that flows quickest has the least viscosity. The one that flows the slowest has the greatest viscosity. At the same time, if there are any gums, rosins or other viscosity producing elements in the oil, they will be apparent by the color of the oil streak on the glass, as these adulterants deposit themselves in the form of sediment. Another way of testing for artificial viscosity producing elements is to drop some of the lubricant on a clean white cloth. A sediment deposit indicates an adulterant.

A good quality of lubricant will not break down, when rubbed between the finger tips, as quickly as a poor oil.

NOTE 2—List of Suitable Greases

These greases have been found suitable for International tractors:

Frazier 3 J, Frazier Lubricator Company, Chicago, Ill.

Purolene, Chainolene Manufacturing Co., Chicago.

Arctic No. 3 Cup Grease, Standard Oil Company.

Ajax Special No. 3, Ajax Lubricating Company, Chicago.

Keystone No. 1, Keystone Lubricating Co., Chicago.

Illust. 52. Titan 10-20. A standard farm tractor meeting all requirements for plowing, belt work and hauling. It has a twin-cylinder valve-in-head medium-speed motor operating economically on kerosene and distillates to 39° Baume, a plowing speed and a faster road speed, stands squarely on four wheels, simple and easy to operate.

Chapter IX
Tractor Requirements

We have thus far considered the power plant of our general purpose tractor. We have determined the kind of fuel we shall burn and the design and construction necessary to secure economical and satisfactory operation on low-grade fuels. Now that we have developed the power, it remains for us to transform this power unto useful work at the drawbar or to the belt pulley. The design of the truck, transmission, speed of the outfit and other important features are still to be considered.

It would be impractical to decide on these important features without considering the requirements up to which we expect a correctly designed general purpose tractor to measure.

General Requirements

Taking all these requirements into consideration, we find that they fall largely under two heads—(1) general requirements, (2) special requirements. The important general requirements are six. The engine must be suitable—

(1) for plowing
(2) for belt work
(3) for hauling
(4) must use cheap fuel economically
(5) must be reasonable in cost
(6) must have a reasonable life

The special requirements are so numerous that we shall not even attempt to mention them.

In our discussion thus far we have already determined upon a design which will meet the fourth general requirement, that is, we have a tractor which will burn cheap fuel economically.

It remains now to determine a design which will fulfill the remaining conditions. Of these the first three are by far the most important —making the tractor most desirable for plowing, for belt work and for hauling.

Plowing Most Important Work

Analyzing these three requirements separately, we find that the plowing requirement should receive the greatest consideration because it is the one most likely to utilize the maximum amount of power developed for the longest continuous time. During this time there will be violent changes of load from light operation in turning at the field ends to the almost instant load of all plows in the ground at once.

Therefore the question of driving speed, size and number of wheels, transmission of power and distribution of weight should be considered from the standpoint of plowing utility.

Best Driving Speed

The amount of power to be developed by the engine, the size and proportions of bearings, the quality of the material as well as nearly every feature of design, must be of the best. From this viewpoint the

Illust. 53. Mogul 10-20. This is another standard farm tractor in the International Harvester line. It has a single cylinder slow speed motor which operates economically on kerosene and distillates to 39° Baume. It stands squarely on four wheels with two drive wheels. Easy to steer, easy to operate, easy to care for. Like the Titan 10-20, it has an ideal belt power pulley arrangement.

driving speed over the ground is the first controlling design point. The methods used in turning over the soil have been developed for years to meet horse speeds, two to two and a half miles per hour. Though higher speeds have been tried, it has been found that, all things considered, horse speeds are the economical speeds for the largest variety of workable soils.

The sensible tractor speeds, then, should range from 2 to 2½ miles per hour.

Size of Wheels

Two features must receive attention in wheel design—the pressure on the ground per square inch, and the grip secured on the ground.

Too much weight per square inch crushes or packs the land, giving undesirable results. By care in the selection of the width of the wheel rim[1] and the wheel diameter, these values can be kept down to between 15 and 16 pounds weight in the tractor to each square inch of pressure area, and with extension rims down to 10 lbs. per square inch. The average horse pressure is 18 pounds per square inch.

As a wheel will sink deep in soft land and ride only on the lugs on hard roads, it is customary to measure the pressure on the ground produced by the tractor weight in the following manner: Taking the weight carried by any one wheel, by running the wheel on a wagon scale for weighing, then assuming that this wheel sinks into the earth ½ inch at its deepest point, we measure the area thus:

Illust. 54. Diagram, showing the method of determining wheel pressures.

Total area over which weight is distributed is length in inches of the rim on the ground by width of rim in inches.

$$\text{Pressure per square inch on earth} = \frac{\text{Weight on Wheel}}{\text{Area (Length by Width)}}$$

NOTE 1—See Note 1 on following page on use of extension rims and lugs

NOTE 1—Use of Extension Rims and Lugs

The width of the tire and the lug equipment has much to do with the amount of traction that can be secured. The wider the tire or the higher the lugs, the greater the traction. This often leads to difficulty. Operators add extension rims or extension angle lugs when traction is needed on soft ground, but they neglect to change this tire equipment when they are working on hard ground or traveling on the roads. Extension angle lugs and extension rims should never be used on hard, uneven ground or on hard roads, because they put too much strain on wheel rims and spokes.

Illust. 55. Three sets of rear wheel extensions needed for this marsh land.

Illust. 55 shows the proper use of extension rims. This tractor is working on what was once the famous Montezuma Marsh near Lake Cayuga, New York. A horse on this land would press his feet through the crust of decayed vegetable matter and mire almost instantly. A tractor with ordinary wheels would also mire, but by the addition of three sets of extensions, the Titan 10-20 was able to plow a furrow 2 feet wide and 18 inches deep of the richest, blackest muck imaginable. The tractor wheels traveling over hard ground or hard roads with these three sets of extensions would be seriously damaged in a short while.

Illust. 56. Titan 10-20 equipped with angle lugs for working in plowed ground.

Illust. 56 shows the correct use of extension angle lugs. This Titan 10-20 tractor is fitting plowed ground for seeding. The slippage would be excessive without these extension angles. The ground is so soft that the projection of the angles well beyond the tire, while it aids in traction, cannot possibly injure the wheels. Were this tractor to do road work, the extension angles should be removed and regular road lugs used.

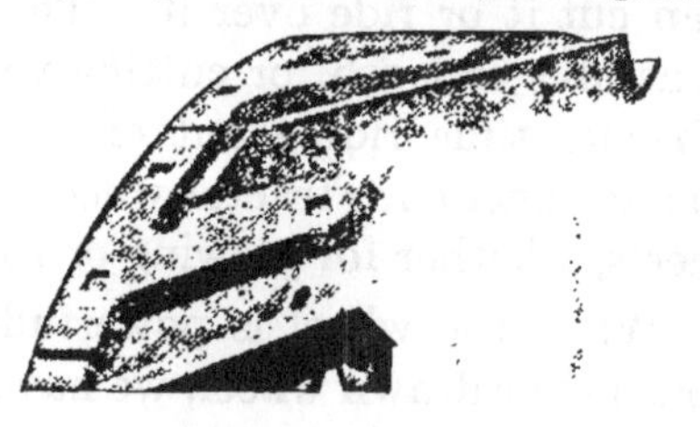

Illust. 56A. Special road lug with angle lugs ready for plowing.

Illust. 57. This illustrates some of the special lugs for securing satisfactory traction. The upper illustration shows the road lug. The lower illustration shows the sand and ice lugs.

Sand lug.

Ice lug.

Illust. 57. Special lugs.

A second point regarding the wheel which has much influence upon the value of the tractor is its diameter. This feature refers to the drive wheels, the front steering wheels, and the rolling coulter on the plow.

The value of any of these wheels lies in its ability to roll, whether on level hard roads or on a soft field, and ride over obstructions. A tractor wheel rides in or out of a furrow, over a log or a stump, under a definite but simple rule—A wheel which is either drawn or pushed will ride easily over an obstruction lying in its path when the obstruction touches the wheel below the 45 degree contact point. Anything touching above this point has a tendency to be pushed ahead, rather than to allow the wheel to roll over it.

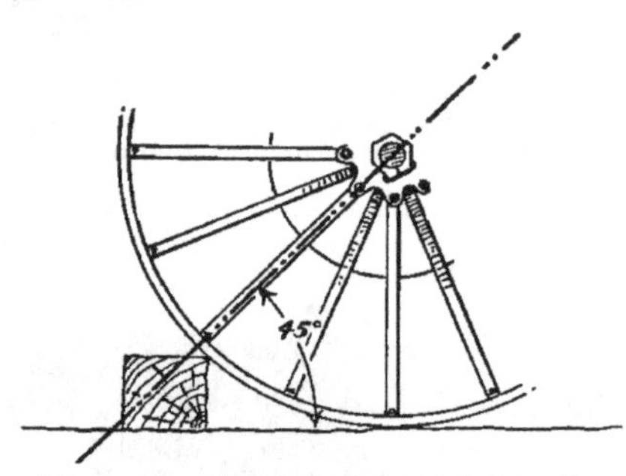

Illust. 58. This shows an obstruction which touches a wheel below the 45° angle. The wheel will go right over this obstruction.

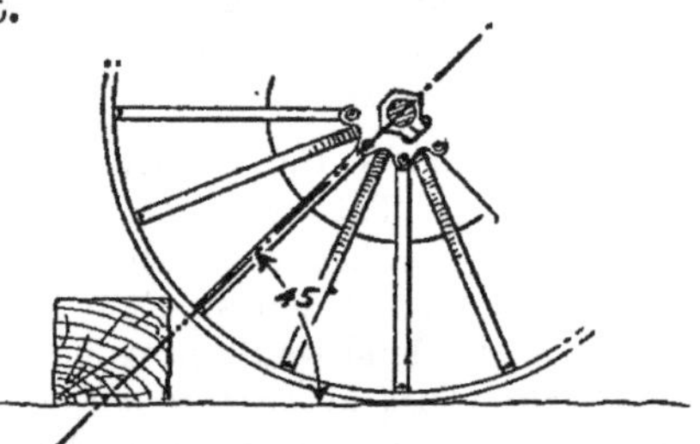

Illust. 59. This obstruction touches the wheel above the 45° angle and is apt to be pushed along ahead of the wheel. This illustrates the advantage of a fair sized drive wheel. The larger the wheels the larger the obstructions that can be run over.

Take the coulter wheel of a tractor plow as an example. If the coulter rides in the ground very deeply, it will push trash ahead rather than cut it or ride over it. The rolling coulter must get a bite on the cornstalks or trash, or cutting will not occur. Also, a small wheel has a harder time riding out of a deep furrow than a larger wheel has. The argument for tractor wheels is evidently, then, for reasonable sized wheels, whether for plowing or road work.

When the wheel is powerfully rotated or driven, as distinct from a pushed or drawn wheel, we have a much better operation in its ability to climb over obstructions or out of mud holes. For this reason a machine provided with two drive wheels is bound to do better than if it had only one drive wheel.

Steering Wheels

The question of whether one front steering wheel, or an axle with two front steering wheels should be preferred, can be argued thus—A much more stable tractor, or one which will not easily turn over when operated under side draft, results when there are two front wheels. This stability is also very much more complete on hillside plowing with four-wheel outfits than with three-wheel outfits. Steering by one wheel is also usually difficult in soft ground.

Number and Arrangement of Wheels

Viewing the numerous tractors with respect to the number of wheels they have, much can be learned. Machines are found with from two wheels up[1]. Patents have even been issued for single wheel outfits. Those which seem to have attracted the designers have usually three or four wheels.

NOTE 1—Number of Wheels

Illust. 60—This is a tractor with three wheels which do not fit any track. It is hard to steer on rough ground or on soft plowed ground, and on short turns the front wheel is apt to skid.

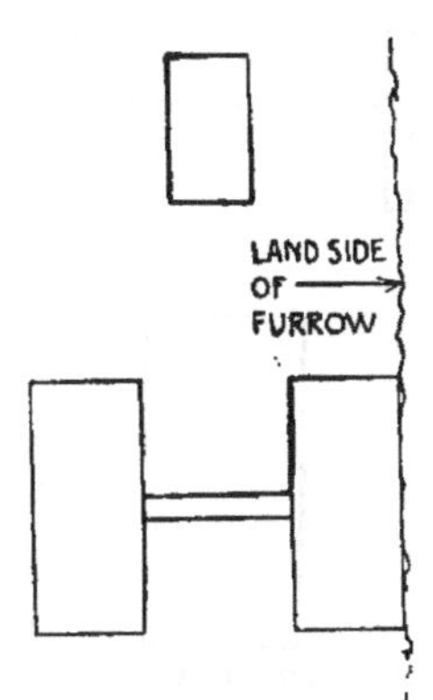

Illust. 60.

Illust. 61—This is another three-wheel tractor with the front and one rear wheel running in the furrow. This packs the sub-soil, tears the last furrow, and sometimes the land-side, and makes a bad-looking job. The machine is not level with two wheels running in the furrow, and this causes excessive wear in the hubs.

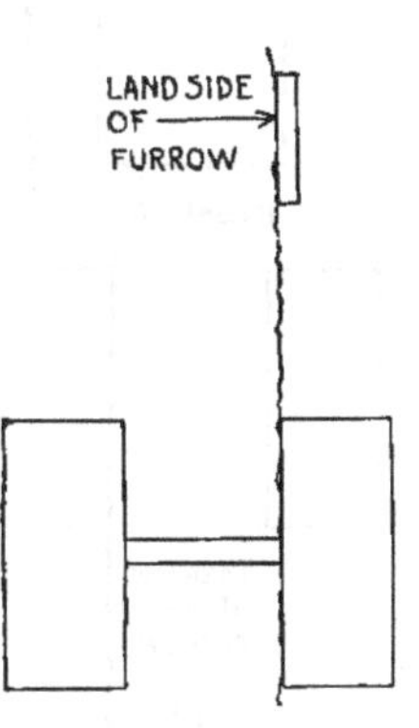

Illust. 61.

Illust. 62—Although this is a four-wheel tractor, it has only one drive wheel. This cuts the chances at the load in half. With both the load and traction on one driver there is soil packing and likewise danger of miring in soft ground. The single drive wheel has a tendency to rack the frame and produce side draft. With the bulk of the weight on a single wheel, the machine is more easily capsized on turns under a load.

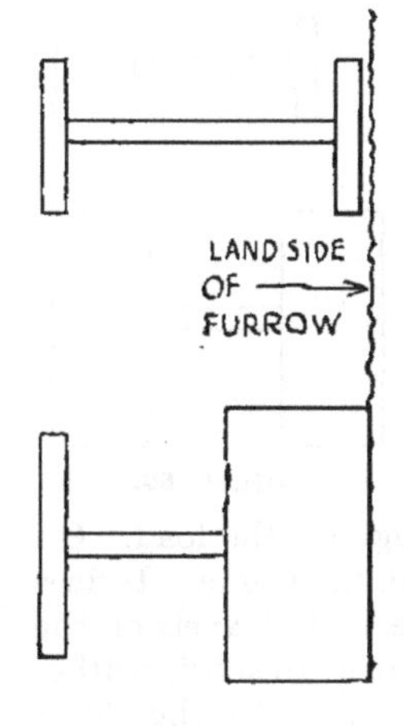

Illust. 62.

Illust. 63—This is another three-wheel type, but it differs from No. 61 in that it has only one drive wheel. The front wheel and the driver run in the furrow. This packs the sub-soil. One driver gives insufficient traction, especially when running in soft plowed ground. Like No. 62, this type of tractor has extreme side draft and is easily capsized on turns. Like No. 61 it is not level when the driver is in the furrow. Also hard to steer.

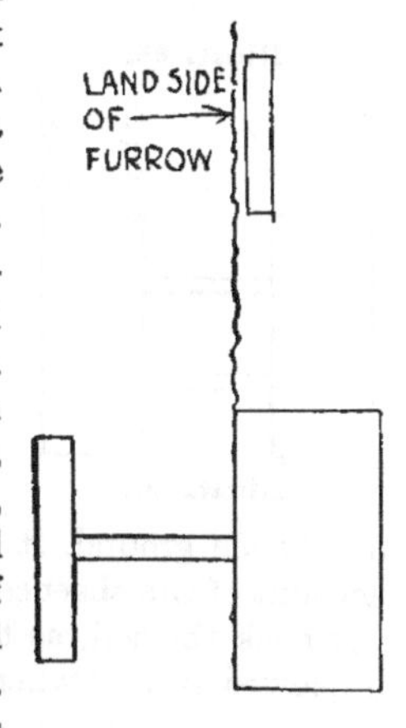

Illust. 63.

Illust. 64—This single driver gives insufficient traction and makes the outfit easily capsized on turns, in fact, it is difficult to turn with very much of a load. One of the front wheels runs in the furrow, which tears the land side and causes excessive wear in the hubs because the machine is not level.

LAND SIDE OF FURROW

Illust. 65—This type has only one rear steering wheel, which makes steering extremely difficult. One of the drivers runs in the furrow, packing the sub-soil and tearing the landside. It is difficult to turn with a load when the power is applied at the front end of the tractor, as in this type.

Illust. 66—This illustrates the endless track type of machine. This type uses an excess of power to operate itself. It has a multiplicity of parts, a very large number of small ones being exposed to dirt, causing excessive wear and high cost of upkeep. This type tears up the ground badly in turning.

LAND SIDE OF FURROW

Illust. 64.

Illust. 67—This illustrates an endless track type with a small steering wheel in front. It is difficult to turn on account of the front wheel's skidding, and it has all the disadvantages of design No. 66.

LAND SIDE OF FURROW

Illust. 65.

Illust. 68—This endless track type has the same points of weakness referred to in designs 66 and, 67 but it has the additional objection of insufficient traction and being easily capsized on turns under load.

LAND SIDE OF FURROW

Illust. 66.

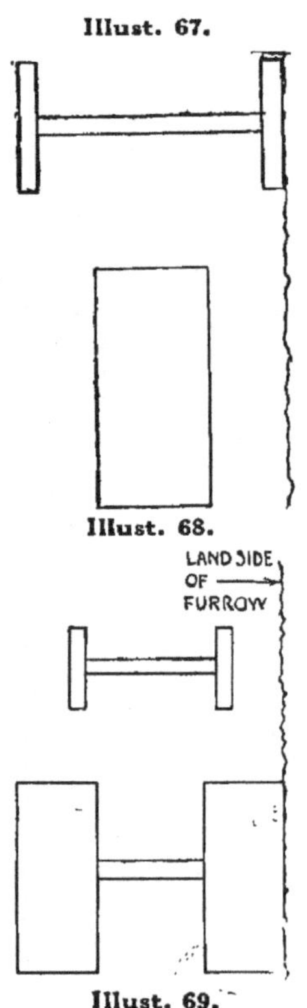

Illust. 67.

Illust. 68.

Illust. 69.

Illust. 69—This is the standard four-wheel type—two steering wheels, two driving wheels. This type has survived the test of years in the design of steam and gas tractors. It produces the greatest traction for the weight, especially on soft ground, and it is the easiest to steer under average conditions. With all wheels high enough to give clearance in soft or uneven ground, it is possible to obtain an excellent leverage on the load. On account of the absence of side draft, there is very little strain on the frame. It does not pack the soil, as the weight is distributed over a large area. It travels on the unplowed ground when plowing, which gives it good footing. It is, in short, neither a freak nor a specialized type, but a safe and sane design accepted by the oldest and most experienced manufacturers.

As the wheels support the engine and frame, it is evident that under all running conditions vibration is bound to take place, except where the support is rigid and the moving parts well balanced. That this can be well carried out and no serious strain come upon any part when the tractor is riding over rough land or hauling a heavy load makes it correct to design the machine with a three point bearing. These points usually are the two rear main bearings or wheels and the third support. This support is the third wheel in a three-wheel outfit, or the pivoted axle bearing between the two front wheels of a four-wheel outfit.

Number of Drive Wheels

One, two, and four drive wheel outfits are offered to the public. While the one-wheel drive and the three-wheel outfit can bring their line of pull near to or in line with the center of the drive wheel, when operating a single plow or a two-plow outfit, they are uncertain in turning under load unless this turn can be made on a wide circle. Its unstable condition results principally from the necessity of placing the engine weight rather high and over the drive wheel.

Driving by the two rear wheels gives far greater certainty of footing, enables the engine weight to be placed low between them, gives fine stability and center draft for plowing or hauling. Also, owing to the differential action between these drive wheels, this design causes less tearing up of roads, sod or soil, upon which the machine is turning[1].

Four wheel drives have been reasonably successful for truck work, and as tractor designers are active in this field, probably something satisfactory will yet result.

Differentials

The purpose of the differential is to enable the wheels which are controlled by it to travel at different speeds in going around a turn.

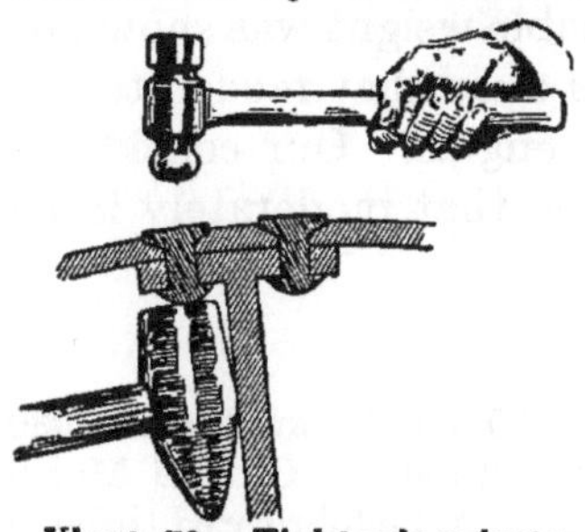

Illust. 70. Tightening rivets on tractor drive wheel.

NOTE 1—Care of Wheels

Special care should be given to spoke rivets of both front and rear wheels. When traveling over crowned roads and hard, uneven ground, tremendous pressure is put on to the wheel rims, causing rivets to work loose. Inspect the wheels carefully and regularly, and if rivets appear loose, tighten them by holding a heavy sledge or weight against the head and pounding the rivet spread down on to the tire until the rivet is solid. Tight rivets prevent cracking of rims and breaking of spokes.

Where the wheels are loose on the axle, like wagon wheels or the front wheels of a four-wheel tractor—they roll separately, going around a turn, while with a machine driving through these wheels, each wheel must do its share of the work. The wheel on the outer circle, or turn, travels farther around than the wheel on the inner circle, which makes it necessary to place between these two wheels a set of bevel gear differentials, or a pair of spur gear differentials, in order to equalize and transport the power to the drawbar. If this provision were not made, excessive slippage of either of the two wheels would occur, similar to the locomotive wheels on a railroad track. The lack of a differential in the locomotive limits the curve which can be used on tracks over which fast trains operate.

Herewith is shown a common bevel gear differential. The sprocket and bevel pinions, forming a unit, receive the chain pull from the engine, and as they convey the power equally on the two large bevel gears, they will enable these gears to carry the power (see Illust. 71) to the drivers. A spur gear differential is sometimes used, but as it requires more room and is of greater weight than the bevel gear differential, it has not been much used except in very large tractors. Other differentiating devices have been devised, though none are as satisfactory as those mentioned[1].

Illust. 71. Chain sprocket and differential gear arrangement on the Mogul 10-20.

Transmission of Power from Engine to Drive Wheels

From the early discussion on engine design, we showed the influence of speed upon weight, and inasmuch as reasonable weight was shown to be necessary in a tractor, our conclusion was clear that moderate engine speeds could and should be used in the engine. Our consideration of tractor wheel sizes led to the conclusion that moderately large sized wheels should be used if possible.

NOTE 1—Lubrication of Differential

This is extremely important. On Titan 10-20, 15-30 and International 15-30 the differential with the entire transmission runs in an oil bath. On the Mogul 8-16 and 10-20 the differential is on the rear axle, but it must be lubricated through grease cups. Lubrication of the differential is very important. Do not overlook it. See your oiling chart for complete instructions.

The transmission of power between these two remains to be considered. The power in the engine reaches the transmission through a clutch[1]. There are various types of power transmission—

1. Spur gear transmission
2. Bevel gear transmission
3. Worm gear transmission
4. Friction transmission
5. Chain transmission
6. Or a combination of these

Spur Gear Transmission

Spur gears are used in every good design, wherever it is feasible to have them, as they are easy to manufacture and usually retain good line contact during a long, hard life. Bearings supporting spur gears can suffer considerable wear without serious inconvenience, nor will a *small* change of distance between their shaft centers seriously affect transmission results. These gears can be operated under heavy duty continously.

Bevel Gear Transmission

Bevel gears are used wherever it is desirable to transmit power at an angle. Usually this is done at a right angle, or 90°. To secure equally uniform results, the tapered teeth are more expensive to make

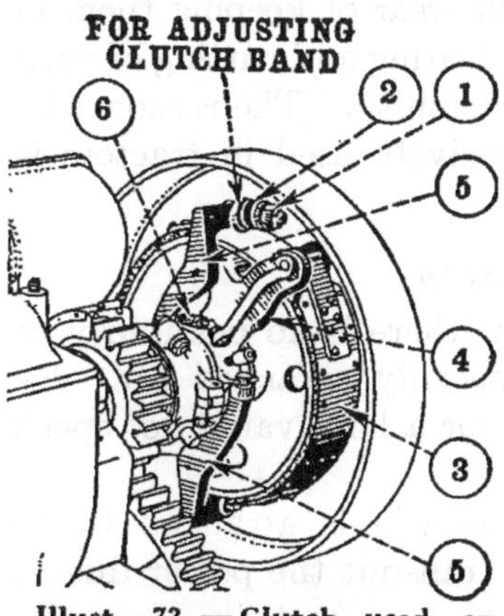

Illust. 72. — Clutch used on Titan 10-20, Mogul 10-20 and International 15-30 tractors.
1. Clutch band adjusting nut.
2. Clutch band spring.
3. Clutch band.
4. Clutch spider.
5. Clutch lever.
6. Clutch lever releasing spring.

NOTE 1—How to Use a Tractor Clutch

The purpose of a clutch on a tractor is to provide a means by which the power can be applied to the drive wheels in such a manner as to start the tractor without any undue strain on the different parts, and it also affords a means of disconnecting the transmission from the engine. It is enabled to transmit power due to the fact that there is friction between the clutch band and the clutch drum. In starting a tractor, then, it is advisable to pull the clutch lever back slowly so as to cause a small amount of friction at first, just enough to start the tractor; then when it is under way, pull the clutch back so that the bands grip the clutch drum without slipping. When this is done, there is no undue strain on the tractor parts.

If the clutch is thrown in quickly, the entire power of the motor throws a terrific strain upon the crank shaft bearing, sprockets, chain, rear axle, rear axle bearings, and frame. By proper handling of the clutch, undue strain will be avoided.

If the clutch is slipping, the clutch band and clutch drum will become heated. If the clutch is not slipping there will be no undue heating of the parts.

If the clutch band slips it should be tightened up until the slipping is overcome. Means are provided for adjusting the clutch band.

than spur gears. These gears are generally used with excellent results where moderately high powers are transmitted continuously.

Worm Gear Transmission

Worm gears are often called screw gears. This type of gear is valuable and used regularly wherever is is desirable to transmit power with large transformation of speed. With spur gears transformation is not desirable in a ratio of more than 5 to 1—although it is possible to have almost any desired ratio; with bevel gears a less ratio than **5** to **1** is usual; whereas with worm gears a ratio of 30 to 1 is not uncommon. It was this ratio idea which caused the inexperienced tractor builder to try to make use of the worm gear. Experience, however, had taught good designers that worm gears are principally valuable in transmitting high ratios of speed but not *high powers* at the same time. This is especially true where these high powers are carried continuously.

Likewise, we have practically a sliding point contact between the teeth in worm gears instead of a line contact, as in bevel and spur gears, making the lubrication of worm gearing unreliable, because few lubricants will stand up against this contact under heavy duty. Again, the possibility of maintaining these gears against wear or keeping them in line is more difficult than with spur gears. Heating and cutting of even very well made worm gears is a constant possibility. The reason why this type of transmission is not more extensively used in tractors is evident from the above.

Friction Transmission

In worm and bevel gear transmission there is no possibility of securing speed ratios other than those specially arranged for. By means of friction gearing we have a chance for a large variety of speed ratios merging one into the other.

The usual friction drive consists of two wheels arranged to be pressed tight against one another and thus transmit the power due to the friction caused by this pressure.

Either straight pulleys similar to spur gears, or bevel gears, are used to transmit a definite speed ratio. When variable speeds are desired, a disk and a wheel pressed against it at right angles, and which can be shifted across the face, is generally used.

For transmitting moderate powers this design is satisfactory. For large powers under long sustained work it is not suitable unless the proportion of parts be very liberal. For tractor work it has been used with fair results, but owing to oil, grease, dirt, rain, and other weathering conditions, along with the necessity of great weight in the parts themselves and high contact pressures, its suitability has been considered so much less than that of spur, bevel, or chain gearing, that few designers will risk their reputations with friction transmission.

Ideal Tractor Transmissions

All International tractors have spur gear transmission from engine to final drive, which in all cases is by chain. On the 8-16 Mogul a planetary type of transmission is used, while on all others a selective gear type is used.

All I H C tractor transmissions operate in an oil bath. It is always essential that this bath be supplied with a sufficient amount of clean oil. On the Mogul 10-20 1½ to 2 inches of oil should be kept in the transmission. On the Mogul 8-16 add one pint twice every day that the tractor is in operation. On the Titan 10-20 and the International 15-30, keep enough good lubricating oil in the transmission gear case to cover the teeth of the smaller compound gear. About 3 gallons will be sufficient, and it may be poured in through filler pipe in the hand hole cover at the front end of the gear casing. The oil level should be about even with the edge of the hand hole opening. It should be watched and oil added only when needed. In warm weather use heavy transmission oil such as 600 or Polarine, and in cold weather use a good light oil.

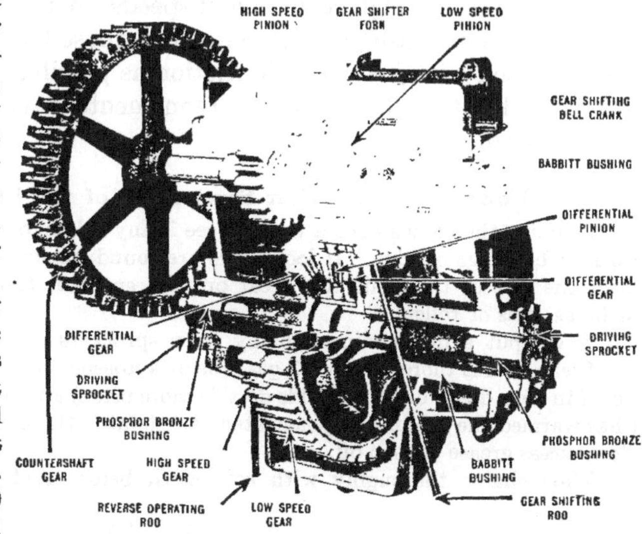

Illust. 73. This shows the Titan 10-20 transmission.

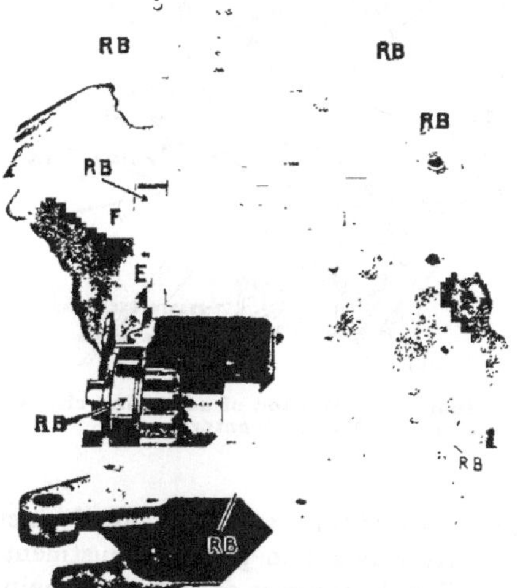

Illust. 74. Mogul 10-20 Transmission. The pinions A and B run loose on the crank shaft. When the clutch is engaged the pinions A and B are locked to the crank shaft. The pinions A and B are always in mesh with the gears C and D which run loose on the countershaft F. The jaw clutch E locks either C or D to the countershaft F. Pinion G is keyed to countershaft F and is always in mesh with gear H. H and sprocket I are securely fastened together. A and C is high-speed and B and D is low-speed. J, the reverse gear, slides over and meshes with gear D. Pinion K is always in mesh with gear H. R B indicates roller bearings.

Chain Transmission

The extensive use of the chain drive on bicycles, automobiles, trucks and tractors has led to very decided and rapid mechanical improvements in this type of transmission[1]. Chain drive has been used first of all to secure high reduction of speeds, such as can be accomplished by the use of worm gearing, but the purpose has been to accomplish this reduction with just as little friction as possible and the longest life attainable for the chain. These refinements have been satisfactorily accomplished.

NOTE 1—How to Get the Most Service out of the Drive Chain

Examine the chains once a week to see if any side bars or rollers have become worn on bushings or pins. If loose bars are found, remove at once, as these will affect the rest of the chain and wear out the sprocket teeth. Remove all worn bushings, pins or rollers.

Never put a new chain on badly worn sprockets.

Clean chains thoroughly with gasoline or kerosene once or twice a plowing season (if in very dusty or sandy fields do this more often) and place in hot tallow until it has warmed the chains and penetrated each joint. Hang chains up at one end to allow excess grease to drip off.

Wipe chains thoroughly with soft cloth before replacing on sprocket. A

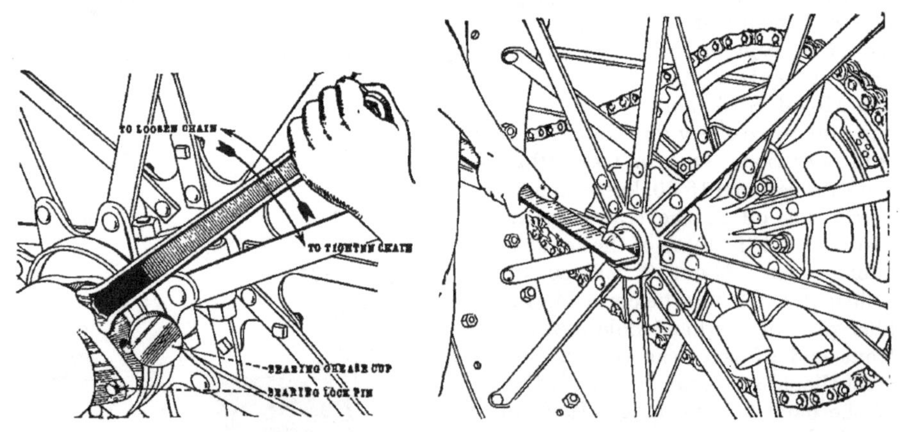

Illust. 75. Method of adjusting chain tension on Mogul tractors.

Illust. 76. Method of adjusting chain tension on Titan and International tractors.

little care of this nature will greatly increase the life of the chain.

Keep chain in proper adjustment.

For the purpose of adjusting chain for proper tension on Titan 10-20, the rear axle bearings have been fitted with eccentric sleeves, which are keyed to the axle. When adjustment is needed, it is necessary to remove the pins from both sides of truck, then take off the right hand cap, washer and pin on outside of hub and turn the eccentric by turning the axle around with a bar until the desired adjust-

Advantages of Chain Transmission

The modern roller chain link, no matter how simple it may appear in construction, is the result of years of study and experimenting to produce a power transmitting medium which has all the qualities of being easily assembled and repaired, a high mechanical efficiency, least friction, greatest flexibility, with extreme durability. A chain drive will stand up under unfavorable working conditions due to the great flexibility of the chain, and due to the fact that perfect alignment so necessary on the gear drive is not necessary on a chain drive. The drive chains designed and selected for International Harvester tractors have a strength to exceed at least ten to twenty times the actual pull of the maximum tractor load.

If materials are properly selected and heat treated, and if the design and specifications of chains and sprockets are carefully watched, the chain drive proves of utmost service.

Illust. 76A. Titan 10-20 Drive. A broken tooth in a gear means a whole new gear, a broken link in a chain means only a new link, not a whole new chain. Chain drives are efficient and durable in service and are easily adjusted and repaired.

ment has been obtained. (See Illust. 76.) Replace the pins in the eccentric and adjustment is complete. Tractor drive wheels may have to be raised from the ground to do this.

Never allow chain to be extremely tight.

For the purpose of adjusting chain for proper tension on Titan and International 15-30, the rear axle bearings have been fitted with plates which can be moved from back to front side of axle.

On Mogul 8-16 and 10-20 the bearings are held by lock pins. Insert adjusting lever; pull lever until pin is loosened and can be removed. To tighten chain, pull lever down or away from tractor, a short distance at a time, alternately on each side, until desired tension on chain is obtained; then replace lock pin and cotter. Be sure lock pins are in corresponding holes on both sides.

☞Never let chains be extremely tight.

Efficiency of Transmission

The amount of horse power which can be transmitted from the engine to the drawbar of any tractor is equal to the power of the engine less the frictional losses due to this transforming of the speed and pressure.

A good transmission, then, is one in which the loss through friction between engine and drawbar has been reduced to the minimum.

These friction losses are divided between the bearings and the gears or chain. They can be reduced by roller bearings and suitable lubrication, but nevertheless there are losses which cannot be overcome.

In any type of gearing, rubbing occurs between the teeth of the gears. as these gears press and work together. This pressure is along a narrow line, thus the pressure is sure to be great enough to squeeze out practically all of the oil.

In a roller chain this contact is better, because the chain roller fits the sprocket teeth over a large area, and the roller also fits the pin of the chain in a similar manner.

While some tests have been made of the efficiency of transmission on tractors, we shall discuss only the general points, using assumed data so as to illustrate the reasons for care in this design and operation.

Percentage of Power Transmitted by Gears

When gears are new and bearings well adjusted, with everything in alignment, any machine should have a certain good efficiency. When a machine has seen considerable service, or is old and gears and bearings are worn out or out of adjustment, there is a lower efficiency of transmission. The usual operating condition is between the good and bad conditions. Again, the design may have finely cut gears running in oil while others are run unoiled and open, exposed to the dirt. We shall take average condition here also.

Illust. 77. Diagram showing power transmission from engine to driver through three sets of gears.

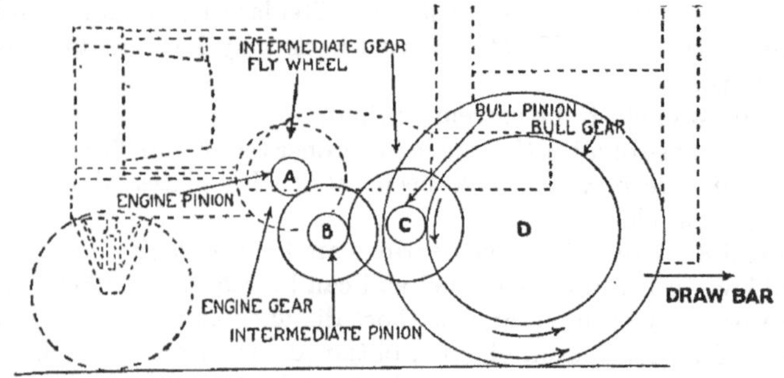

Illust. 77 shows a geared tractor. The engine is geared through the shafts A B C to D to the drawbar. Arrows show the directions of rotation. We shall assume that the gear on the engine shaft and the gear with which it meshes are cut gears, likewise those on B and C are cut, but those on C and D, the bull pinion and gear, are cast gears.

If, for convenience, we start with 100-h.p., at the engine, what shall we have at the drawbar?

Cut gears and good bearings will transmit about 90 per cent of the power given to them, cast gears and bearings about 80 per cent. With these values, let us reckon the drawbar results in horse power. Starting with 100-h.p. at the engine shaft A, shaft B receives 90 per cent of 100-h.p., or 90-h.p., shaft C would receive 90 per cent of 90-h.p., or 81-h.p., shaft D would receive 80 per cent of 81-h.p., or 64.8-h.p. By this means we are enabled to show the following table:

Table XI.

Efficiency of transmission between shafts	Power of Engine shaft A	Power Delivered to Different Shafts					
		to shaft B Cut Gears		to shaft C Cut Gears		to shaft D Cast Gears	
		%	H.P.	%	H.P.	%	H.P.
Engine new and in prime condition..	100-h.p.	95%	95-h.p.	95%	90.25-h.p.	85%	76.7-h.p.
Bearings and gears in good condition	100-h.p.	90%	90-h.p.	90%	81 h.p.	80%	64.8-h.p.
Bearings and gears in worn condition.	100-h.p.	85%	85-h.p.	85%	72.25-h.p.	75%	54.2-h.p.

The influence of cast gearing and worn parts, or even lack of care in keeping the tractor well adjusted and lubricated is very evident. The above is of course taken from designs prevailing some years ago and caused the change to one shaft instead of three between engine and drawbar.

Many machines have been designed with more than three sets of gears and shafts between engine and drawbar, but it must be evident that the fewer geared reductions of speed we have, the higher the possible efficiency. also the fewer the number of shafts we have, the fewer bearings and higher the efficiency.

These high losses have caused designers to carefully observe these points in tractor design.

Whenever gearing is used, it is worth while to have the best of cut gears, run in oil and enclosed, made of the best material and liberally designed. The bearings must be large, well lubricated, few in number and of a quality to insure long life.

Drawbar Efficiency Increasing

One of the results of trying to increase the efficiency by reducing the number of gears and bearings is the larger use of high grade chain gearing. This along with high class bearings, such as genuine babbitt or roller bearings, produces very high transmission efficiencies. Where formerly tractors made by reliable concerns were able to deliver to the drawbar from 40 per cent to 50 per cent of the available power in the engine, they now are able to deliver 65 per cent to 83 per cent, results which any good operator can maintain over a long period if he only does his part.

Distribution of Weight in a Tractor

The distribution of weight in tractor design is very important, especially so because of the unexpected, sudden, enormous loads likely to come upon the outfit, such as result when the plow strikes a hidden

Illust. 78. International 15-30. For the man who wants more power than can be delivered by an 8-16 or 10-20 tractor, this International 15-30 meets every requirement. It has a four-cylinder valve-in-head motor, burning kerosene and other cheap fuels economically. It is water cooled, of medium speed, stands squarely on four wheels, has selective gear transmission to final chain drive, easy to operate and take care of.

stump, or a large stone, neither of which the operator sees. Heavy pull from the side and the working on hillsides creates conditions which are unsafe for both engine and operator, unless provided for in the tractor design.

To get the greatest pull on the drawbar it is quite necessary to have much of the weight on the rear drive wheels. Again, in order to steer well there must be a reasonable weight over the front wheels. Too much weight in front means hard steering.

For all practical purposes we can say that the main weight is brought together into one point, which is the "weight center" of the machine. Should this weight center be too far in front of the axle, the front wheels will carry more than they should. Good practice has shown that the weight center should be about one-third of the way in front of the rear axle, thus leaving the rear wheels two-thirds of the total weight of the tractor and the front wheels one-third of the weight. This, of course, applies to the general four-wheel type of tractor.

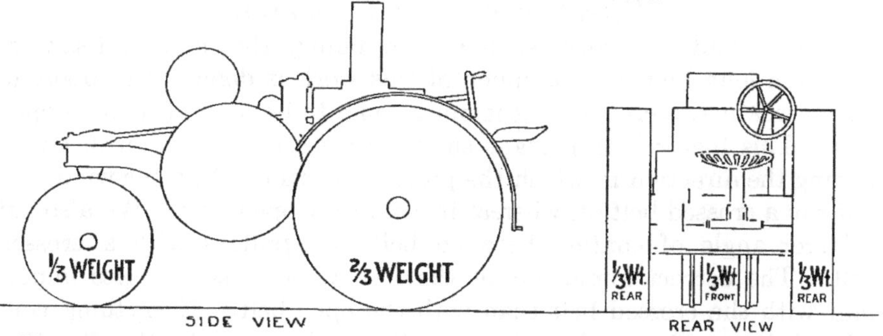

Illust. 79. Side and rear view of tractor showing sensible distribution of weight.

Viewed from the rear, this weight center should be found about midway between the wheels. Further, the height above the ground is a very important point. If too high, the tendency to overturn is greater than if set lower.

Belt Work Requirements

Next to the drawbar requirements of a tractor comes its suitability for belt work.

The large amount of belt work which can be done with a tractor makes it necessary

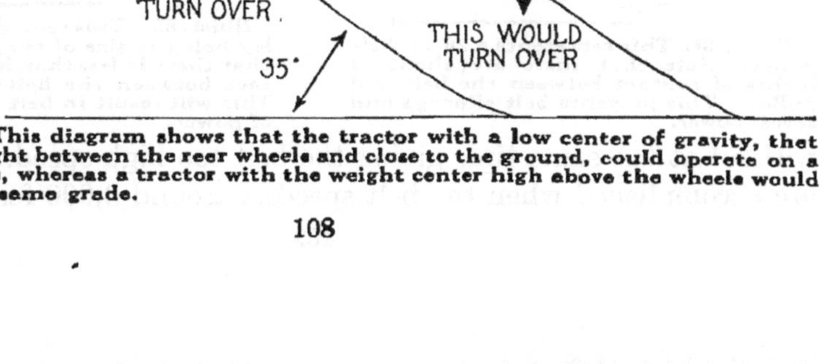

Illust. 80. This diagram shows that the tractor with a low center of gravity, that is, with the weight between the rear wheels and close to the ground, could operate on a 35 per cent grade, whereas a tractor with the weight center high above the wheels would tip over on the same grade.

to have the (1) position of the pulley, (2) the direction of rotation, (3) the size of the pulley, (4) the speed of rotation, given careful consideration in the engine design.

Position of Pulley

The position of the pulley must be such as to enable the operator readily to back into the belt and easily line up his pulley. This naturally means that the pulley shaft should be set across the frame, or across the direction of transmission of the machine. Numerous machines have the pulley set at right angles to the above requirement. This makes the problem of lining up very difficult and unsatisfactory.

Direction of Pulley Rotation

Some kinds of work, such as silo filling, threshing and sawing, require a long belt and, as much of this work is done out of doors in windy weather, a crossed belt is much more to be desired than an open belt. This factor is important enough to deserve attention in determining the direction in which the pulley is to run. A strong wind cannot run a crossed belt off whereas it would an open belt. We also get a larger angle of contact between belt and pulleys with a crossed belt. The correct alignment of the two pulleys is also less important with the crossed belt than with the open belt. Everything considered, it would seem best to have the pulley turn in the direction which a crossed belt calls for.

Size of Pulley

The size of the pulley, especially its diameter, is important. This should be as large as convenient, to make the belt pull small

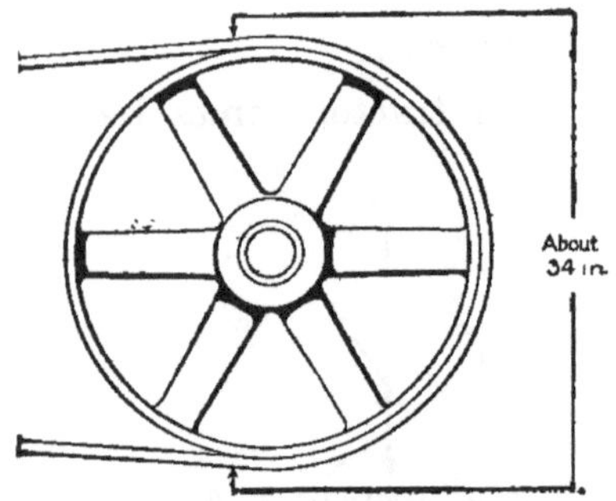

Illust. 81. This represents a 20-in. belt pulley. Note that there are about 34 inches of contact between the belt and pulley. This prevents belt slippage and saves power.

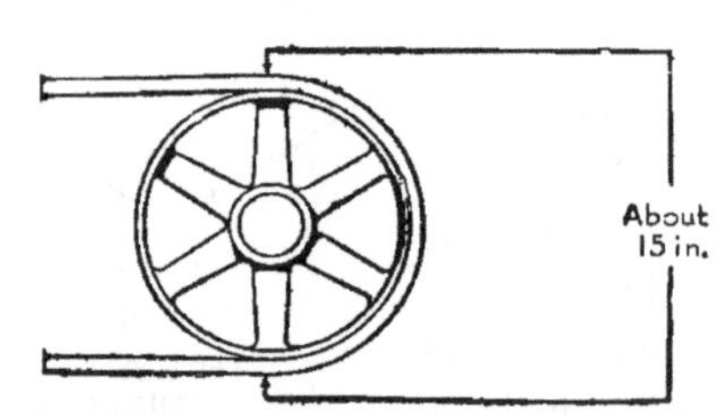

Illust. 82. This represents a 10-in. pulley half the size of the large one. Note that there is less than half as much contact between the belt and the pulley. This will result in belt slippage and loss of power.

without at the same time giving the belt too high speed. Best results are accomplished when the belt speed is around 3,000 feet per minute.

The pulley width should not be too great, a fault often offered to offset a small pulley. Belting is expensive equipment and its life depends upon little bend, reasonable tightness, and speed[1].

Pulley Speed

The speed of rotation shows a wide variation, particularly because of the use of high speed engines. Medium speeds are most desirable[2].

Illust. 8[illegible]. This shows a Titan 10-20 operating a McCormick husker and shredder. Note the crossed belt, the large diameter of the pulley, and its excellent location. Backing into or out of the belt with an outfit of this kind is a simple matter.

NOTE 1—Information on belts

Leather belts must be protected against moisture. Rubber belting gives best satisfaction where belt is exposed to weather. It is desirable to run the grain (hair) side of leather belts next to the pulley. Belts should be kept soft and pliable. For this purpose blood-warm tallow dried in by heat is advised. Castor oil dressing is good. The diameter of the pulleys should be as large as possible. Large pulleys reduce belt slippage. The pulley should be a little wider than the belt. When it is convenient to measure the length required, apply the following rule: Add the diameter of the two pulleys together, divide the result by 2, and multiply the quotient by $3\frac{1}{4}$, then add this product to twice the distance between the centers of the shafts and you have the length required. To figure belt speeds apply this rule: The circumference of the pulley in feet times the r.p.m.

NOTE 2—Use and Care of Friction Clutch Pulley

Although the friction clutch pulley is a simple piece of mechanism, it requires some attention. There are two positions for the clutch, viz., the in and the out position. When the clutch is out, the toggle arms which force the clutch band against the inner band of the pulley are loose and if the tractor is operated with the clutch in this position, the toggle joints will become worn and will need to be replaced. When the tractor is used for drawbar work, the clutch should always be pushed in so that the toggle joints will be held tight and there will be no wear caused by the toggle arms playing back and forth, which they will do if the tractor is operated with the clutch out.

Hauling With a Tractor

The third important feature of a tractor is its adaptability to hauling on the road.

Two Speeds Advisable

Owing to the powerful drawbar pull, and the small friction of wagons on a good road, long trains can be pulled at the slow plowing speed. Since as much time is occupied in returning empty as when hauling loaded where one speed only is available, the demand for the two speed tractor resulted. Under all conditions on a good road the one-speed tractor can pull with ease a great number of wagons. It therefore has become good practice to use higher speed than plowing speed both in going and coming on the road, leaving the low speed principally for use in climbing hills or under bad road conditions.

Good Brake Essential

Road hauling also brought out the necessity of having more suitable facilities for applying a brake to the machine. The earlier types were clamped rigidly for belt work. The plowing engine seldom required the use of a brake, but hills on the road demanded an easily applied brake. Since the hauling practice has increased, we find a positive need for brakes, not only for the tractor but also for the trailing outfits, which have a tendency to overrun the tractor. Many accidents are liable to occur if care is not used in arranging hitches, and with wagon trains by not having proper brakes on wagons[1].

Serious consideration of the hauling problem calls attention to the methods of hitching the various devices to the tractor[2], hence we see developed rigid yet adjustable and easily managed hitching equipment.

Special Road Lugs

In many countries the road laws demand that the evil effect of gripping tractor wheels on the road shall be the very minimum. Where macadam or fine gravel roads are extensively used, tractor manufacturers have designed and offered suitable lugs for attachment to the drive wheels to meet these conditions.

NOTE 1—Care of Brakes

Brakes should be inspected occasionally to make sure that the brake lining is in good condition. To put in new lining, take off the brake band, cut rivets, and remove old lining. Replace it by a new lining and rivet with new rivets that are hammered down so that they come well below the surface of the lining.

NOTE 2—Tractor Hitches

Write for our special book on tractor hitches.

Chapter X
Materials Used in Engines and Tractors

When the first engines of the internal combustion type were developed, available materials were not of the variety, suitability or quality which it is now possible to obtain and use. The earlier engines and many of the cheap ones of today are made from simple cast iron and stock steels. Well-built engines today are made of irons and steels of such special composition and so treated as to safely take the strains and stresses we learned about in previous chapters.

As iron forms so large a part of the engine in some form or other it is well to know its sources, the general processes of manufacture, and the methods of treating it to bring out a variety of valuable products. Iron is one of the elements dug from surface or deep mines. As it comes from the ground it is full of impurities. Iron ore consists

Illust. 84. To insure a suitable supply of raw material, the Harvester Company has its own iron mines. This shows the Agnew Iron Mine near Hibbing, Minnesota, a surface mine from which the ore is taken by steam shovels, loaded on to the ore boat, Tha Harvester, and delivered to the Harvester Company's Steel Mill at South Chicago, Illinois.

mainly of iron oxide, or, in simple language, iron rust. The impurities are removed by burning this ore in a blast furnace. The process in the blast furnace consists of removing the oxygen from the iron ore and freeing the iron. This is accomplished by the use of a cheap substance which will chemically attract the oxygen away from the iron. Limestone is used for this purpose. The iron ore and the limestone must be brought under sufficient heat in a large cupola or furnace in which heat is produced through coke so that the iron is freed and runs off as a crude iron product into sand beds, where it cools as pig iron.

The general chemical formula showing the changes which follow is this:

$(O+N)+Fe_2O_3+CaCO_3+C=CaO+CO+CO_2+Fe+N.$

Which reads without going into quantities:

Air+Iron Oxide+Limestone+Coke=Slag+Carbon Monoxide+Carbon Dioxide+Iron+Nitrogen.

About 60 per cent of the gas going off is nitrogen, 28 per cent is carbon-monoxide and 11 per cent is carbon dioxide. The 28 per cent of carbon monoxide gas used to be wasted but now is used in blast furnace gas engines where it furnishes enormous power.

The molten iron as it runs from the blast furnace is not pure iron, but has trapped within it small quantities of other substances. These were contained in the ore, limestone and coke placed in the furnace, such as the following:

Carbon, silicon (like sand), manganese (a metal), phosphorus (a metal) and sulphur.

Of these substances the desirable and useful ones are the carbon, silicon, manganese. The undersirable ones are sulphur and phosphorus; their presence in various quantities require further treatment before we can make full use of the iron.

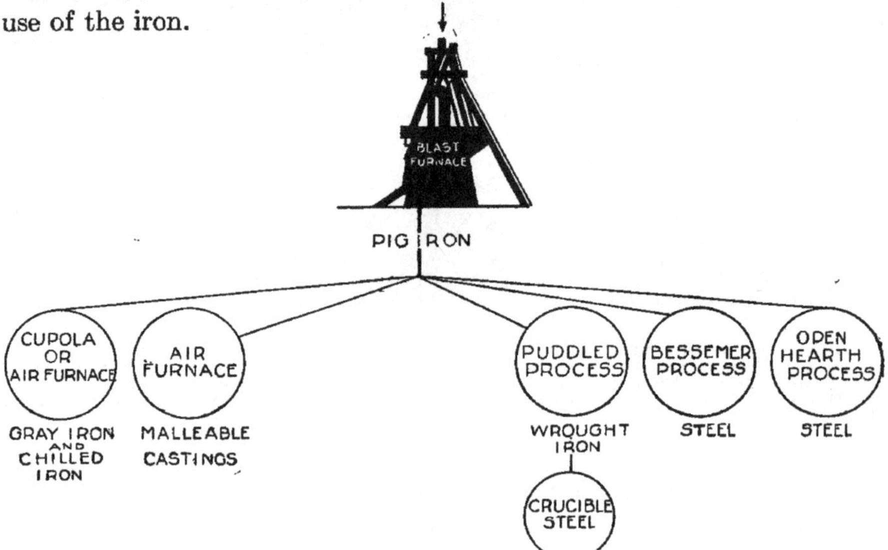

Illust. 85. Diagram showing process in the making of iron and steel.

In Illust. 85 note that ore from the mine is put into the blast furnace and converted into pig iron. The next step consists in remelting this pig iron and mixing it in such a way as to produce the proper character of iron or steel that we desire for each special purpose. Note in the diagram that the pig iron might be taken to the grey iron foundry, melted in the cupola, and cast into grey iron castings, or the pig iron which comes from the blast furnace might go from the malleable furnace into a reverberatory furnace and then be cast into malleable parts.

Small percentages of carbon, silicon, manganese, sulphur and phosphorus influence considerably the quality and properties of irons and steels. For example, if in any foundry producing grey iron castings the coke used to melt the iron should contain in one carload lot more sulphur than ordinarily, there would in all probability be an excess of sulphur in the resulting castings. The effect of the sulphur is to weaken the strength of the castings by making them brittle. To avoid such a possibility it is necessary for the chemist who usually controls the melts to analyze or check up just what goes into the furnace, and then check up each day the result of the mixing. Only the greatest care at all times will result in uniform castings.

Illust. 86. An illustration in the foundry at the Titan tractor factory. This is one of the best equipped foundries in the United States.

Grey Iron

Grey iron is commonly known as cast iron. It has a crystalline structure, can be molded into almost any shape, and is used very extensively in the building of many kinds of machines. Melting pig iron with a percentage of scrap iron and refining it at the same time gives a molten metal suitable for grey iron castings. The analysis of the iron depends upon the purpose for which the casting is to be used, whether it is to be machined, to stand wear as in a bearing, or to be especially strong and tough. The crank case, flywheels, pistons, cylinders and heads of engines are made of grey iron.

Malleable Iron

Malleable iron is made from a pig iron of special analysis in a furnace known as a reverberatory furnace. The process is designed to give iron of great fluidity, producing a casting which can be easily

Illust. 87. Reverberatory furnace in the malleable foundry.

annealed. When the casting comes from the sand, it is extremely brittle. By a seven days' annealing (baking) process carbon is removed, the structure of the iron is changed and made more uniform, the castings become malleable and withstand breakage to a considerably greater extent than common grey iron castings.

The Difference Between Steel and Iron

Iron, as noted above, is one of the chemical elements. Steel is produced from iron ore, so that steel is iron, the construction of which

Illust. 88. International Harvester Steel Mill at South Chicago where most of the steel for I H C machines is made. At this mill they have specifications for more than thirty different qualities of steel of over 800 sizes and shapes. No tractor manufacturer in the world has a greater variety of specially adapted steels from which to select his materials.

has been changed by the addition of carbon and other chemicals or elements which toughen and strengthen it in varying degrees. On a basis of quality or composition, authorities no longer call any steel standard, so that steel is now known better by the name of the process used to produce it, as Bessemer, open-hearth, etc., than by the proportions of the elements from which it is made up. In the case of alloy steels, however, the metals or alloys which have been added determine the character and properties of the steel. Alloy steels are composed of iron and carbon and either one or two other metals or elements, such as chrome, nickel, silicon, manganese, or nickel-chromium, tungsten-manganese, tungsten-chromium, and nickel-manganese.

Effect of Carbon When Combined with Iron

All iron contains at least a trace of carbon, and as stated above this element is the most important constituent of steel. Although of itself carbon does not possess strength or hardness (except in the diamond form) it confers both of these properties when present in iron up to a certain point. Iron free from carbon has a tensile strength of up to 40,000 pounds per square inch, is soft, and has practically no hardening power. By the addition of the correct amount of carbon the tensile strength is increased to 125,000 pounds per square inch, and the material becomes hard with maximum hardening capacity.

Illust. 89 gives some conception of the effect of carbon when combined with iron. The first section represents commercial iron free from carbon. The dark spots represent slag, while the grain represents the granular or crystalline structure somewhat enlarged. This iron has a low tensile strength, is soft and ductile with no hardening power, that is, if heated to a high temperature and then quenched in water it will show no appreciable hardness.

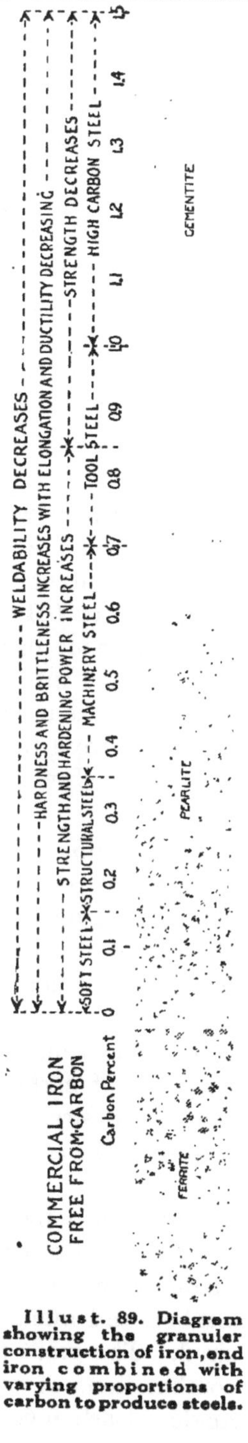

Illust. 89. Diagram showing the granular construction of iron, and iron combined with varying proportions of carbon to produce steels.

With the addition of carbon to iron, the strength, hardness, brittleness and hardening power increase, while ductility and weldability decrease. The point .85 per cent is the point at which iron is thoroughly saturated with carbon. Any carbon added beyond .85 per cent is surplus carbon and collects at the boundary lines of the grains, which is indicated by heavy lines surrounding the grains in the last section. The addition of carbon beyond the saturation point or beyond .85 per cent increases the hardness and brittleness proportionate to the amount of carbon added.

It thus appears that carbon combined with iron is the predominant element governing the various grades of steel, depending upon their base (iron) and their method of manufacture.

High and Low Carbon Steel

Frequently we hear steel referred to as high carbon steel or low carbon steel. As shown in Illust. 89, high carbon steel indicates a carbon content of from 1 to 1.5 per cent, while low carbon steel varies from 0.03 to 0.3 per cent. High carbon steel is used only in places where extreme hardness is desirable. Low carbon steel, when heated and plunged into water, will not harden to excess, and can be easily welded. It is used in drop forgings, and some gears, cams, valves, etc., are made from it and then carbonized, that is, hardened by a special process which will be described later.

Bessemer Steel

The name Bessemer no longer indicates the quality of steel, but merely the process by which it is made. This process involves the taking of a quantity of molten iron into a converter and blowing air through it to burn out impurities, including carbon, and reduce the quantity of phosphorus as much as possible. When reasonably pure iron remains, there is added to the molten mass a known quantity of good grade iron, such as ferro-manganese, in which there is the desired quantity of carbon. This gives us a steel with the carbon content that we desire. The carbon content of Bessemer steel varies from 0.06 to 0.24 per cent.

Open Hearth Steel

Like Bessemer, the name open hearth no longer indicates quality but merely a process. Instead of air being blown through the molten metal, as in the Bessemer process, air is blown over the top of the metal. Carbon and manganese are added to produce the quality of steel desired. The great flexibility of the open hearth furnace enables many combinations of carbon with steel and a large variety of alloys to be made. Carbon content is up to about 0.25 per cent.

Tool Steels

The tool steels are of considerable importance in our industrial development, so that a brief description of the method of manufacture will not be out of place. These steels are known as crucible steels, deriving their name like Bessemer and open hearth steels, from the process by which they are made. This steel, instead of being made from pig iron, as are Bessemer and open hearth, is made from wrought iron. The more expensive grades are made from Swedish iron. Either the wrought iron or the Swedish iron is cut up into small sections and placed in a crucible. Charcoal, pig iron or other carbonizing elements are added in proper proportion on top of the crucible. These carbonizing elements are used to impart hardening power and other desirable characteristics to the steel. In the case of special steel, alloying elements such as metallic nickel, manganese, tungsten, chromium and vanadium are placed in the crucible in proportion to the quality and grade of steel required. These elements impart characteristics such as hardening power, wearing and cutting properties to the steel, and in certain combinations produce such qualities as unusual strength, toughness, resistance to shock and vibrations. The crucibles are then placed in the furnace, covered over with lids, and subjected to heat enough to thoroughly melt the contents. The crucibles are then removed from the fire, the slag taken off, and the molten metal poured into ingot molds.

The carbon content of tool steel varies from 0.07 per cent to 1 per cent. The average tool steel contains 0.09 per cent.

These alloy tool steels are used in the manufacture of milling cutters, lathe tools, dies and other parts requiring qualities of great strength, hardness, and resistance to wear.

Nickel Steel

The most important of all alloy steels is nickel steel. The carbon varies from 0.2 to 0.5 per cent, while the nickel runs from 1.25 to 4.5 per cent. Nickel gives this steel wonderful strength along with remarkable toughness. Its most important use today is in the manufacture of armor plate. It possesses, to a great degree, the impact-resisting quality desired.

Magnet Steel

This steel is of interest because magneto bars are made from this stock. It contains about 0.6 per cent carbon and 5 per cent tungsten, and has the property of retaining magnetism exceedingly well.

How the Quality of Steel is Designated

The percentage of carbon together with the name of the alloy added usually designates the quality and properties of steel. For example, 40 carbon steel means steel with 0.4 per cent carbon, 70 carbon steel indicates 0.7 per cent carbon alloyed with some constituent which is necessary to get the full value of the high carbon. One and one-half per cent nickel open hearth steel would indicate 1.5 per cent carbon alloyed with nickel made by the open hearth process.

Phosphor Bronze

Phosphor bronze is an alloy of copper and tin, phosphorus only being combined with it as a purifying factor. The purity of phosphor bronze must be above suspicion. There can be nothing cheap in the way of phosphor bronze. Some bearings in tractor transmission, piston pin bearings in small engines, and principal bearings in cream separators are made of phosphor bronze,

Babbitt

Babbitt metal, white metal, or anti-friction metal, as it is sometimes called, is composed of tin or lead, zinc and antimony, and sometimes a small per cent of copper. The name Babbitt does not indicate quality or composition of the metal. The cheaper grades may be almost entirely lead and the higher grades largely tin. The quality of Babbitt metal is generally understood to vary directly with the proportion of tin used. It is possible, therefore, to make Babbitt metal which costs more than phosphor bronze, as at the present market prices tin is.worth nearly double the price of copper. The duty imposed upon the bearing determines the use of Babbitt or phosphor bronze. Babbitt metal of various grades is used in the majority of engine bearings.

BABBITTING GUIDE FOR FIELD WORK

Clean out the old babbitt in the bearing housing and clean the housing of all dirt and moisture. See that the shaft is in good shape to receive the babbitt, and be sure to have the shaft in perfect alignment in every respect. Block the shaft so it will stay in this alignment throughout the babbitting operation. If possible, heat the shaft and bearing housing in order to pour a perfect bearing. Be sure and plug the ends so that you provide an escape for the air and gases and also insure a perfectly filled bearing. Heat the babbitt to the point where it will char or blacken a dry pine stick, and then pour as fast as possible to insure a good bearing. For a solid bearing, or in cases where a shaft, and housing cannot be heated, wrap one thickness of thin writing or other paper around the shaft, this leaves clearance for removal. In pouring half bearings be sure to insert enough liners to allow for future adjustments. In fitting bearings be accurate and careful, and provide oil grooves for bringing oil or grease to all parts of the bearings. The edges of each half bearing should be trimmed down far enough so as not scrape the oil off the shaft. Be sure to clean and lubricate bearings thoroughly after fitting.

Chapter XI
Processes in the Handling of Metals

Annealing

This is a treatment to which parts are subjected for removing strains due to uneven cooling or chilling, to make the crystal formation of iron and steel more uniform, and to increase the strength of the parts. The parts, usually castings or hardened machine parts, are heated up above a point where the size of the crystal is established, after which it is allowed to slowly cool. The resistance to shock is thus greatly improved. Annealing is frequently used in connection with the process of malleablizing.

Case Hardening

Case hardening is a process of putting a hard shell or surface on soft steel to enable parts to resist extreme wear and yet retain toughness. It is a process which gives a glass hardness to the outside and still retains the strength and resistance to breakage of low carbon steel. A common method of doing this is to heat a piece red hot, touch it to a piece of cyanide of potassium, allowing the cyanide to run over the surface of the metal, and then while the piece is still hot, plunging it into cold water. This transforms the outer shell of the part from a low carbon steel to a high carbon steel, and changes the crystal formation, which is coarse on the inside, to a very fine formation on the outside.

Carbonizing

Carbonizing is a process similar to case hardening, except that the hardening process penetrates more deeply into the metal. This is accomplished by first forming the part in soft, low carbon steel, followed by sealing the part in an air-tight case of iron, but surrounded by charcoal or similar carbon containing substance. The part is then heated up to a temperature reaching about 1700° fahr., to which it remains subjected for some twenty-six hours more or less, according to the desired penetration. The case and parts are then slowly cooled within the furnace, the parts removed from the case are heated again to a temperature around 1700° fahr., and plunged into a water or oil bath. A tempering is often desirable, following the above treatment, by reheating the parts to about 400° fahr., in a bath of hot oil. Several quenchings are frequently made for special effects.

Roller and ball bearings and their cases are treated as above—also gears, cams, or other parts requiring extreme hardness with support of soft material.

Chilling Process or Chilled Surfaces Production

When some portion of a casting requires extreme hardness over a small area, a process known as chilling is used to force a rapid cooling on that surface, while the rest of the casting has time to cool slowly. This is accomplished by casting the molten iron against a chill, which can absorb heat rapidly from the metal next to it. The result is peculiar in that the carbon, which is present in the cast iron, does not have time to separate out and remains in the iron as combined carbon, instead of being present as free carbon or graphite. A broken section showing a chill looks white and crystaline, beneath which is the grey iron appearance. The depth of the chill is affected by the amount of heat absorbed quickly. Car wheel treads, brake bands, cams and similar parts can be chilled. If need be, the finish is made by grinding, since it otherwise is too hard for a tool to cut it.

Cold Rolled Steel

Cold rolled steel is rod stock steel which has been passed through a set of steel rolls under severe pressure, while still cold. The effect produces a smooth, hard surface with a softer core. Stock of this kind can run true to size within a few thousandths of an inch. The strength also is greatly improved against twist. Rods, studs, pins, shafts, axles, are pieces usually made of this stock.

Crystalizing

When parts break, showing a section where the crystal effect has both large and small crystals, the expression is often heard—"The piece got crystalized," meaning that the continued shock or strain to which the part was subjected caused the crystals to change size. As this is a mistaken idea, the correct explanation should be understood.

Parts do break due to continuous shock or vibration, but the crystals do not change in size, unless the part has been subjected to a heat above what is called the "Critical temperature," which is a good red heat.

The best explanation of so-called crystalization under vibration or shock would be this—that steel is made up of numerous crystals bound together, the impurities such as carbon, sulphur, phosphorus, silicon, etc., filling the intervening spaces, unless they be directly combined chemically with the steel crystals. When under constant vibration these particles of impurities become loosened a break results.

So-called crystalization in rolled stock might also result from rolling in slag which had not been properly removed from the steel.

Drop Forging Process

By means of this process we are able to produce irregular shapes in small parts, which duplicate castings in form, but which possess the strength of steel and are capable of the finest tooling. The parts are heated to a bright red heat, placed on a die and hammered by a die from above. The shaping is done in several stages when the form is complicated.

For drop forgings low carbon or mild steel is used, which, after being forced into shape, is carbonized or treated as required. Cams, cams on cam shafts, gear blanks, ignitor electrodes, draw bars, crank shafts, connecting rods, are made in this way. The uniformity and strength of the product are notable, so this method is being more and more extensively used by reliable manufacturers of high grade goods.

Grinding Process

This is one of the surest methods of producing a fine finish on parts which should fit well to the thousandth part of an inch. The effect of the grinding is such as to give a true surface, yet one which will hold oil. Such parts as crank shafts, pistons, valves of the present high standard, could not be produced without this process.

Hardening Process

This process was devised to enable us to define the type of crystal we wished and also secure the desired hardness. The means consists of heating the piece up to or slightly above the critical temperature, and then suddenly cooling it by plunging into a substance which absorbs heat quickly, such as oil or water.

Tempering or Drawing

This may be called the toughening process. The temperature to which the piece is raised must be below the critical temperature at which the size of the crystals is defined. The expert who handles this work causes a bright spot to be formed on the surface of the metal during the cooling process and then watches the variety of colors that pass over it, straw yellow, brown, blue, as it cools. He catches and holds the one he wants by sudden cooling in water or oil.

Heat Treatment

All pistons for engines from 4-h. p. up are heat treated in the following manner:

Piston castings are machined, all but the grinding finish. These pieces are then placed in an oven, and according to size are exposed to a temperature from 800° to 1200°, the object being to put them in a temperature which will raise them to a dull red heat. This temperature is just visible in the dark. Following this they are left to cool off in the oven and given the final finish of grinding, etc. The above treatment has the following effect:

First, it thoroughly anneals the piston, taking out all strains caused by chilling or cooling, making it softer without hard spots, causing it to wear more uniformly and with less danger of scratching or injuring the cylinder, which part is, of course, more expensive to repair.

The second purpose of heat treatment, and really the principal one, is to warp the piston as much as it will ever be possible for it to warp. It is a well-known fact that castings which have varying thicknesses of metal, thick and thin parts close together, have a tendency to change shape when the outer shell is removed by machining. This change of shape is increased by working under high temperatures, such as are necessary with low grade fuel engines.

Manufacturers who do not pay attention to this point must provide a large clearance between the cylinder and piston to allow for this warping effect, with the result that gases blow by the rings and the pistons, causing a great deal of trouble.

By the treatment outlined above, the clearance between the cylinder and piston can be reduced to the very minimum that will allow for expansion and give sufficient room for lubricating oil, but will allow no gases to blow by.

Illust. 90. A view in the chemical laboratory at one of the Harvester Company tractor works. Here is made a scientific analysis of all metals, likewise of various heat treating processes. Materials and parts are constantly tested and analyzed under varying conditions, and the manufacturing department is given the benefit of all investigations, so that when the product is finally completed it will be known just what can be expected of every part and every material.

The Strength of Iron and Steel

Without going into too great detail in a very wide and intricate subject, it is well to realize what can be done in the manufacture of materials by close and careful attention to the rules and regulations of nature.

One material only will be discussed—the irons—from which the general laws can be understood to apply in every way to other materials.

The simplest way to realize differences made by mixtures and processes upon the irons, is to take equal sized bars of one square inch cross section and put each one under a measured pull to see how much strength it has. Testing machines for this purpose are specially made, so the strength of materials can be measured with great exactness. Of the commercial irons and steels Table XII shows normal values. By carelessness in manufacture, values will often run away below the figures here given, but extra attention to details will increase these values in some cases considerably.

The steels and irons indicated in the list below started from the same source and had the same possibilities in them. The point of most interest is that we have here available a splendid variety of materials adapted to make the highest grade machines. Proper choice of these materials enables us to build machines that will outlast by many years machines which may look as well in the paint, but which may be constructed of improperly chosen, inferior, unsuited material.

Table XII
Strength of Various Irons and Steels

	Commercial Samples per Square Inch
Grey Iron, Common	15,000 lbs.
Better Grade	20,000
High Grade	30,000
Wrought Iron	42,000
Extra Soft Steel	45,000
Soft Steel	50,000
Medium Steel	60,000
Hard Steel	70,000
Steel Forgings	78,000
Steel Castings	80,000
Best Iron Wire Hard Drawn	90,000
Bessemer Steel Wire	92,000
Nickel Steel—Structural	100,000
Rail Steel	110,000
Nickel Steel—Good Grade	120,000
Spring Steel	135,000
Galvanized Telegraph Wire	192,000
Spring Steel—Oil Tempered	200,000
Vanadium Steel	232,000
Crucible Steel Wire	270,000
Extra Quality Crucible Steel Wire	360,000

For example, a manufacturer might be using rod steel stock one inch in diameter for studs, pins, and rollers. If he were building cheap engines he could use one quality of steel which would fit all three different requirements fairly well, but he cannot do so well for the customer as could the manufacturer who selects special analysis stock best suited for each of these requirements, which, of course, would cost considerably more. This point explains, in part, why it is economical to buy a machine with all parts built of materials best adapted to the work they are required to do. Such a machine must be a better product than one not so built, must do better work and last longer.

Some machinery parts should be hard, others soft. Some should be made of steel, others of iron, brass, bronze, babbitt, sheet steel, wood, or leather. The careful designer is the one who knows these differences and the suitability of various materials and makes use of them accordingly. He will design a machine it will pay a customer to buy. The most desirable product, considering price, service, and everything else, would be that in which just the right material was used for every part—nothing which would tend to either cheapen the price or increase the cost.

Illust. 91. The big testing machine at the Mogul factory that enables experts to determine the strength of material. There is no guessing at any of the Harvester Company tractor works. The testing machine shown above is capable of exerting several hundred thousand pounds of tension or compression to the square inch on the material being tested. Accurate reports are kept. These records enable the manufacturing department to use only such material as is best adapted to the purpose.

Chapter XII

Finding a Safe Load for the Tractor

Many a good tractor has gone to the junk heap years before its time for the sole reason that from the beginning it was overloaded. A good farmer would not think of working his horses until they fell in their tracks. The warning given by their heaving and panting would not pass unheeded. But with a tractor the heaving and panting—slowing down of the speed, knock or pound in the cylinder, killing the engine by a load it cannot overcome, seem to go unheeded. As a result, one part after another gives way, until the farmer finds himself all too soon with a worn out tractor.

A misunderstanding of how much a horse can do and how much a tractor should do undoubtedly accounts for many an overload. We probably think one horse gives us one horse power, three horses, three horse power, and a tractor rated at 10 horse power on the drawbar more than three times as much power as a three-horse team.

Does it? The average horse can exert a pull of about 200 pounds traveling at 2 miles per hour.

200 lb. × 10,560 ft. (2 mi.) = 2,112,000 ft. lb. in 1 hour.

2,112,000 ÷ 60 = 34,200 ft. lb. in 1 min.

1 horse power = 33,000 ft. lb. per min., therefore a horse pulling 200 lb. is developing a little more than 1 mechanical horse power.

How much plowing could horses do exerting just this amount of power? The average resistance to the passage of a plow through the soil is about 5 lb. per sq. in. of the perpendicular cross section of cut. This resistance varies with different soil types and conditions as shown in the table herewith:

Table XIII

In sandy soil	2 to 3 lb. per sq. in.
In corn stubble	3 lb. per sq. in.
In wheat stubble	4 lb. per sq. in.
In blue grass sod	6 lb. per sq. in.
In June grass sod	6 lb. per sq. in.
In clover sod	7 lb. per sq. in.
In clay soil	8 lb. per sq. in.
In prairie sod	15 lb. per sq. in.
In virgin sod	15 lb. per sq. in.
In gumbo	20 lb. per sq. in.

(The soil resistance per square inch of furrow slice turned varies greatly in different sections of the country. Tests made by the Hyatt Roller Bearing Company showed that Texas cornstalk stubble required an average of 8 pounds to the square inch of furrow slice turned, while Bermuda sod required 11 pounds to the square inch of furrow slice.)

Suppose we used 14-inch plows and plow 6 inches deep. A cross section of this plow would be 14×6 or 84 square inches. At an average pressure of 5 lb. per sq. in., we have 5×84 or 420 lb. per plow. Two plows would require a pull of 2×420 or 840 lb. We found previously that at 2 mi. per hour a horse pulled about 200 lb. and exerted a little over 1 horse power. If the horse had exerted only 188 lb. pull it would have been exactly 1 horse power. Dividing 840×188, we find that we need practically 4½ mechanical horse power to pull the two 14-inch plows 6 inches deep.

As the plows start into the soil the horses must overcome 1,200 to 1,500 lb. resistance, or they must exert from 6 to 8 horse power. They can do this for a short time. After the plowing is well started the resistance lowers until it reaches normal, or about 840 lb. or 4½ horse power. Suddenly the plow strikes a root or a stone or hard pan. Up goes the resistance again to 8 horse power.

It must be apparent from this that it wouldn't be safe to go into a field with plows needing 4½ h. p. for ordinary work unless you had at least again as much power in reserve to take care of emergencies. A horse capable of pulling 1 horse power on an average can exert from 4 to 5 horse power for a short pull. It is this reserve power which enables horses to get through with the work.

The same reserve power is needed in a tractor. If 4½ horse power ordinarily would handle the load, your tractor should have 4½ more in reserve, or a total of 9 horse power. There are times in plowing when the resistance is doubled. When those times come, if you have no reserve, you put on an overload, and in just a few moments do an untold amount of injury to your tractor.

A throttle governed tractor with plenty of reserve power is no more expensive to operate than one working up to full capacity all the time. Throttle governed tractors use fuel only in proportion to the load, consequently a 10 horse tractor with a 5 horse load uses no more fuel than a 5 horse tractor with the same load. When an overload comes your reserve power will take you through without any change in the engine speed or any excessive strains.

Find the safe load for your tractor. The ideal way would be to try the tractor on various parts of your farm with a dynamometer between the tractor and the plow, so that you can get the average soil resistance per plow bottom. Knowing the rated horse power of your tractor and its speed and the average soil resistance of your farm, by using the method of figuring given above you can easily tell how many and what size plow bottoms to use to avoid all danger of overload.

Government Experts Caution Against Overloading Tractors

The United States Government, in Farmers Bulletin No. 719, makes some very important statements along this line, as follows:

"It does not pay to overload a tractor any more than it does to overload a horse. Three plows behind a two-plow tractor will cover only a little more ground, as a rule, than will two plows, because the tractor usually will travel a little slower, partly because the motor is overloaded and does not maintain its proper speed, and partly because the drive wheels will slip more with a load heavier than the machine was designed to pull. As a result, delays on account of small holes or slight grades will be more common, as will also mechanical difficulties."

Symptoms of Tractor Overloading

In running a tractor the operator soon gets to recognize the sound and regularity of the exhaust as an indication of its speed and running condition. An overload reduces the normal speed of the motor which in turn cuts down the number of exhaust sounds per minute. Any load which slows the tractor down in this manner is an overload and is more than the prescribed amount it should pull with safety.

A common practice when the motor of a tractor slows down under an overload is to disengage the clutch and allow the motor to regain its normal speed, then engage the clutch again, relying upon the momentum of the heavy flywheels to "pull her through." This is dangerous practice for the almost irresistible power of the flywheels throws excessive strain on the other parts of the tractor and something must give way sooner or later. In cases of this kind it would be better and safer to ease up the load in starting and until the tractor can handle it and still

Illust. 92. Attempting to pull an overload by speeding up the power before the load is engaged.

Illust. 93. The effect of attempting to pull an overload by increasing the momentum of power before the load is engaged.

keep up the normal speed of the motor. To illustrate the point, imagine a team of horses hitched to a rope that in turn is attached to some heavy object. Suppose the horses were started into a gallop as the slack was taken out of the rope (Illust. No. 92). Then the terrific strain of the load would very likely throw the horses off their feet, injuring them as well as tearing the harness to pieces (Illust. No. 93).

Variation in kinds of soil, degree of moisture and topography of land make it impossible to state how many plows a certain tractor will pull. In view of this fact, and in view of the fact that the average operator of any size tractor almost invariably tries to get more out of his machine than it was built to do, he is taking the same chances that he would take if the tractors consisted of so many horses that he was taxing to their limit for the sake of turning over a few more furrows daily. The sensible thing to do with any machine, and especially the tractor which represents a rather larger investment than the average farm machine, is to treat it considerately with respect to the amount of work required daily.

The Tractor Not to be Compared with the Automobile

Everyone knows how rapidly the automobile depreciates in value. At the end of four years' time an automobile is worth only about 30 per cent of the original investment. A small fraction of this is due to its being "out of date" yet the same rule applies to standard makes of cars whose manufacturers do not change materially their models from year to year. Such cars, on the average, have a maximum speed of 50 to 60 miles per hour. They run, possibly, at an average speed of 15 to 20 miles per hour when used throughout these four years. Under ordinary conditions only 30 per cent of their rated horse power is used. It is only under unusual road conditions, such as in mud or sand, climbing hills, or when a maximum speed is desired, that the automobile is taxed to its limit. Notwithstanding the fact that the automobile is not taxed to its capacity for any length of time, yet it is common knowledge that its value, due to wear and tear upon the motor and upon the car in general, causes a falling off in value of 70 per cent in four years.

The tractor, on the other hand, is designed to do heavy work to the limit of its rated capacity all the time. It has no great surplus of power as the automobile has for getting out of tight places except by means of additional lugs for handling its prescribed load. It is not expected that the power of the tractor will be abused or overtaxed because this only leads to dissatisfaction later when the owner finds by his persistent overloading, that he has decreased the period of service of his machine.

TABLE XIV

Pounds Draft a Tractor May Be Expected to Pull at Different Rates of Speed

Miles per Hour	Rated Drawbar Horse Power								
	8 H.P.	10 H. P.	12 H. P.	15 H. P.	18 H. P.	20 H. P.	25 H. P.	30 H. P.	40 H. P.
	Lbs.	Lbs.	Lbs.	Lbs.	Lbs.	Lbs.	Lbs.	Lbs.	Lbs.
1.00	3,000	3,750	4,500	5,620	6,750	7,500	9,360	11,250	15,000
1.25	2,400	3,000	3,600	4,500	5,400	6,000	7,500	9,000	12,000
1.50	2,000	2,500	3,000	3,750	4,500	5,000	6,250	7,500	10,000
1.75	1,710	2,150	2,580	3,200	3,860	4,300	5,360	6,450	8,600
2.00	1,500	1,880	2,230	2,820	3,390	3,760	4,700	5,650	7,500
2.25	1,335	1,670	2,000	2,500	3,000	3,340	4,180	5,000	6,700
2.50	1,200	1,500	1,800	2,250	2,700	3,000	3,750	4,500	6,000
2.75	1,090	1,360	1,630	2,040	2,450	2,720	3,400	4,080	5,450
3.00	1,000	1,250	1,500	1,875	2,250	2,500	3,125	3,750	5,000

The figures in this table are worked out according to this formula: The pounds of draft of any tractor = the rated drawbar horse power × time × 33,000 ÷ distance in feet. For instance, an 8-16 tractor is rated at 8 horse power on the drawbar. It travels 2 miles or 10,560 feet per hour, therefore 8×60 min. × 33,000 = 15,840,000 ÷ the distance or 10,560 feet (2 miles) = 1,500 lb. which is the drawbar pull in pounds of that tractor at 2 miles per hour. At one mile per hour the tractor can pull just twice as much, or 3,000 pounds, while at 3 miles per hour it can pull only a two-thirds as much, or 1,000 pounds. Knowing the rated drawbar power of your tractor and its speed, you can easily determine from this table what its drawbar pull is on average footing with a tractor in average condition. By referring to Table XIII showing the power required to turn a square inch of furrow in various soils, you can easily divide your tractor drawbar pull by the plow pull and determine a safe load for your tractor.

TABLE XV

Determining The Tractor Speed

Miles Per Hour	Feet Per Minute	Yards Per Minute	Total Feet	Total Yards
1.0	88	29–1	5,280	1,760
1.25	110	36–2	6,600	2,200
1.5	132	44–0	7,920	2,640
1.75	154	51–1	9,240	3,080
2.0	176	58–2	10,560	3,520
2.25	198	66–0	11,880	3,960
2.5	220	73–2	13,200	4,400
2.75	242	80–2	14,520	4,840
3.00	264	88–0	15,840	5,280
4.00	352	116–4	21,120	7,040

This table gives the relationship between miles per hour, feet per minute and yards per minute. This is a handy table when following a tractor if you wish to know the speed at which it is traveling. Take out your watch, count the 3-foot steps the tractor will make in a minute. Supposing it makes 66; by referring to the table above in the third column you will note 66 yards per minute on the same line with the 2.25 miles per hour. This means that the tractor traveling at the rate of 2.25 miles per hour covers 198 feet per minute, or 66 yards. The total distance in feet that the tractor will travel in an hour is shown in column 4, 11,880 or 3,960 yards, shown in column 5.

Knowing the speed at which the tractor is traveling, by referring to Table XVI it is easy to reduce the figures to the number of acres that are being plowed per hour.

TABLE XVI

Rate of Plowing in Acres Per Hour

Miles per Hour	1–8 in. Disk Plow	1–12 in. Mouldboard Plow	1–14 in. Mouldboard Plow
1.0	.0808	.119	.142
1.25	.101	.148	.177
1.5	.123	.184	.213
1.75	.143	.206	.247
2.00	.163	.236	.284
2.25	.183	.266	.317
2.5	.203	.298	.353
2.75	.223	.328	.388
3.00	.243	.357	.426

Knowing the rate of speed at which your tractor is traveling, it is easy from the above table to determine just how much land you are plowing each hour.

Effect of Grades on the Power of a Tractor

Each one per cent of rise in grade—rise of 1 foot in 100 feet—adds one per cent of the weight of the tractor and plows to the draft.

This addition of one per cent of the weight of tractor and plows to the draft for every one per cent of grade is equivalent to a reduction in the engine power of 3 per cent. In other words, a 10 per cent grade implies that the tractor has available for load 30 per cent less power than on level ground.

It can be readily seen that the number of plows that can be pulled will depend largely upon the elevation and condition of the land. The footing of the tractor, weight of the plow gang, the elevation above sea level, and other points should be taken into consideration in figuring on tractor outfits.

Chapter XIII
Cold Weather Hints

Cold weather offers certain problems to all tractor owners. These are not much of a handicap to the experienced tractor operator, but are likely to be to the man who is wintering his tractor for the first time. In order of their importance these problems are:

First—Danger of the water in the cylinder and head jackets freezing with consequent cracking of the cylinder and head.

Second—Faulty lubrication due to the sluggish action of oils when cold.

Third—Difficulty in starting the tractor.

Fourth—Storing the tractor for the winter months.

Danger From Freezing

The reasons why engine cylinders and heads can be damaged so easily in cold weather are not hard to understand. Iron gives off heat rapidly and therefore reaches the temperature of the surrounding air very quickly. The sheet of water in the water jacket around the cylinder is very thin, consequently it is also quickly brought to the same temperature as the walls of the jacket. This water has been known to freeze at times when a pail of water standing near the engine would not even have a film of ice on its surface. This is due to the very rapid evaporation of heat from both the iron cylinder and this thin sheet of water. They reach a freezing temperature in a surprisingly short time.

A man may forget to drain his tractor or he may not think it is going to be cold enough to freeze the water in the cylinder jacket. No matter how the water happens to be left there, the result is invariably a cracked cylinder followed many times by an extensive outlay for repairs.

To avoid anything of this sort, there is one simple precaution to take during cold weather, that is, to drain the water out of the cooling system at the end of every run. Where a tractor is to be left standing idle for a few hours, it should be drained. Where it is to be left standing for an indefinite winter period, it should be drained. Where a tractor operator has finished using his tractor, although at time the weather may not be freezing, he should take care to drain his tractor because when the freezing weather does come, he will have forgotten that he left water in the cooling system.

How to Drain a Tractor

Every International tractor is equipped with the proper number of drain cocks for drawing off the water. These should all be opened and care taken to see that the water drains properly through each one. Stoppage anywhere may result in the very thing we wish to avoid. It is a good plan to open all the drain cocks just before the tractor is shut down. Where tractors are equipped with water pumps, care should be taken that these be also drained. A water pump freezes up very quickly, and the pump bracket is often broken on account of the pump plunger being held fast in the pump.

Another important point to be observed is to leave all drain cocks open until ready to fill up the cooling system for another run. This is especially important where the tractor is left in the open. A rain can refill the cooling system, especially of the hopper-cooled type, enough to do serious damage if the drain cocks are not left open.

Anti-Freezing Solutions Not Recommended for Tractors

Anti-freezing solutions are not to be recommended for tractors on account of the rapid evaporation of the water in the cooling system. This causes a wide variation in quality of any anti-freezing mixture. By reason of this rapid evaporation, tractors must be refilled more often than automobiles, making it impossible to maintain an efficient, uniform, anti-freezing solution. Pure water is the best cooling medium. Proper care in draining the tractor during the winter months requires but a few minutes' time and prevents any damage to the tractor. **Be sure to drain your tractor at the end of each period of work during the winter months or freezing weather.**

Repairing Cracked Water Jackets

While the ounce of prevention method should be used in draining tractors yet some tractor owners may be careless enough to allow their tractor cylinders and heads to freeze up and crack the water jacket as the result. Where this takes place, it is seldom that the cylinder itself is injured. It is usually only the outer casing, or water jacket so-called, that really bursts. There are two general methods of patching cracked water jackets.

The "Rust Joint" Method

Where the crack is a very small one, not over a thirty-second of an inch in width, the patching can be done by means of what is termed a "rust joint." After the ice has been melted, drain off all water, then close the main drain cock. Put a coat of putty or tallow over the crack being careful not to fill the crack with it. Fill the jacket high enough to cover the crack with a salammoniac solution (one pound to a gallon of water), let stand thirty minutes, drain, and run engine five minutes to warm jacket. Stop engine, put solution back into jacket and repeat the process three or four times. If the crack is not too wide, you will thus form a rust joint that will never leak.

The Cement Method

The second method of mending a cracked water jacket can be used to advantage where the crack is too wide for the system outlined above to be used. This method is by filling up the crack with cast steel cement or "Smooth On" No. 1. These cements can be bought in small quantities at small cost and can be obtained from hardware stores, machine shops, or from International branch offices, and should be mixed according to directions upon the cans in which they come. In preparing a crack for this kind of a patch, both edges of the crack should be beveled off with a sharp chisel back about one-eighth of an inch on each side to serve as a funnel for forcing in the cement. In beveling the edges of this crack, care must be taken not to break off a portion of the jacket by using too much force on the hammer and chisel. When the crack has been thus dressed down, the paint should be scraped off to a distance of a quarter of an inch on both sides. Then this mixture of cement should be forced down into this crack by using a putty knife or common steel case knife until it is filled. When the crack is full throughout its length and depth, the surface of the cement should be smoothed over and the patch allowed to harden for several hours or a day if convenient. When once hard, this metal cement takes on the properties of the metal around it. It will contract and expand with changes of temperature and generally prove very satisfactory.

Faulty Lubrication in Winter Weather

That there is a positive danger through poor lubrication in cold weather has been demonstrated over and over again. It is common knowledge that oil does not flow as fast in cold weather, and for this reason unless special care is taken will not get to the working parts in time to prevent serious wear and tear on bearings and pistons when tractors are first started. The same custom which old steam engineers observed, of heating their lubricating oil on frosty mornings, should be followed by tractor operators. A little warm oil added to what happens to be already in the lubricator will make the entire supply more easily handled by the automatic pump. In addition to this, every operator is urged, before starting his tractor in freezing weather, to turn the hand crank of the oiler from sixty to seventy-five revolutions. This will insure a sufficient quantity of oil on all working parts to prevent serious trouble. Observance of this precaution will increase the life of the tractor by preventing undue wear.

Cup Greases Affected to a Greater Degree by Cold

Cup grease stiffens to a greater degree than lubricating oil when cold. There are some grades of grease that actually freeze when subjected to zero weather. This is due to the presence of water in the grease. Cup greases so hardened require considerable heat to make them again efficient, and unless they receive this heat within a reasonable length of time after a tractor has been started, risks are taken of damaging such parts as are lubricated by greases. Take special pains to see that all grease cups are not only kept filled with a good, light grease, but are also screwed down several turns more at the start during cold weather.

Difficulty in Starting

It is common knowledge that all internal combustion engines are harder to start in cold weather because all grades of fuel become less easily vaporized at the lower temperatures. The greatest difficulty comes from using a poor grade of gasoline for starting purposes. A poor grade of gasoline produces an extremely aggravating situation for the tractor operator who does not know there are different grades on the market.

Owners of International tractors are urged, especially on account of the very small quantity of gasoline needed for starting purposes, to buy a few gallons of the very highest grade of gasoline on the market, testing not less than seventy degrees Baume. By using a high grade of gasoline for priming, the chief difficulty in starting will be eliminated.

If a tractor operator will put a bucket or two of warm water into the hopper or cooling system of his tractor just before he wishes to start, he will find it an advantage. This warm water in the water jacket raises the temperature of the cylinder up to a point so that it does not have the same condensing and chilling effect upon the vaporized gasoline that it otherwise would have. There will also be a saving in fuel consumption, for it takes a large portion of the fuel just to heat the cold engine and the water.

In starting kerosene tractors that are still hot from the previous run, it will be found satisfactory to start on kerosene rather than by the use of gasoline. Gasoline is needed, in most cases, only when the tractor is cold.

Chapter XIV

Storing and Overhauling the Tractor

Overhauling Season

The tractor owner should take advantage of a lull in his work and look his tractor over with the aim of putting it in first-class condition for next spring's work. Nothing should be overlooked at this season of the year that will prevent another season's good work. The old saying, "A stitch in time saves nine," should mean much to every tractor owner.

Order Repairs Early

All parts should be carefully examined for wear, and if replacements are needed they should be ordered early. Tractor owners frequently make the mistake of postponing the ordering of repairs, thinking that they have ample time in which to get them. If there is ample time to get the repairs, it is always wise to give this time to the manufacturer who must supply the part. Thus if your description of the part wanted should not be complete, the manufacturer would have time to write you and verify your orders. If you wait until the last minute before ordering, the manufacturer does not have this opportunity, and must take a chance on sending you the right piece. He has an even chance of sending the right piece but he may possibly send the wrong one, then you suffer a delay which may prove serious. It is the part of wisdom to order the repairs early, so that should there be any delay in shipping or interruption of transportation facilities, you will still get the part in ample time for your work.

Care of Tractors in Storing

Where a tractor is not to be used for a period of time it should be stored in a dry place.

All water should be drained from the cooling system and the drain cocks left open. Be sure that the tractor is level for thorough draining.

In order to prevent rust forming upon the working parts of the tractor, each tractor owner should pump, by means of the hand crank on the lubricator, a fresh supply of oil to the bearings, piston and cylinder.

The operator should then turn the engine over a few times in order that this oil may be spread over all wearing surfaces.

The lubricator should then be refilled to its limit. This will prevent the polished mechanism of the pump in the lubricator tank from rusting.

Chapter XV
Engine Troubles Classified

DIFFICULT STARTING

With Satisfactory Fuel, Compression and Spark, Any Internal Combustion Engine Can Be Started. All Starting Troubles Can Be Traced to These Three Points

Cause	Testing For	Remedy
1. **Defective Magneto**—Race, brushes or distributor points dirty and gummed from too much oil.	See page 35, "Testing for Spark."	See page 39, i, j, m, and page 37 "Adjusting Breaker Points."
2. **Defective spark plug**—points or core short-circuited by water or carbon, or gap too small or too large.	See page 40, "Testing Spark Plugs."	See page 40, "Care of Spark Plugs" and m, on page 39.
3. With make-and-break ignition, speed of brake too slow due to dirt or weak igniter spring or rust.	Turn movable electrode by hand. If it doesn't move freely, clean.	See pages 42, 4, b. Remove igniter, clean in kerosene or gasoline.
4. With make-and-break ignition stationary electrode short-circuited.	Take out igniter, connect wires, and test for spark. If no spark, correct.	Remove electrode, clean in gasoline. If necessary, tighten mica. Dry and replace.
5. With make-and-break ignition, igniter points may be worn or points short-circuited by dirt.	Test same as No. 4.	Clean points with fine emery cloth or replace.
6. Sparking mechanism of make-and-break igniter out of adjustment.	See page 41, b, c, e, f.	See page 41, b, c, e, f.
7. Wiring incorrect, broken, short-circuited, disconnected or loose at binding post.	If no spark, trace wiring and see that it corresponds with wiring diagram for your particular engine or tractor. See if wires are tight at connections.	For 10-20 Titan follow diagram, page 37. For 10-20 Mogul follow diagram, page 38. For 8-16 Mogul follow diagram, page 41. For 15-30 Titan and International follow diagram, page 38. For other systems, see pages 42, 43, 44, 45 and 46.

Difficult Starting—Continued

Cause	Testing For	Remedy
8. Engine out of time.	See page 42, e, and page 43, g. Timing for late ignition for starting I H C 8-16, 10-20 and 15-30 tractors is indicated by ignition timing marks on outside face of flywheel. Spark for late ignition must occur with spark lever in retard position on Mogul tractors when ignition timing mark is on inner horizontal center; on Titan and International tractors, on upper vertical position. If spark does not occur in time engine must be retimed with magneto.	To time Mogul 8-16 with low tension ignition set trip rod to contact with trip lever when crank has traveled in on compression stroke about 45° to 50°, then be sure that rod is set and adjusted so that when flywheel is turned trip occurs when ignition timing mark is at horizontal inner center. Engine timing for Mogul 10-20 must be so that spark occurs when the crank is on the inner dead center of compression stroke or ignition mark on flywheel is in same position on compression stroke. On Titan 10-20 and 15-30 and International 15-30 crank is in same position but ignition timing mark is at upper vertical center. See Magneto Timing, No. 9.
9. Magneto not timed with engine.	If engine timing is correct but spark is not right, check up magneto timing with engine. For checking K W high tension rotary magneto timing (Titan 10-20, Mogul 10-20, Titan and International 15-30), see page 36. Timing of Magneto, 37, 38 and 39.	See pages 36, 37, 38 and 39. On low tension oscillating magnetos, see pages 40 and 41.
10. On rotary magneto with impulse starter impulse spring may be too weak.	Will cause magneto to operate as rotary too soon so it cannot generate electricity enough for good spark.	Tighten spring adjusting screw E, Illust. 18, page 36, until impulse starter pawl will hook up when engine is at half normal speed.

Difficult Starting—Continued

Cause	Testing For	Remedy
11. Poor compression.	Turn flywheel against compression. If compression weak, examine valves and piston rings. If the leak is past the piston because of poor lubrication or worn rings, you will ordinarily hear a blowing, hissing sound. If the leak is not past the piston, then the valves leak.	To remedy leaky valves, see page 12, Note 1. For leaky piston rings, see page 15, Note 1, and page 16, Note 4.
12. Cold engine and fuel.	This difficulty which occurs in cold weather most frequently prevents starting, especially with low grade fuels.	Heat fuel in hot water for priming charges or prime with one part petroleum ether and two parts gasoline, or start on special high grade gasoline or heat igniter or spark plug. If cold not too severe, fill cylinder jacket with hot water. See page 133.
13. Engine primed too freely or not enough.	Open petcocks and see if fuel runs out.	If over-primed, open petcocks, turn flywheel against compression until overcharge exhausted, then prime in moderation with right kind of fuel for conditions. Where no petcocks are provided, turn flywheel backwards, which opens exhaust valve when piston returns to head and cleans out overcharge. It may also be necessary to clean igniter or spark plugs before starting.
14. Feed water not turned off before stopping engine, or feed water needle valve open at starting.	Open petcocks and turn flywheel against compression.	Turn flywheel against compression to force water out of petcocks. It may also be necessary to remove igniter or spark plugs and wipe thoroughly.

Difficult Starting—Continued.

Cause	Testing For	Remedy
15. Fuel carelessly handled, unstrained and mixed with water.	Lack of fuel may indicate clogged fuel pipe, strainer or needle valve passage. To test for water put sample of fuel into a clear bottle and look for distinct hairline between water and fuel, or pour out a small quantity of fuel on a smooth surface. The fuel distributes itself evenly over the surface, the water collects in drops.	Strain fuel and clean fuel pipe, strainer and mixer. To remove water strain through chamois skin. If water is present in quantity, pour off fuel from top of water. See Note 3, page 25.
16. Intake and exhaust valve operation restricted—out of time or not fully opened or closed.	Examine valves for opening as described on pages 21 and 22.	See pages 21, 22 and 23.
17. Improper adjustment between governor and throttle valve.	Insufficient fuel may be due to throttle valve not opening in time or far enough.	Adjust the connection between the throttle valve and the governor arm so that when the engine is at rest throttle valve is fully open, and when engine reaches normal speed throttle valve is closed. These two positions of the throttle valve are carefully marked on the throttle valve shaft and hub.
18. Fuel needle valve not open.	Examine.	Open needle valve.
19. Gasoline supply cup empty.	Examine.	Fill.
20. **Lack of fuel.**	Lack of fuel may indicate clogged fuel pipe, strainer or needle valve passage. To test for water put sample of fuel into a clear bottle and look for distinct hairline between water and fuel, or pour out a small quantity of fuel on a smooth surface. The fuel distributes itself evenly over the surface, the water collects in drops. Also examine fuel supply tank. Fuel pump may be out of order.	See Note 1, "Care of Fuel Pump", and Note 2 "Pump Check Valves", page 25.

Difficult Starting—Continued

Cause	Testing For	Remedy
21. Dirt in feed cup.	See No. 20 above.	Strain fuel and clean fuel pipe, strainer and mixer. To remove water strain through chamois skin. If water is present in quantity, pour off fuel from top of water. See Note 3, page 25.
22. Defective ignition.	See No. 1, 2, 3, 4, 5, 6, 7, 8, 9, 10, under "Difficult Starting".	See No. 1, 2, 3, 4, 5, 6, 7, 8, 9, 10, under "Difficult Starting".
23. Too much fuel.	Causes sluggish running engine, flooded cylinder and black exhaust smoke.	Feed less fuel.
24. Too little fuel.	Back-firing or muffler explosions may indicate too weak mixture.	Open needle valve wider to feed more fuel.
25. Feeding too much water.	Causes engine to stop.	Adjust water needle valve until hard knock in cylinders is eliminated. See pages 80 and 81, and 27 to 31 incl.
26. Engine overheated due to improper lubrication.	Indicated by slowing down of engine, and pre-ignition.	The first thing to do is to supply sufficient lubrication of the right quality. Read carefully every word on pages 47 to 53, inclusive, 62, and 88 to 90, inclusive.
27. Engine overheated due to imperfect water circulation.	Indicated by pre-ignition and slowing down of engine.	See pages 63, 64, 65 and 66.

LOSS OF POWER

No point in engine operation is more destructive of its power, life and service, and to the reputation of its manufacturer than the continual operation of the engine with late spark. Many an engine condemned because it did not produce power or did not operate satisfactorily was absolutely O. K. in every respect, but its failure to deliver power was due solely to the fact that the spark was too late. Don't operate your engine with a late spark. It will prove disastrous in the end.

It reduces engine efficiency
It reduces engine power
It reduces thermal efficiency
It increases fuel consumption
It destroys piston and cylinder lubrication
It overheats cylinder and piston
It causes carbon deposits in cylinder, on valves and in ports, on piston and rings and ring grooves
It overheats engine so cooling system is prevented from performing its function
It increases water consumption
It destroys exhaust valve seat and burns stem
It destroys life and shortens working life of cylinder and piston
It shortens life of wrist pin and bearing
It destroys igniter and spark plug points
It causes movable electrode to stick and tends to destroy insulation of stationary electrode and spark plugs
It causes igniter and spark plugs to short circuit
It causes undue wear to valve mechanism because of added pressure at exhaust valve opening

Cause	Testing For	Remedy
28. Defective ignition, especially late spark.	Check up with timing marks on flywheel. If spark occurs with crank on or about dead center, **spark is too late for normal working conditions.** See e, page 42, and g, page 43.	When working up to load, spark lever adjustment should be such that you get full spark advance throw on magneto. See Nos. 2, 3, 8 and 9 under "Difficult Starting". **Retarded spark is used for starting only, early spark for working.**
29. Lack of fuel.	Lack of fuel may indicate clogged fuel pipe, strainer or needle valve passage. To test for water, put sample of fuel into a clear bottle and look for distinct hairline between water and fuel, or pour out a small quantity of fuel on a smooth surface. The fuel distributes itself evenly over the surface, the water collects in drops. Also examine fuel supply tank.	See Note 1, "Care of Fuel Pump," and Note 2, "Pump Check Valves", page 25.

Loss of Power—Continued

Cause	Testing For	Remedy
30. Over-feeding of fuel and water.	Causes sluggish running engine, flooded cylinder and exhaust smoke. Causes engine to stop. See Nos. 54, 55 and 56.	Feed less fuel. Adjust water needle valve until hard knock in cylinders is eliminated. See pages 75 and 76, and 27 to 31 incl.
31. Loss of compression.	Turn flywheel against compression. If compression weak, examine valves and piston rings. If the leak is past the piston because of poor lubrication or worn rings, you will ordinarily hear a blowing, hissing sound. If the leak is not past the piston, then the valves leak.	To remedy leaky valves, see page 12, Note 1. For leaky piston rings, see page 15, Note 1, and page 16, Note 4.
32. Overheated cylinder and piston, causing frictional overload.	Late spark, poor lubrication, insufficient cooling water, gases escaping past piston rings or pre-ignition, cause overheating, which is indicated by loss of power due to slowing up of engine speed and a sluggish, laboring action. Escaping gas is indicated by hissing noise, pre-ignition by a decided pound.	To correct late spark see No. 28. To correct poor lubrication see No. 26. To correct cooling see No. 27. To correct leaky piston rings see No. 11. To correct pre-ignition see pages 80 and 83.
33. Outside load too great for engine power.	Engine labors and loses speed. See pages 126, 127, 128 and 129, "Finding a Safe Load."	See pages 126, 127, 128 and 129, "Finding a Safe Load."
34. Overload due to slipping clutches.	If clutch drum is worn or hot, clutch is slipping. **Clutch drum never heats when it is not slipping.**	See Note 1, page 100, and Note 2, page 110.
35. Belt too weak to transmit power, too short or slipping.	Check up with belt information on pages 109 and 110.	See Note 1, page 110.

Loss of Power—Continued

Cause	Testing For	Remedy
36. Belt pulleys too small.	Check up with information on page 109, "Size of Pulleys."	See page 109, "Size of Pulleys."

EXCESSIVE FUEL CONSUMPTION

Cause	Testing For	Remedy
37. Overload on engine.	Engine labors, loses speed and uses excessive fuel. See pages 126, 127, 128 and 129, "Finding a Safe Load."	See pages 126, 127, 128 and 129, "Finding a Safe Load."
38. Defective ignition, especially late spark.	Examine ignition timing as explained in Nos. 8 and 9.	Correct as explained in Nos. 8, 9 and 28.
39. Loss of compression.	Turn flywheel against compression. If compression is weak, examine valves and piston rings. If the leak is past the piston because of poor lubrication or worn rings, you will ordinarily hear a blowing, hissing sound. If the leak is not past the piston, then the valves leak.	To remedy leaky valves see page 12, Note 1. For leaky piston rings see page 15, Note 1, and page 16, Note 4.
40. Incorrect mixture—too much fuel or water.	Too much fuel is generally indicated by excessive black or grey exhaust smoke. See No. 17.	Throttle fuel needle valve down to the point where engine will handle load with least fuel regardless of marking on needle valve disk. Never use more water than is absolutely necessary. Throttle the water valve also to the closest running point. See pages 27 to 31 incl.
41. Engine runs too cold or too hot.	Take temperature of cylinder jacket water, which should be from 200° to 212° Fahr. for kerosene.	See pages 63, 64, 65 and 66.

Excessive Fuel Consumption—Continued

Cause	Testing For	Remedy
42. Engine parts slipping and binding.	Bearings become hot.	See page 24, Note 2, "Care and Adjustment of Bearings."

POUNDING

Cause	Testing For	Remedy
43. Pre-ignition.	A decided metallic pounding or knock in cylinder. See page 80, Note 1, and pages 83 and 84.	If caused by overheated cylinder and piston, see No. 32. If caused by glowing carbon or metallic points in cylinder, see page 84, Note 1. If caused by deep sand holes in exhaust valve, disk, cylinder or piston head, plug holes with steel, iron or copper. If caused by uncertain ignition, correct ignition timing as explained in No. 28.
44. Looseness of some engine part.	A loose main bearing causes a deep, hollow pound once every revolution. A loose connecting rod or wrist pin bearing produces two short knocks every revolution. A loose flywheel or one with a cracked hub or spoke causes more of a grating sound. If there is lost motion in any other parts, detect by inspection.	Readjust bearings, tighten flywheel hub and take up lost motion in loose parts. If flywheel hub or spokes are cracked, should be replaced.

POOR SPEED REGULATION

Cause	Testing For	Remedy
45. Defective ignition.	Check up with timing marks on flywheel. If spark occurs with crank on or about dead center, **spark is too late for normal working conditions.** See e, page 42 and g, page 43.	When working up to load, spark lever adjustment should be such that you get full spark advance throw on magneto. See Nos. 2, 3, 8 and 9 under "Difficult Starting." **Retarded spark is used for starting only, early spark for working.**
46. Governor out of adjustment.	Inspect. See No. 17.	Take up lost motion in moving parts, clean and lubricate. Be sure that both governor springs have same tension and that the collar is free to act. It must not be obstructed or restricted in its movement.

BACK FIRING

Delayed Burning of the Previous Fuel Charge

Cause	Testing For	Remedy
47. Mixture too weak.	Explodes back through mixer.	Open needle valve and feed more fuel.
48. Spark too late (still burning when new charge is admitted).	If feeding more fuel does not remedy, examine spark timing.	Advance spark, see No. 28.
49. Feeding too much water may cause slow burning.	Test for 47 and 48 first.	Feed less water. See pages 27 to 31, incl.

HEAVY EXPLOSIONS AT END OF EXHAUST PIPE

Cause	Testing For	Remedy
50. Defective ignition causing misfiring.	Check up with timing marks on flywheel. If spark occurs with crank on or about dead center, spark is too late for normal working conditions. See e, page 42, and g, page 43.	When working up to load, spark lever adjustment should be such that you get full spark advance throw on magneto. See Nos. 2, 3, 8 and 9 under "Difficult Starting."
51. Mixture too weak to burn at all times.	Check up fuel feed.	Open fuel needle wider to feed more fuel.
52. Mixture too rich, causing incomplete combustion.	Check up fuel feed.	Feed less fuel.
53. Leaky exhaust valves.	See that the exhaust valve is well seated.	To remedy a leaky exhaust valve, see page 12, Note 1.

SMOKE

Cause	Testing For	Remedy
54. Fuel mixture too rich.	Black smoke at end of exhaust pipe.	Feed less fuel.
55. Excessive lubrication.	Blue smoke at end of exhaust pipe.	Use less lubricating oil, but exercise care.
56. Excessive water in kerosene.	Grey smoke at end of exhaust pipe.	Throttle down water and kerosene.
57. Leaky piston rings.	Excessive smoke at open end of cylinders.	To remedy leaky piston rings, see page 15, Note 1, and page 16, Note 4.
58. Overheating of piston and cylinder.	Late spark, poor lubrication, insufficient cooling water, gases escaping past piston which may cause excessive fuel consumption and excessive smoke at the open end of cylinders.	To correct late spark, see No. 28. To correct poor lubrication, see No. 26. To correct cooling, see No. 27. To correct leaky piston rings, see No. 11. To remedy pre-ignition, see No. 43.
59. Poor lubrication (excessive and of poor quality).	Excessive smoke at open end of cylinder.	Use only recommended grades of oil and lubricate with care. Read every word on pages 47 to 62 and 88 to 90, inclusive, and **follow instructions.**

Chapter XVI
Miscellaneous Tractor Information

HOW TO START, RUN AND STOP A TITAN TRACTOR

1. See that gear shift lever is in central (neutral) position of its quadrant. In this position no transmission gears are in mesh.

2. Be sure to disengage tractor clutch.

3. If using belt pulley, see that its clutch is disengaged. Belt should never be tight when trying to start engine. If convenient, belt should be removed.

4. **Important. Do Not Engage Tractor Clutch Before Getting Into Seat.**

5. Turn crank on mechanical oiler forty to fifty times when starting engine to make sure that cylinder, crank shaft and piston are getting sufficient oil.

6. Put some cylinder oil on gland of kerosene pump, disengage side rod from pump arm and pump by hand until feed cup on mixer is full.

7. Set magneto for starting engine. To do this, throw small lever out of position so that pawl will fall into notch A. Illust. 22.

8. Adjust magneto timer lever on mixer to position marked "Late" on quadrant. This gives a late spark.

9. Place two-way valve in a vertical position, this being position for running on gasoline. Illust. 14.

10. Open needle valve to marked position.

11. Open relief cocks on bottom of cylinders by means of compression relief lever.

12. See that water valve on mixer is closed.

13. Leave cold air inlet in mixer open.

14. Prime engine with gasoline, using spring bottom oil can shipped with tractor.

15. Crank engine until first explosion occurs, then remove starting crank and close relief valves on bottom of cylinder.

16. Adjust fuel needle valve and air damper until engine runs smoothly.

17. As engine gains in speed, advance the spark by setting magneto lever for early ignition.

18. Let engine run on gasoline for a few minutes and then change to kerosene by opening needle valve a little wider and placing the lever in two-way valve in a horizontal position. **Leave needle valve open slightly beyond running mark until engine is warm.**

19. When engine begins to pound or knock, slowly open water needle valve. Feed just enough water to stop pounding. Too much water will cause engine to miss explosions or stop.

20. Air inlet damper can be regulated by lever to provide hot air to vaporize kerosene when starting engine in a cold room, or for running on light loads. Never allow mixer to become so hot that you cannot hold your hand upon it. Turn on cold air before it becomes this hot. As a general rule use hot air as little as possible for steady running.

21. As engine becomes heated up, it may become desirable to slightly retard the spark. Adjust magneto timer lever.

22. To stop tractor, turn off the water supply to mixer.

23. Then change fuel to gasoline by turning two-way valve on mixer and allow engine to run a few minutes.

24. Close kerosene needle valve.

25. Release tractor clutches, thus throwing all load off engine.

26. Close oil cups for crankshaft pinion.

27. Open relief cocks.

28. If engine is to stand for some time, be sure that intake and exhaust valves are closed.

HOW TO START, RUN AND STOP A MOGUL TRACTOR

1. See that gear shifting levers forward and reverse are in neutral position.

2. Push clutch lever forward as far as possible, thereby disengaging tractor clutch.

3. Do not engage tractor clutch before getting into seat.

4. Turn crank on mechanical oiler forty to fifty times when starting to make sure that cylinder, crankshaft and piston are getting sufficient oil.

5. Open gasoline needle valve about three-quarters of a turn or to point indicated. Illust. 15g and 15h.

6. Put air damper in position marked "Start."

7. Move relief lever towards flywheel to relieve compression for starting.

8. Set spark advance lever at retarded or starting position and set impulse starter on magneto.

9. Now turn flywheel, top of wheel towards front of tractor until engine starts off under its own power.

10. As soon as engine starts, put relief valve in its original running position at once.

11. Put air damper at position marked "Run."

12. Advance spark by moving spark advance lever to position indicated.

13. Adjust gasoline needle valve to point where engine runs best and gives greatest power.

14. As engine increases in speed, advance spark. To get best results spark should be advanced as much as possible without causing early ignition, indicated by a bumping or knocking in the cylinder.

15. If spark is not advanced to proper position, engine will not develop full power, too much fuel will be used and exhaust valve will be subjected to extreme heat, which is objectionable. As engine becomes heated up it may be desirable to slightly retard spark.

16. The engine having been started by using gasoline and cylinder well heated, the change from gasoline to kerosene may be made. Simply open fuel needle valve and shut off gasoline needle valve.

17. Open water needle valve and adjust to give engine just enough water to prevent bumping or knocking in cylinder.

18. To stop engine, take all the load from engine, and in cool and cold weather open hopper and cylinder drains and allow all water to run out.

19. Then close water needle valve.

20. Close fuel needle valve.

21. Retard spark lever to starting position.

22. Open pet-cock in bottom of cylinder.

23. Put relief lever in same position as for starting.

24. Close pet-cock in bottom of cylinder.

25. If engine is to stand for some time, be sure that intake and exhaust valves are closed.

HOW TO STOP A TRACTOR TO FACILITATE STARTING

1. If using water with fuel, shut it off when load is off.

2. Switch over to gasoline from kerosene just before stopping. This will aid in cleaning inside of cylinder.

3. Shut off gasoline or kerosene.

4. Open pet-cocks or release before engine stops to aid cleaning cylinder.

5. If weather warrants, or if tractor is to stand idle for any period above a day, it is advisable to drain out water completely. This will help to prevent lime deposits or other sediments from forming in tank, jacket or passages.

6. When possible, be sure to have engine set with all valves closed.

7. When engine is still warm it is a good time to check up valve and ignition timing.

8. Examine the ignition system and put in shape if needed.

9. Examine the whole tractor, and if anything is found enough out of order to need correction, do it and clean the tractor.

10. Close pet-cocks or release, and where possible draw in a priming charge, letting piston remain at end of suction stroke. Then if valves are seated and the piston and rings are in good condition and well lubricated, the fuel charge admitted will stay in cylinder and gasify, ready to start at first cranking.

FORMULAS

DEFINITION OF A MECHANICAL HORSE POWER

A mechanical horse power is the power required to raise 33,000 pounds one foot in one minute. This, according to James Watt, inventor of the steam engine, is about the power of the average horse. On this basis a 1500-pound horse, traveling at 2½ miles per hour and pulling one-tenth of its weight, would be pulling exactly one mechanical horse power.

RATED HORSE POWER

$$\frac{\text{Bore}^2 \times .7854 \times \text{stroke in inches} \times \text{r. p. m.} \times \text{No. of Cyl}}{\text{13,000 to 15,000 cu. in. piston displacement}} = \text{Guaranteed or rated horse power}$$

NOTE—We do not find it advisable to attempt to produce a brake or delivered horse power on kerosene by using less than 11,000 cubic inches of piston displacement per horse power. In the formula above, by using 13,000 to 15,000 cubic inches for every rated horse power, we have a safe working surplus in all cases. **I H C** engines rated on the above basis are therefore very conservatively rated.

Titan 10-20 — A Twin-Cylinder Valve-in-Head Kerosene Tractor

Motor—A twin cylinder valve-in-head kerosene-burning motor that is silent, smooth running, and a giant for power.

Mixer—Uses without change of parts gasoline, benzine, naphtha, kerosene and distillate down to 39° Baume. Valve, after being opened, automatically supplies water in proportion to the amount of fuel being consumed.

Governor—A flyball throttling governor controls the amount of fuel entering the cylinders in proportion to the load.

Ignition—A high tension magneto furnishes current for jump spark ignition. No batteries needed.

Lubrication—A six-feed mechanical oiler keeps essential parts well oiled. Transmission is lubricated by an oil bath.

Cooling—Motor is cooled by water circulating from a tank having a capacity of 40 gallons.

Transmission—A spur gear, selective type transmission, transmits power from engine to final chain drive. Gears run in oil.

Chain Drive—Double chain drive to rear wheels.

Steering—The steering gear is of the automobile type with wheel convenient to driver. Worm and gear completely enclosed.

Four Wheels—Stands squarely on four wheels, two large, broad-faced drive wheels for traction and two front wheels to make it steer easily.

SPECIFICATIONS TITAN 10-20

Rated H. P. Belt	20
Rated H. P. Drawbar	10
Bore	6½
Stroke	8
R. P. M.	500
Capacity Cooling System	40 gallon
Fuel Tank Capacity	16 gallon
Width	60 inches
Length	147 inches
Height	66¾ inches
Diameter, Rear Wheels	54 inches
Diameter, Front Wheels	36 inches
Face, Rear Wheels	10 inches
Face, Front Wheels	6 inches
Forward Speeds—1.85 and 2.5 miles per hour	
Friction Clutch Pulley, Diam.	20 inches
Friction Clutch Pulley, Face	8½ inches
Weight (Approx.)	5710 lbs.

Mogul 10-20—A 3-Plow Kerosene Burning Tractor

Motor—Simple, low-speed, long-lived and efficient motor, made in the Mogul factory.

Enclosed Crank Case—Keeps dust, dirt and grit out of working parts.

Hopper Cooling System—No pump; no radiator troubles; no small passages to become clogged with sediment or lime, or to freeze.

High Tension Magneto—Motor starts and runs on the magneto. No batteries are needed.

Fuel Saving Governor—Regulates the volume of fuel to the load and also keeps the speed of the motor uniform.

The Oiler that Never Forgets—The force feed oiler on the Mogul gives the main bearings and working parts the proper amount of oil. It is always on the job.

Serviceable Transmission—Is enclosed in a dust-proof case and runs in oil. It is of the selective type with large, accurately cut gears of hardened steel, fitted with high grade roller bearings. Two speeds forward and one reverse.

Flexible Drive Chain—Power is transmitted to the two drive wheels by a strong, flexible, high grade roller chain—the best known way to transmit power on a tractor. There is no binding, no getting out of alignment.

Two-Wheel Drive—Both rear wheels are drive wheels. The pull is straight ahead.

SPECIFICATIONS MOGUL 10-20

Rated H. P. Belt	20
Rated H. P. Drawbar	10
Bore	8½
Stroke	12
R. P. M	400
Hopper Capacity	35 gallon
Fuel Tank Capacity	13 gallon
Width	56 inches
Length	135 inches
Height	70 inches
Diameter, Rear Wheels	54 inches
Diameter, Front Wheels	36 inches
Face, Rear Wheels	10 inches
Face, Front Wheels	6 inches
Forward Speeds	1.8 and 2.5 miles per hr.
Friction Clutch Pulley, Diam.	20 inches
Friction Clutch Pulley, Face	10½ inches
Weight (Approx)	5500 lbs.

International 15-30—A Medium Weight Tractor That Operates on Kerosene

Four-Cylinder Motor—The engine is of the four-cylinder type, set horizontally, so that power is delivered direct to transmission through spur gears without bevel gears. Completely enclosed. Dust-tight crank case with removable cover.

Mixer—One mixer with four fuel needle valves and a single water needle valve is used, which reduces adjustments to the minimum. This mixer will handle any of the cheap fuels, such as kerosene, distillate down to 39 degrees Baume, gas oil, solar oil, motor spirits, gasoline or naphtha.

Governor—A fly-ball throttling type governor controls amount of fuel entering cylinders in proportion to the load.

Ignition—The ignition is jump spark, current being furnished by high-grade gear driven magneto—no battery required.

Lubrication—Motor is lubricated by automatic force feed oiler with twelve feeds. Transmission is lubricated by an oil bath.

Cooling—The motor is water-cooled, circulation through cylinders, tank, and a vertical tube radiator being secured by a belt-driven rotary pump.

Transmission—Two speeds forward and one reverse, all controlled by a single lever. Roller bearings. Gears run in oil. Double chain drive to rear wheels. Chains tightly encased.

Steering—Automobile type.

SPECIFICATIONS 15-30

Rated H. P. Belt	30
Rated H. P. Drawbar	15
Bore	5¼
Stroke	8
R. P. M	575
Cooling System Capacity	40 gallon
Fuel Tank Capacity	24 gallon
Width	80 inches
Length	160 inches
Height	118 inches
Diameter, Rear Wheels	66 inches
Diameter, Front Wheels	40 inches
Face, Rear Wheels	14 inches
Face, Front Wheels	7 inches
Forward Speeds	1.8 and 2.4 miles per hr.
Friction Clutch Pulley, Diam.	18 inches
Friction Clutch Pulley, Face	9 inches
Weight (Approx)	8700 lbs.

Chapter XVII

Plow Adjustments, Care and Operation

Our reasons for taking up plow adjustments, care and operation is because we find that many of the so-called tractor troubles can be traced directly to plow difficulties. These plow difficulties arise through the operator's lack of knowledge of the principles involved in the adjustment, care and operation of plows.

The practical hints outlined herewith are general and refer to the successful operation of practically all tractor plows. It is safe to say that if all plow adjustments are properly made the tractor outfit will operate with less fuel expense, less power, and with less wear and tear on all parts.

Read Instructions

First, read the instructions carefully for assembling the plow and see that it is properly put together and that all bearings, cams and gears are well oiled.

Oiling

The grease cups should be filled with good cup grease, turned down, and refilled when starting a new plow. Also put grease on gears and clutch cam, drive chain and other parts.

Remove the Varnish Before Starting Plow

Plow bottoms, rolling coulters, and other parts of implements finished with a high polish are usually varnished before leaving the factory to prevent rust. Good work cannot be accomplished until the varnish is removed.

For this purpose use a regular prepared varnish remover which can be obtained from almost any hardware or drug store handling a line of paints, or use ordinary concentrated lye mixed with water, making a liquid strong enough to remove the varnish. The lye may be applied by attaching cloth or waste to the end of a stick. After applying the lye, let it stand for about fifteen minutes; then, if necessary, repeat the operation.

Be sure that all varnish is removed before putting the plows into the ground.

Adjustment of Hitch

Adjust the hitch up or down as nearly as possible in the line of draft from engine to plow. The lateral adjustment of the hitch is also important, and this should be set as nearly from the center of the plow as possible. The center of the tractor must also be taken into consideration, as sometimes it is necessary to hitch off to one side of plow in order to get somewhere near the center of the tractor. The front end of the draft rod should never be lower than the point at which it is attached to the plow if adjustment can possibly be made to overcome this.

If the hitch is too high on the vertical clevises or too low on the tractor, it will put too much weight on the front wheels, which is liable to break the wheels or bend the axles. It will also cause the plow bottoms to run on the points and the front bottom will run deeper than the rear bottoms, resulting in an uneven furrow bottom. At the same time, it will pitch the moldboards forward at the top, which will prevent the moldboards from turning the furrow correctly. The plow bottoms are liable not to scour and the cutting edges of the shares will wear off rounding on the under side, making it difficult to keep the plow in hard ground.

When the plow is attached to a tractor that has a very low hitch and the hitch on the plow is not low enough to make the weight equal on both furrow wheels, the front end of the plow will run too deep and the rear end of the plow will raise off the furrow bottom and thus cause very unsatisfactory work. Correct this by raising the hitch on the tractor.

The correct plow hitch to the tractor is very necessary for good work and is also essential if you wish to operate the tractor on minimum power and with a low fuel consumption.

Setting the Plows for Width

See that each plow cuts the proper width and runs level, that is, full depth of landside. This adjustment is made at the coupling pin of each plow by unlocking and turning malleable notched eccentric with spanner wrench furnished with plow for this purpose. It will be necessary sometimes to get the proper adjustment, that is, both the proper width of land and the level of furrow, to turn both eccentric couplings at either end of coupling pins.

Setting the Plows for Suck

To adjust the plow for proper suck, loosen the bolts that hold the plow bottoms in suck alignment and drop the head for less suck or raise it for more. A plow should not have too much suck or it will run on its nose in hard land and put unnecessary weight on the gauge wheel in soft land. The plow should, if properly set, run with the heel of the landside down on the bottom of the furrow.

Plow Should Run Level

To do the best work with the least draft, the plows should be adjusted so that they will run level when plowing the required depth. For example—if six inches is the depth you wish to plow, give the bottom suck enough to penetrate that depth, and then regulate the pitch of the standard by raising or lowering the point of the plow so the heel of the landside touches the bottom of furrow when plowing at that depth. If this is done, it will relieve the pressure on the gauge wheel and the plow will run steady.

How to Adjust the Combination Rolling Coulter and Jointer

Attach coulter crank shank to plow so center of coulter blade is from 1 to 3 inches back of point of plow bottom, and adjust crank of shank so coulter blade will cut from ¼ to ½ inch wider than plow bottom, and never set a rolling coulter below 45° angle point, for if set below that point it will push trash before it in place of cutting it.

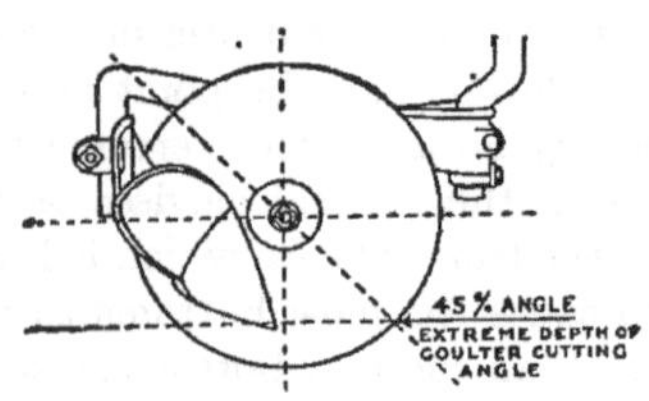

Illust. 94. Diagram showing extreme cutting angle of a rolling coulter.

If the ground is soft and free from trash and the plow is running from 5 to 6 inches deep, the coulter blade can be adjusted down just low enough to swing over plow point. When set this way, the plow can be turned in either direction at the corners of the field.

The jointer bottom should be set just deep enough to cut the furrow loose, sc it will roll down in the furrow bottom.

For hard and trashy ground and deep plowing, the coulter blade should not be set as low as for soft ground as the coulter will raise the plow bottom up and take the weight off the plow wheels and the plow will not run steady. At the same time, it will be difficult to get the plow in the ground.

For extremely hard ground, have the crank of coulter shank to the rear and the coulter blade raised high enough so the plow bottom will have a chance to enter the ground in advance of the coulter blade.

The angle of the jointer can be changed by adjusting jointer arm in the pivot arm for coulter. This will give much better results under the different conditions than if set in a fixed angle.

Always keep the rolling coulter clamping bolt tight and the bearing full of hard grease. In adjusting jointer bottom on jointer arm, always keep a space 1/16 inch between point of jointer share and rolling coulter blade. This is necessary in order to keep the rolling coulter blade from wearing on jointer bottom. If at any time the rolling coulter blade rubs on the jointer bottom, adjust jointer on arm so they will not rub together. When the bearings get worn too much, so the coulter blade does not run true, renew necessary parts.

The pivot for coulter arm should always be adjusted so the arm will pivot freely. If too loose, the coulter will not run steady.

By removing jointer arm from coulter pivot arm, the coulter can be used independent of the jointer.

When adjusted correctly, the jointer will turn any reasonable amount of trash under and the coulter blade will leave a fine bank and furrow for the front furrow wheel to run it.

How to Free the Plow Bottoms from a Stump or Stone

First reverse the tractor and back the plows far enough to free then from the obstruction, then force the front furrow wheel lever to the rear until it reaches the rear notch in sector; this will raise the plow bottoms up so they will pass over the obstruction; and as soon as the plow bottoms have passed the obstruction, put the lever back in its original position.

Care of Plow

Never leave the plow in the ground even though you expect to resume work in a short time. When through plowing for the day, be sure to clean and grease moldboard and shares to prevent rust.

Tractor Hitches for Farm Machines

It is the combination of farm tractor and farm machine which makes a working farm unit. The tractor without some machine to operate is of little value. A farm machine cannot do its work without power. The tractor hitch, usually forgotten altogether until after the tractor is purchased, is really the connecting link which, when right, enables the combination to work to the best advantage.

Recognizing the importance of having the hitch right, the Harvester Company has worked out the following tractor hitches which can be purchased for use with their tractors and machines. In addition to these manufactured hitches, the Harvester Company has many suggestions for home-made hitches to adapt most farm machines to tractor power. These suggestions can be had upon written request to the Chicago office. State specifically what implements you wish to draw, the order in which they are to be arranged, and what hitches or parts of hitches you have on hand at the present time. Information regarding the hitches listed herewith can be had from the local dealer, from the nearest branch house, or from the general office in Chicago.

Tractor Hitch for One Grain Binder

Deering stub tongue tractor hitch suitable for one New Ideal or Ideal Deering binder alone (ZDA-104).

McCormick stub tongue tractor hitch suitable for one flat frame binder only, either right or left hand (Z-1367).

Milwaukee stub tongue tractor hitch suitable for one No. 10, No. 12 or New 12 Milwaukee binder alone (Z-1368).

Tractor Hitch for First Grain Binder of Two

Deering stub tongue tractor hitch suitable for first binder of two. Fits New Ideal or Ideal Deering binders (ZDA-103).

McCormick stub tongue tractor hitch suitable for first binder of two. Fits either right or left hand binders of improved flat frame type (Z-1353).

Milwaukee stub tongue tractor hitch suitable for first binder of two. Fits Milwaukee No. 10, No. 12 or New 12 binder (Z-1368).

Tractor Hitch for Second Grain Binder of Two

Deering (Type F) steering tongue tractor hitch suitable for second binder of two. Fits New Ideal or Ideal Deering binders (ZDA-101).

McCormick steering tongue tractor hitch suitable for second binder of two. Fits right or left hand improved flat frame binders (ZA-1130).

Milwaukee steering tongue tractor hitch suitable for second binder of two. Fits No. 10, No. 12 or New 12 binder (A-1369).

Tractor Hitch for Three or More Grain Binders

When a tractor hitch is to be used for a large tractor (larger than 10-20-H. P.) for pulling grain binders, it is necessary that the first binder be equipped with a steering tongue tractor hitch. The steering tongue tractor hitch is needed on the first binder because a stub tongue tractor hitch may not permit the first binder to cut a full swath. A steering tongue tractor hitch will also be needed on each of the other binders after the first.

Tractor Hitch for Deering or McCormick Mowers

Stub tongue tractor hitch suitable for first mower (Z-1352).

For Second or Additional Mowers

Steering tongue tractor hitch (Z-1328).

Tractor Hitch for Deering or McCormick Push Machines

Deering tractor hitch for push binder or header (ZDA-105).

McCormick tractor hitch for push binder or header (Z-1295).

Tractor Hitch for Spreaders

Stub tongue tractor hitch for manure spreaders (same for all I H C spreaders).

Tractor Hitch for Disk Harrows

Stub tongue tractor hitch for Deering or McCormick disk harrow (J-9908).

Tractor Hitch for Wagon, Short Turn Trailer Gear and One or More Grain Drills

In addition to the above hitches, we can supply suitable hitch for one short turn trailer gear or for one or more grain drills. These can be ordered by name without number.

One-Man Binder Control Tractor Hitch

Made for operating Deering or McCormick binders from the tractor seat. The levers are placed so that the man driving the tractor can operate them without leaving his seat. They control the platform, binder attachment and bundle carrier. For McCormick Improved left hand binder, order 1 Z-1402 and 1 Z-1403. For Deering New Ideal left hand binder, order 1 Z-1402 and 1 Z-1404.

One-Man Tractor Control Hitch

One-man tractor control hitch can be used on Deering and McCormick binders for guiding and controlling either the Mogul 10-20 or the Titan 10-20 kerosene tractor. The operator sits on the binder seat and steers the tractor by means of an extended steering device. A suitable device is also supplied for throwing the clutch of the tractor in and out from the binder seat. For McCormick Improved left hand or right hand and Deering New Ideal binders, the Mogul hitch is No. 8854-T. For McCormick Improved left hand or right hand and Deering New Ideal binders, the Titan hitch is No. 6910-TM.

For Two Binders

If a one-man tractor hitch is to be used on the first binder of two of the same line (both Deering or both McCormick) a steering tongue tractor hitch and supplementary hitch parts must be ordered as shown below:

For McCormick Improved left hand or right hand binders, 1 ZA-1130 and 1 Z-1455 supplementary tractor hitch parts.

For Deering New Ideal binders 1 ZDA-101 steering tongue tractor hitch and 1 ZDA-106 supplementary hitch parts.

If two binders are to be pulled together, we recommend a one-man (binder control) tractor hitch for the first binder.

The Farm Tractor and Its Relation to Other Machines

In farming operations many different machines are required. Each machine has certain definite work to perform, and it is seldom that one machine can take the place of another. However, in one respect practically all of these machines are alike—they all require power for their successful operation. From the power standpoint they can be grouped in two classes—those which require a motive power to carry the machines over the field or on the road, and those which require a power transmitted by belt for the operation of internal mechanism.

Up to the time that the farm tractor was introduced, the uptodate farmer had two kinds of power—horses for field work or to pull the first class of machines, and usually a stationary or portable engine to drive the second class, that is, the belt machines. The modern farm tractor is designed to supply power to both classes of machines. If the tractor is properly built there can be no question regarding its economy in both instances.

In this connection it is well to remember that this new power—the farm tractor—is of little or no advantage unless it is used with some farm machine. In itself, it is only half an outfit. Likewise the many different farm machines which require power are perfectly useless without power. It is always the combination of tractor and machines connected by a suitable hitch or belt which does the farm work. This fact should never be forgotten.

Since this is true, it is the part of wisdom to select both power and machine from lines which are adapted to each other. It is equally wise in selecting a tractor to be sure that the power will handle both classes of machines.

In view of this very close relation between power and machine, we are listing herewith the drawbar and belt machines found in the International line which can always be satisfactorily hitched and operated by an International Harvester farm tractor.

Drawbar Machines in the I H C Line For Use with Kerosene Tractor Power

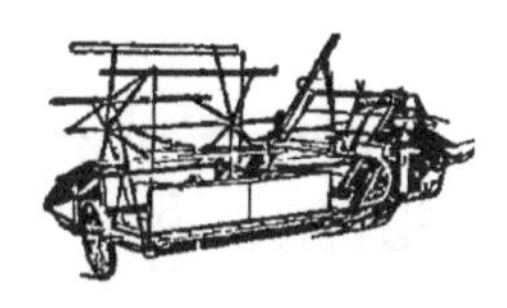

Grain Binders

Deering, McCormick and Milwaukee. Sizes 6, 7 and 8-foot. Tongue trucks, bundle carriers and transport trucks can be supplied. Special type for harvesting rice. International shocker attaches to binder. Shocks grain automatically.

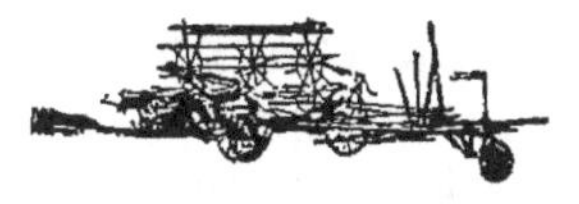

Push Binders and Headers

Deering and McCormick. Sizes, push binders, 10, 12 and 14-foot; headers, 10, 12 and 14-foot. Push binders can be supplied with elevator for converting them to headers.

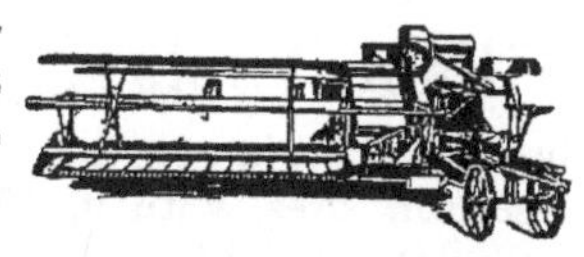

Harvester-Threshers

Deering and McCormick. Cut 9-foot swath. Harvest and thresh at one operation 15 to 20 acres per day. A 15-30 tractor or 8 to 12 horses and 2 men required. Can be used as a stationary thresher.

Mowers

Deering, McCormick and Milwaukee. One and two-horse, regular and vertical lift; 3½, 4½, 5, 6 and 7-foot cutter bars. Reaping attachments and clover bunchers extra.

Hay Loaders

International and Keystone Windrow loaders, single cylinder, elevate hay 10 feet; cylinders 6 feet wide. Gleaning cylinder on special order. Double cylinder loaders elevate 9½ feet; cylinders 8 feet wide. Gearless or rake-type loaders elevate hay 9 feet high, direct from swath 8 feet wide. All loaders unhitched from top of load. International Harvester loaders are the greatest time savers in the hay field.

Side-Delivery Rakes

International and Keystone. Combined side-delivery rake and tedder and regular side-delivery rake. Raking width, 7¼ and 8-foot. Left-hand delivery. 8-foot size suitable for beans.

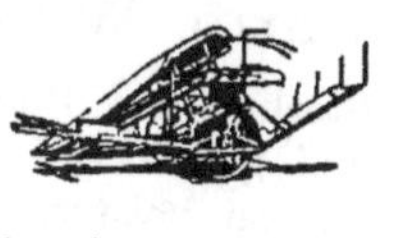

Corn Binders

Deering, McCormick and Milwaukee. Cut and bind 5 to 7 acres per day. Have devices that get down corn. Special style for short corn. All equipped with bundle carrier. Elevator to load bundles on wagon or special conveyor bundle carrier supplied at extra cost.

Corn Pickers

Deering and McCormick. Pick and husk 5 to 7 acres per day. Elevator delivers husked corn into wagon driven along side of the picker. Tractor or five horses and one man are required for picker.

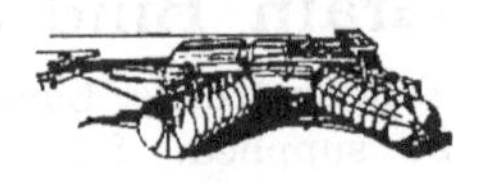

International Leverless Tractor Disk Harrow

Something entirely new. No levers. First exclusively tractor implement since the self-lift plow. Gangs angled by tractor. Straightens automatically when backing.

Disk Harrows

Deering, McCormick, and International. Horse and tractor styles. Sizes 4, 5, 6, 7, 8, 9 and 10-foot, with 16 or 18-inch disks. Tandem attachments, forecarriage, and transports at extra cost. Special type for orchard work. Exceptionally strong. Two and three-lever styles.

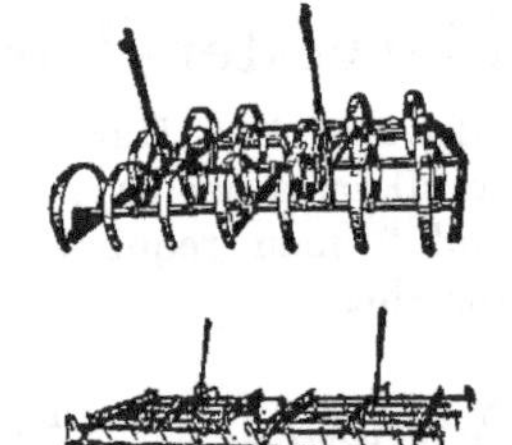

Tillage Tools

Deering, McCormick and International. Spring and peg-tooth harrows. Spring-tooth harrows are built in 1, 2, 3 and 4-section sizes, with 9, 15, 17, 23, 25, 33 and 35 teeth. Sulky attachment extra.

Peg-tooth harrows are made in 25, 30 and 35-tooth sections. Sulky and orchard guards extra. Soil pulverizers in 5, 6, 7, 8, 9 and 11-foot. Tongue truck extra.

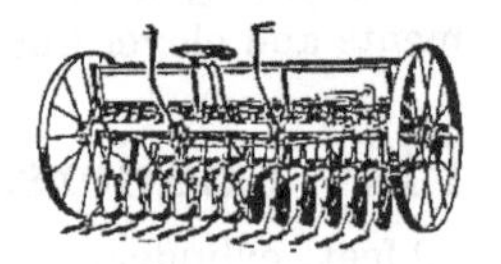

Grain Drills, Fertilizer and Lime Sowers

Hoosier, Kentucky and Empire, Jr. Sizes, 5 to 24 furrow openers; 4, 6, 7 and 8-inch spacing. Single disk, double disk, spring trip and pin break hoes, or plain shoes. Also press drills or press wheel attachment. Sow all kinds of seed from flax to peas and beans. Also complete line of fertilizer drills, lime sowers, grass seed and alfalfa drills and broadcast seeders.

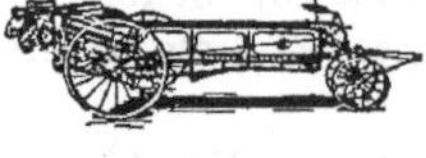

Manure Spreaders

Low 20th Century, Low Corn King, and Low Cloverleaf. Three sizes each—light 2-horse, medium 3-horse, and large 3-horse. Endless or reverse apron. Choice of spiral wide spread or double disk wide spread; low, narrow boxes, wide spread, light draft steel frame, worm drive, roller bearings for main axles and apron and steel beaters.

Farm Wagons and Trucks

Weber, Columbus, Sterling and Buckeye. One and two-horse. Standardized and guaranteed. Guaranteed carrying capacities stamped on rear bolster. Logging gear, steel and wood wheel farm trucks; grain tanks. A style and size of wagon or truck to meet all requirements.

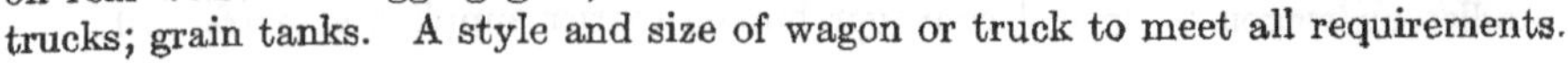

Belt Machines in the I H C Line For Use with Kerosene Tractor Power

Hay Presses

International. One and two-horse, motor and belt power styles in sizes 14x18, 16x18 and 17x22-inch bale chambers. Horse presses, capacities 6 to 15 tons per day. Motor presses equipped with 6-h. p. engine, capacities 12 to 20 tons per day. Motor presses have self-feed and automatic block setters. Engine can be disconnected for other work. Belt power presses, capacities 15 to 30 tons per day. Six-horse power required. 17x22 size has self-feed and automatic block setter; others have pan type block setter and self-feed.

Ensilage Cutters

International. Made in four sizes. Capacities 3 to 25 tons of cut fodder per hour. Reliable safety devices. Force feed, large throat and heavy fly wheel give large capacity at low power cost. Power required varies from 6 to 25-horse power depending on size and capacity.

Corn Shellers

International, Keystone and Keynote. Mounted and down styles. Sizes, 1, 2 and 4 hole. For hand or power operation. Adjustable to all sizes of ears. Capacities, 150 to 2,500 bushels per day. Power required, 1 to 8-h. p. A suitable size for every condition.

Huskers and Shredders

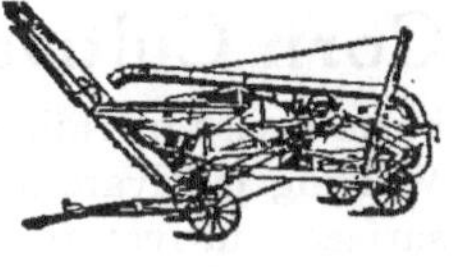

Deering and McCormick. Sizes, 2, 4, 6, 8 and 10-roll. Small sizes for individual farm use or large ones for custom work. Require 8 to 25-h. p.

Feed Grinders

International Type B grinds corn on the cob. Three sizes, 6 to 45 bu. per hr. Power, 2 to 12-h. p. Type C grinds small grain. Two sizes, 6 to 45 bu. per hr. Power, 2 to 12-h. p. Type D grinds corn in the husk. Two sizes, 10 to 45 bu. per hr. Power, 3 to 12-h. p.

Meadows Stone Burr Mills

Grind corn meal, buckwheat, graham or whole wheat flour. Eliminate weevil and trash before corn is ground. Automatically dries meal and cools burrs. Made in five sizes with capacity from 2 to 25 bushels per hour, 2 to 20 h. p. required. Can be equipped with sacking or wagon elevators, flour and grits bolters at extra cost.

Threshers

International, New Racine and Sterling. Sizes, New Racine 20x32, 24x40. Sizes, International 22x38, 28x46. Sizes, Sterling 21x28, 21x33, 26x33 and 30x37. New Racine and International can be equipped with self feeders, wind stackers and various grain measuring elevators and loaders. Thresh all grains, seeds and peanuts.

Other Machines in the I H C Line

Rakes

Deering, McCormick and Milwaukee. Sizes, 8, 9, 10 and 12-foot. Self-dump, steel construction, interchangeable wheels, removable bearings and reversible dump rods.

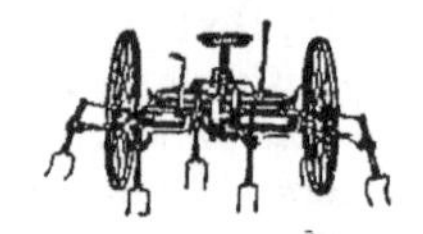

Tedders

Deering, McCormick and International. Sizes, 6-fork and 8-fork. All steel construction, center drive, fork relief springs, fork angles adjustable.

Sweep Rakes and Stackers

International. Six styles and sizes of sweep rakes —side hitch, rear hitch, two, three and four-wheel.

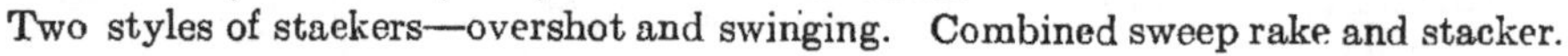

Two styles of stackers—overshot and swinging. Combined sweep rake and stacker.

Corn Planters and Drills

International and C B & Q two-row planters and drills, Hoosier, Kentucky and Empire one-row drills. Six types of International and C B & Q—regular, narrow row, wide row, high wheel, drill and wire drive. Open or closed wheels. Sled runner, stub runner, single and double disk furrow openers. Fertilizer attachments, combination corn and pea attachments, special plates for large or small seed, power drop attachments for hill dropping without wire on special order. Hoosier, Kentucky and Empire one-row drills with shoe, hoe or disk furrow openers. Fertilizer attachments can be supplied.

Corn Cultivators

International. Pivot pole, pivot axle, rigid pole and rigid beam styles of riding cultivators. One and two-row cultivators. Walking cultivators with heavy or light beams. Also disk and surface cultivators. Tread adjustable from 28-inch to 48-inch rows. 4, 6 or 8-shovel beams can be used. Shovels 3 to 5 inches wide. Three sizes of spearhead or semi-surface shovels can be supplied. Can be quickly adjusted to cultivate shallow so as not to injure roots after corn has developed.

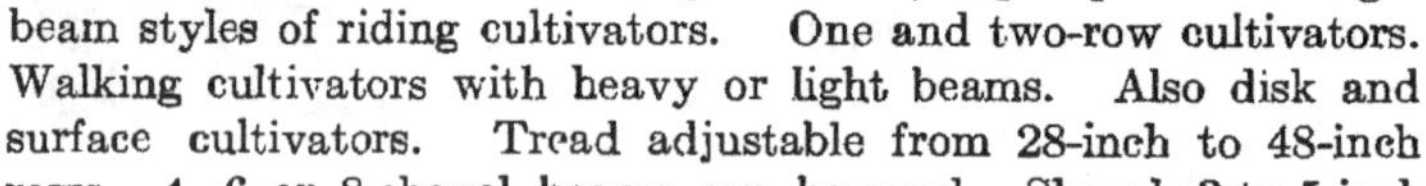

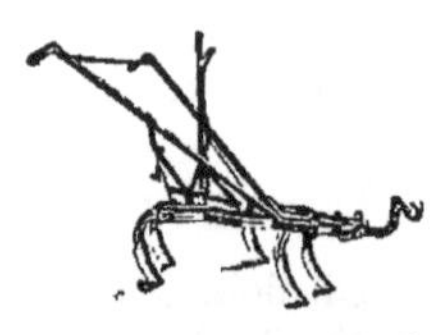

One-Horse Cultivators

Built with 5, 7 and 9 shovels, also 7, 9 and 14 teeth. Can be equipped with special shovels or sweeps, depth regulators, potato hillers, beet shovels, goose-foot teeth, and double-pointed teeth.

Motor Cultivators

International. Have 8, 12 and 16-shovel equipment. Cultivate two rows. Motor is placed back of driver directly over drive wheels, which run between corn rows. Driver steers machine by pivoting the cultivator wheels as he shifts the gangs with his feet. Complete variety of shovels.

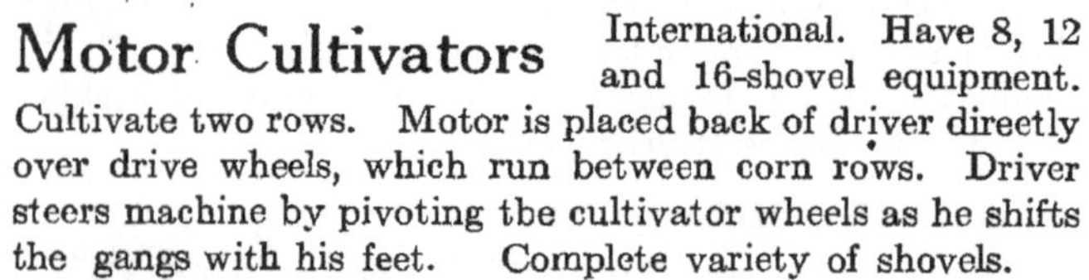

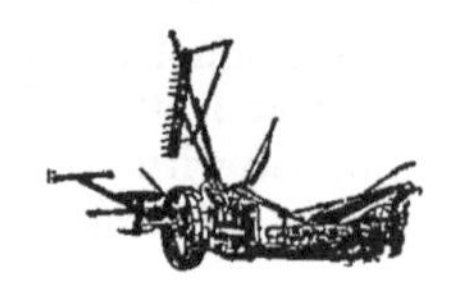

Reapers

Deering, McCormick and Milwaukee. Sizes, 5 and 5½-foot. Useful on small farms and in mountainous countries. Cut grain and lay it in gavels or bunches. Also used for harvesting grass seed crops.

Stalk Cutters

International. Sizes, 7 or 9 blades; 26 inches long. Chopping action cuts every stalk, making it easy to plow stalks under, and have a clean field. International has steel wheels, staggered spokes, non-clogging knife head, angle steel frame, dust proof bearings, handy foot lever, shock absorbing hitch and other features.

Kerosene Tractors

Mogul, Titan and International. Sizes, 8-16, 10-20 and 15-30. Guaranteed to operate on kerosene and other low-cost fuels down to 39° B. as well as on gasoline.

Kerosene Engines

Mogul and International. Low cost of operation and reliable quality are their outstanding features. Burn kerosene and other low-grade fuels as well as gasoline. Sizes, 1 to 15-horse power. Stationary, skidded, mounting and portable types. An engine for every purpose.

Motor Trucks

International. Sizes, ¾, 1, 1½ and 2-ton capacities. Four-cylinder, block cast, heavy duty engines, three-speed transmission and famous International internal gear drive rear axles. No matter what you have to haul, there is an International built to haul it. It is more economical, more flexible in rush season, and places the owner in reach of a much wider range of territory for marketing all products.

Cream Separators

Primrose and Lily. Four sizes, capacities 350, 450, 650 and 850 pounds of milk per hour. Close skimmers. Great money savers. Turn easily. Built to last. Any man with three average cows can pay for a cream separator in a few months with the extra cream it gives him. Besides he has fresh, warm skim milk to feed to his young stock. Better have three cows and separator than four cows and no separator.

Twine

Deering, McCormick, Milwaukee and International. Made in six grades—Sisal, Standard, Standard Manila, Manila, Superior Manila and Pure Manila. The fibres used are high grade, every step in manufacture is carefully watched, tests are made for strength and size.

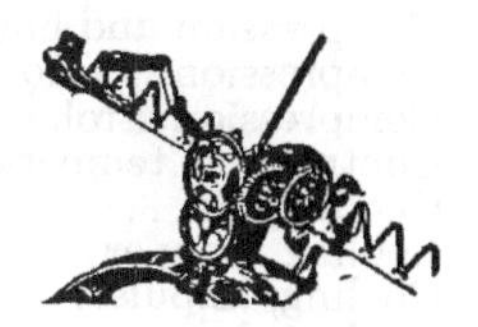

Knife Grinders

Deering, McCormick and Milwaukee. Equipped with stones shaped to grind mower knives. Flat stone for general tool grinding extra. Attach to bench or implement wheel.

INDEX

United States Branch Houses of

International Harvester Company of America

(Incorporated)

Aberdeen, S. D.
Albany, N. Y.
Atlanta, Ga.
Auburn, N. Y.
Aurora, Ill.
Baltimore, Md.
Billings, Mont.
Birmingham, Ala.
Bismarck, N. D.
Boston, Mass.
Buffalo, N. Y.
Cedar Falls, Ia.
Charlotte, N. C.
Chicago, Ill.
Cincinnati, Ohio
Cleveland, Ohio
Columbia, S. C.
Columbus, Ohio
Council Bluffs, Ia.
Crawford, Neb.
Davenport, Ia.
Denver, Colo.
Des Moines, Ia.
Detroit, Mich.
Dubuque, Ia.
East St. Louis, Ill.
Eau Claire, Wis.
Elmira, N. Y.
Evansville, Ind.
Fargo, N. D.
Ft. Dodge, Ia.
Ft. Wayne, Ind.
Grand Forks, N. D.
Grand Rapids, Mich.
Green Bay, Wis.
Harrisburg, Pa.
Helena, Mont.
Hutchinson, Kan.
Indianapolis, Ind.
Jackson, Mich.
Jacksonville, Fla.
Kankakee, Ill.
Kansas City, Mo.
Knoxville, Tenn.
Lincoln, Neb.
Little Rock, Ark.
Los Angeles, Cal.
Madison, Wis.
Mankato, Minn.
Mason City, Ia.
Memphis, Tenn.
Milwaukee, Wis.
Minneapolis, Minn.
Minot, N. D.
Nashville, Tenn.
New Albany, Ind.
New Orleans, La.
Ogdensburg, N. Y.
Oklahoma City, Okla.
Omaha, Neb.
Parkersburg, W. Va.
Parsons, Kan.
Peoria, Ill.
Philadelphia, Pa.
Pittsburgh, Pa.
Portland, Ore.
Quincy, Ill.
Richmond, Ind.
Richmond, Va.
Rockford, Ill.
Saginaw, Mich.
St. Cloud, Minn.
St. Joseph, Mo.
St. Louis, Mo.
Salina, Kan.
Salt Lake City, Utah
San Francisco, Cal.
Sioux City, Ia.
Sioux Falls, S. D.
South Bend, Ind.
Spokane, Wash.
Springfield, Ill.
Springfield, Mo.
Terre Haute, Ind.
Toledo, Ohio
Topeka, Kan.
Watertown, S. D.
Wichita, Kan.
Winona, Minn.

Address the nearest branch house or the general offices of the Company at Chicago for information.

Canadian Branch Houses of

International Harvester Company of Canada, Limited

WEST

Brandon, Man.
Calgary, Alta.
Edmonton, Alta.
Estevan, Sask.
Lethbridge, Alta.
N. Battleford, Sask.
Regina, Sask.
Saskatoon, Sask.
Winnipeg, Man.
Yorkton, Sask.

EAST

Hamilton, Ont.
London, Ont.
Montreal, Que.
Ottawa, Ont.
Quebec, Que.
St. John, N. B.

Write the nearest branch house for catalogue and complete information on any of the machines and implements sold by the International Harvester Company of Canada, Limited, as listed below:

GRAIN MACHINES

Binders
Reapers

HAY MACHINES

Mowers
Rakes
Tedders
Side Delivery Rakes
Hay Loaders
Hay Presses
Sweep Rakes
Hay Stackers

CORN MACHINES

Planters
Cultivators
Binders
Ensilage Cutters
Huskers and Shredders
Shellers

TILLAGE

Disk Harrows
Tractor Disk Harrows
Cultivators
Spring-Tooth Harrows
Peg-Tooth Harrows
Plows
Tractor Plows
Scufflers
Land Rollers
Land Packers

GENERAL LINE

Kerosene Engines
Kerosene Tractors
Motor Trucks
Farm Wagons and Trucks
Manure Spreaders
Cream Separators
Grain Drills
Seeders
Feed Grinders
Feed Crushers
Threshers
Democrats
Bob Sleighs
Knife Grinders
Binder Twine

CPSIA information can be obtained at www.ICGtesting.com
Printed in the USA
LVOW01s1601300714

396753LV00025B/1835/P

9 781313 123372